COMPUGIRLS

DISSIDENT FEMINISMS

Elora Halim Chowdhury, Editor

*A list of books in the series appears
at the end of this book.*

COMPUGIRLS

*How Girls of Color Find
and Define Themselves
in the Digital Age*

KIMBERLY A. SCOTT

**UNIVERSITY OF
ILLINOIS PRESS**
Urbana, Chicago, and Springfield

Library of Congress Cataloging-in-Publication Data
Names: Scott, Kimberly A., author.
Title: Compugirls: how girls of color find and define
    themselves in the digital age / Kimberly A. Scott.
Other titles: COMPUGIRLS
Description: Urbana: University of Illinois Press,
    [2021] | Series: Dissident Feminisms | Includes
    bibliographical references and index.
Identifiers: LCCN 2021012056 (print) | LCCN
    2021012057 (ebook) | ISBN 9780252044083
    (Cloth : acid-free paper) | ISBN 9780252086137
    (Paperback : acid-free paper) | ISBN
    9780252053023 (eBook)
Subjects: LCSH: Educational technology—United
    States—Case studies. | Multicultural education—
    Curricula—United States—Case studies. |
    Education, Secondary—Curricula—United States.
    | Minority high school students—United States. |
    Teachers—In-service training.
Classification: LCC LB1028.3 .S3788 2021 (print) |
    LCC LB1028.3 (ebook) | DDC 370.117—dc23
LC record available at https://lccn.loc.gov/2021012056
LC ebook record available at https://lccn.loc.gov/2021012057

Dedicated to my mother, Dr. Beverly Norine Dunston Scott, who encouraged me not simply to live in this world but to transform it for our daughters' sakes.

Contents

Preface

Writing. It has been and probably always will be a challenge for me. Good writing requires an author to reveal a certain level of vulnerability. For academic writers, this poses an issue. Scholarly writing is supposed to be objective, clinical, and nonpersonal. I was taught to defend my thoughts with empirical proof, not emotion or beliefs. And as an African American female professor, the stakes are even higher. Revealing too much of yourself suggests lack of intellect and can quickly lead to suspicion about abilities; revealing too little feeds into the commonplace narrative of being a cold Black woman. Focusing on program development and putting everything I learned throughout the years into building a sustainable enterprise would be easier, more exciting, and less intimidating than writing. At least this is what I thought after completing my doctorate in education. So, why did I spend the better part of the last eight years writing this book? Beginning with my childhood, my life's chapters provide a partial answer.

Growing up in the 1980s, my parents stressed the importance of education. Given that they both were first-generation college graduates and later earned their doctorates, my sister and I learned that erudition was the key to success. No one can ever take away your education, they taught us. We were to learn from every experience, no matter where, and from every individual, no matter that person's title or lack thereof. This unspoken but very significant expectation carried through in our nonacademic lives.

As I attended school and various church activities, I also participated in an array of community groups. Girl Scouts was great for building a sense of an empowered girl; the YWCA taught me leadership skills. At church, my friends provided me a sense of belonging, and the elders illuminated how educators need not be teachers. Altogether, I felt beholden to something and many people beyond myself. However, I had not yet begun the episode in my life story to know what to do with this sentiment.

Fast forward to the first decade of the new millennium. After observing one too many stressed urban educators yell at students who looked like me, I adopted a new mantra: Comfort the disturbed, disturb the comfortable. This was risky but propelled me to pursue my master's and doctoral degrees and focus on underserved communities. I committed myself to designing projects that positioned girls to be innovative change agents. I resolved to develop education projects that counter stereotypes of and biases against girls of color. My efforts were often questioned.

Academia values published work, not necessarily the effort behind the writing. This mindset comforts academia, distinguishing "real" research from service (which is far less important to many scholars in higher education). However, I could not in good conscience depart from my commitment. The neighborhoods surrounding my university's campus housed individuals who led lives very similar to mine in my early upbringing. Yet, many of the most respected academic works captured stories of deficiency and underperformance. Sadly, once I moved across the country to a new academic position, the same images and discourse of "those people's" inferiorities appeared. In my new context, the marginalized populations were not predominantly Black, but the stories of Latinx and Native American students were similarly depressing. Biased narratives encouraged me to do more than build programs. I began writing a book describing how I developed COMPUGIRLS, but that story quickly became insufficient. Instead, I wrote this book to document the results of my efforts. I hope that it will invite individuals to join the dialogue about and initiatives for girlhoods of color in this digital age. Together, we can deconstruct simplistic images of girls of color. We can collectively provide girls contexts in which to wrest control over their narratives and lives. Collaboratively, we can prepare them to cultivate a more just future in which they can flourish. Those goals required me to disturb my writing demons and my comfort.

This book is for a diverse audience. I hope that both academic and non-academic readers will understand that there should be far more attention paid to how broadening technology participation efforts affect girls in more ways than simply boosting their ability to replicate current skills or navigate troubled pathways. Equally important, this book is also for the girls who have privileged me with their stories. While I followed my institution's review board procedures and gained approval to collect and analyze their narratives, I did not feel this was sufficient. Always mindful of Jackie Jordan

Irvine's assertion that too many scholars treat marginalized communities like plantations,[1] I developed a member checking system with the girls that relied on multiple years' worth of communication. I shared drafts of the subsequent chapters with many past participants, some whose stories appear and others who were part of a cohort with whom I maintained contact via e-mail, Facebook, or phone. I asked the "stars" of this book to provide their own pseudonyms. For those who did not, I still changed their names to maintain confidentiality. Nevertheless, involving the girls in the process of analysis and taking seriously their input were essential research dimensions, ensuring a higher level of credibility. This project cannot be owned solely by adult professionals. If the narratives reveal anything, it is the importance of persistence and the constant need to adapt as participants and investigators work in concert to reimagine reality.

I am incredibly grateful to a host of individuals. Dawn Durante, a fabulous and unfathomably patient editor, always made me feel as if there was hope in completing this book. My friend and colleague Sarane Boocock taught me how to approach book writing in the first place and regularly talked me off the writer's ledge. Many others allowed me to share drafts with them: Patricia Garcia, Kristin Ellwood, Steve Elliott, Chun Tao, and Tara Nkrumah are among the rising academic stars who graciously provided feedback along this journey. Megan Berry, Tori Jackson, and Sierra Fales kindly assisted with gathering data to substantiate and contextualize my work. And my father, Dr. James Scott, has always been a fantastic editor for me. I am grateful for his loving pushes.

Finally, I want to dedicate this book to my mother, Dr. Beverly Norine Dunston Scott. She passed away before I completed the volume, but she visited COMPUGIRLS many times. A woman who was the epitome of a change agent, she inspired me in more ways than there is room to describe. I owe a big debt to her as the first Dr. Scott in our family—always a model, always a mentor, and in a distinct way, forever a part of COMPUGIRLS.

COMPUGIRLS

Introduction

AT THE START OF THE twenty-first century, the United States experienced some considerable developments, and setbacks, related to education, technology, and digital inclusion. Microsoft was found violating anti-trust laws; Hillary Clinton became the first former First Lady to win a U.S. Senate seat; the space shuttle *Columbia* exploded, killing all seven astronauts; and the war on terror began after the World Trade Center was attacked. The nation's education system was experiencing a back-to-basics push with Congress approving and President George W. Bush signing into law the No Child Left Behind Act. School vouchers became more popular following the U.S. Supreme Court ruling in the *Zelman v. Simmons-Harris* case. Within this fury of conservatism and political machinations, some progressive ideas emerged.

Around this time, I learned about the Reggio Emilia approach. Beautifully described by William Corsaro and Luisa Molinari,[1] I—like other educators— marveled at the way teachers in a northern Italian school centered children's experiences as early as age three. Irrespective of the youngsters' family lives, parents were invited as important agents in a child's educational journey. Small group work was the norm, with teachers creating rich settings that would provoke thought and dialogue. Teachers also served as "documenters," establishing portfolio-like systems so students could visualize the progression of their learning. As a former fourth-grade teacher, I appreciated how Reggio Emilia educators had time to reflect on their teaching and work collaboratively with their colleagues. The Reggio Emilia approach to education appeared to many as a better way to improve academic performance of students. And with this possibility, I began to dream out loud.

Why shouldn't U.S. students from districts economically stressed experience a curriculum that values their knowledge? Why should standardized tests become the exclusive force, driving teachers' practices to "teach to the test"? How is Reggio Emilia able to institute such a humane approach to education while the United States engages in empirically unsupported strategies? Answers to these questions eluded me for quite some time. Yet, I noted the incredible activity outside of schools that would eventually change our pedagogy and cause me to link theory to praxis.

While the education system tried to manage federal policies, the twenty-first century ushered in a time of great technological advancements. In 2001, the first iPod was released. Phones began to have cameras (2003), and Google Maps launched (2005). USB flash drives became more ubiquitous and floppy disks were quickly forgotten. Game consoles became more like entertainment units, with PlayStation 2 introducing the capacity for DVDs and game disks. For game players no longer interested in competitive scenarios with a distinct end, The Sims appeared, allowing players to build and "live" in a self-created world. This was an era where more massively multiplayer online role-playing games (or MMORPG) boomed and individuals began collaborating across geographic divides. Social networking sites emerged with MySpace (2003) and Facebook (2004). At the center of all these developments remained the iconic image of a White male creator, hacker, and entrepreneur.

Girls of color—African American, Latina,[2] and Native American in particular—were invisible in this early part of the digital age. Yet, our invisibility did not equate to our inactivity. Indeed, as early as 1975 the American Association for the Advancement of Science held a meeting with and about underrepresented women in STEM (science, technology, engineering, and mathematics) fields.[3] However, until 2008, few articles and published pieces appeared about women of color and STEM, and organized events including this cohort were rare.[4]

I was acutely aware of how poorly, in far too many instances, our daughters were treated. In the early 1990s I was a fourth-grade teacher in what was then called a "special needs school," meaning one economically disadvantaged and with a disproportionate number of African American kids. I taught students interested in all the new developments indicated above, hungry to learn more about the impending digital developments. Students in this supposedly deficient setting read both local and national newspapers to follow the current events. But many teachers inflicted on students their beliefs about youngsters' perceived inferiority and provided far less than the minimum instruction. Principals and school administrators often stated that my standards were too high for "these kids." Why would I expect them to learn foreign languages, study World War II, or read books normally assigned to students in the district's high school? I was able to form responses to these questions during my graduate program.

While completing my doctorate in education, I served as a teaching assistant. In this role, I interacted with hundreds of eager preservice teachers. Repeatedly, these students expressed their worry of how to reconcile what I sermonized as theoretically and empirically grounded pedagogy with increased pressure to teach to standardized tests. Regularly, I called attention to Geneva Gay's and Gloria Ladson-Billings's work on culturally responsive pedagogy . Their works were guiding stars, I told my adult students, to effectively engage youngsters from "special needs" districts. Weekly, we theorized how centering students' cultural backgrounds as assets on which to build was the ideal teaching method. Yet, theory and practice remained separate in the minds of these would-be teachers. Countless times I heard, How will culturally responsive pedagogy protect my job, since I will be judged on my students' performance? No matter what my answer, I observed many well-meaning preservice teachers opt for employment in well-resourced schools or apply their skills in out-of-school programs. The perceived ineffectiveness of a well-known framework such as culturally responsive pedagogy was outweighed by the supposed deficits of students navigating low-income, urban schools.

This malaise moved me. As a classroom teacher and later as a junior professor, I knew that if provided access to opportunity and resources, students would achieve. I believed that if educators could recognize students' interests and value their background—unrelated to their parents' socioeconomic level, the color of their skin, their geographic location, or their hair texture—then they could use these as stepping stones to further youngsters' learning. At the same time, I understood that standardized testing looms large. Urban classrooms were squeezing in more and more youngsters, and few college students yearned to become teachers. Pre- and in-service teachers felt great pressure. I wanted to respect their attitudes and avoid placing any more requirements on overtaxed, underpaid urban educators. Out-of-school experiences arranged by community organizations seemed like important spaces to engage students. Equally important, in-service teachers are not the only adults who can effectively educate youngsters.

In the late 1990s and into the next decade, more out-of-school programs emerged that were focused on engaging kids from economically strapped areas. Organizations such as the YWCA developed Girls Empowerment After-School Programs, providing girls activities and lessons in coding, science, and art. Lesser-known initiatives such as danceLogic also appeared. Targeting African American girls, participants engaged in both dance and coding. Kids-in-Tech ran a girl-centered STEM program, offering girls from underserved communities opportunities to explore STEM through experiments and research. Sisters4Science was one of the earliest initiatives. As an after-school program for middle and high school girls, women of color scientists interacted with girls as role models, discussing their pathways and building girls' leadership skills. Techbridge appeared around the same time. A program for girls in low-income communities in California and the Pacific Northwest and around Washington, D.C., it works with girls to develop STEM, social, and emotional skills.

As the decade continued, more programs emerged. Girls Creating Games: Cafe Universo worked with Latina middle school girls from California. It was an after-school program that mixed astrobiology and computer science in order to encourage girls to explore science and information technology. They were enrolled in the program for two years at a time and developed and released games about life in space. Techbridge created an extension program called Girl Go Techbridge. Math and activism were part of the curriculum, along with hands-on science experiments. Again, the focus was on girls from economically troubled settings. Yet, save for a program led by the University of Maryland, Baltimore County, which worked in underserved middle schools to increase the interest of girls in information technology, few efforts had partnerships with postsecondary institutions.

Regardless of technological advancements, between 2004 and 2008 there were conflicting education trends for women of color. In 2004, for example, 16,602 African American female college freshmen declared their interest in majoring in computer science. By 2008, that number dropped to 13,381. Native American female freshmen, however, saw the reverse: in 2004, 405 women belonging to this social category stated the same interest; by 2008, 1,574 indicated the desire for a computer science degree. For Hispanic women, 851 earned their bachelor's degree in computer science during 2005; that number decreased to 551 in 2008. What was happening? More importantly, what could a college or university do to address these statistics?

The out-of-school programs at that time focused on providing girls from under-resourced areas skills for the workforce—admirable intent, but a step was skipped. What about the best avenue to get to the workforce? Attending and graduating from a college or university would prepare students to be much more successful than if they simply had skills to be a worker. Few programs focused on leadership, and the scarce number that did sought to develop girls' leadership skills to work in an industry without changing it. Why would Black girls want to lead a field that increasingly excluded Black women? Why not provide girls those skills that the White male technologists possessed, which could ultimately change the world? Why not nurture girls' abilities to be change agents who will construct and own a new system?

Clearly, the success of White male technology leaders was not only about technical knowledge. In collaboration with others, these creators wielded mighty swords. Yes, they were White men whose power and privilege allowed them access to forms of capital from which many of us were and are precluded. These leaders had more than skill. Indeed, many of the leading technologists did not major in computer science or engineering, and they instead attended liberal arts colleges pursuing English, philosophy, or some other nontechnical degree.[5] And these juggernauts were constructing technologies that were culturally responsive to communities that looked like and privileged them.

Posing academic questions was never the driving force in my work. Trained as a sociologist of education, I was committed to rigorously designing research projects to gain potential answers to questions. This professional identity was informed by and intersected with my positionality as an African American female educator. But I felt obligated to provide what I call under-anticipated students the same opportunities as their affluent counterparts. That this would benefit students of color made the work even more meaningful. No more could I stand by and watch youngsters who looked like me be left out of the digital age. I was confident that continued disenfranchisement would have lasting, generational effects. Our exclusion was the newest manifestation of every ism I had studied, observed, and experienced. Combining my academic knowledge about social structures, methods to analyze them, and strategies to challenge their power dynamics with my personal experiences positioned me to do more than research a perceived problem. I yearned to develop a sustainable structure that would produce solutions.

COMPUGIRLS' Birth and Adolescence

Focusing on girls seemed logical. Even though my initiative occurred well before the Girl Effect program[6] demonstrated that any significant social change needs to begin with girl-children, my personal experiences graduating from an all-girls high school and an all-women's college had taught me this fact long ago. I sought to realize that any and every girl-child, if given access to digital opportunities and support, could be a technologist, and not at the expense of her community. I believed that the pursuit of becoming a technologist begins with girls furthering their communities, envisioning themselves as agents to change their settings with technology as a manipulative tool. Thus, I put all of these ideas and theories into a program called TLC—Teaching, Learning, and Community. With an emphasis on e-zines (which were relatively popular at the beginning of the new millennium), parental civic engagement, and mentoring, this early attempt at a digital inclusion program served as an important launching pad. Once recruited to move across the nation and join a top public research university, I seized the opportunity to transplant myself and recreate TLC.

What an opportunity, I told myself. To draw on the lessons learned from building and managing three years of TLC and expand its breadth and depth in partnership with leading academic voices seemed like a chance I could not dismiss. Equally important, I wondered how the program could support the journeys of girls to whom I had not had access while at my previous institution, especially due to geographic location—namely, girls identifying as Native American. These ponderings encouraged my decisions both to go farther west of the Mississippi River than anyone in my family and to develop a new program.

It is short-sighted to believe that the creation of a program for young women can rest on the shoulders of any one person. While COMPUGIRLS may be seen as my "brain child," the concept, implementation, and research methods were the fruits of multiple people's labor, intellect, and faith. In partnership with leading computer scientists and engineers, TLC's focus on e-zines shifted to computer science skills such as programming and design thinking. A colleague in girl gaming joined the effort, thereby ensuring participants in this new initiative learned game design essentials. Given the inclusion of girls from local tribal sovereign lands and my continued desire to ensure girls recognized the relevancy of their work to their communities, I enlisted the support of an expert in Indigenous knowledge systems. And to make certain that our programmatic decisions would ultimately affect girls' self-perceptions in both their current and future perspectives, a social psychologist joined our collective to support quantitative research designs. Finally, an external evaluator with a long history in education programs became instrumental in this endeavor, documenting whether we were meeting our programmatic objectives. Together, we constructed the program centering this book and organized the first COMPUGIRLS cohort in 2007.

Leading this interdisciplinary, diverse group required a considerable amount of dialogue. Although all of us, except the evaluator and social psychologist, had experience building programs for students in secondary or postsecondary schools, our personal and professional positionalities sometimes collided. In retrospect, I believe our challenges had to do with the tenor of the time. Thanks to the support of a local community organization, the Arizona Community Foundation, our team began working toward developing the 2007 COMPUGIRLS curriculum in 2006. It was in 2008 that a large federal grant[7] provided five years' worth of funds for the further development, research, and evaluation of curriculum to support multiple COMPUGIRLS cohorts. Each team member was well aware of the statistics and confusing trends stated above. Our collective desire to actively engage in building an enterprise that would alter the seeming decline of girls of color majoring in computer science united us. Yet, interdisciplinary efforts were relatively new at that time.

Those research team members with technical knowledge of computer science principles and design thinking were not necessarily well versed in how girls of color navigated life. Research team members who understood self-efficacy and self-concept often struggled with how learning how to code could impact these ideas. And game designers did not have many occasions to consider how to appropriately capture life on sovereign tribal lands. For me, I theorized how these seemingly disparate views and disciplines could join forces but, admittedly, was not sure how to put my beliefs into practice. Even with these uncertainties, we all remained committed to creating an innovative program for girls we knew had been, and continued to be, undervalued by their schools. We worked hard to broaden participation by underrepresented groups in our individual programs. Our collective seized the opportunity to do so at a larger scale than our individual efforts could afford.

As a group, we had witnessed the 1990s debate about the digital divide and the ensuing efforts addressing it.[8] We knew that simply providing access to equipment and software was insufficient. We envisioned COMPUGIRLS as a gateway to postsecondary school and a way to encourage girls of color to cocreate their learning in the fast-paced digital age while maintaining close ties to their communities. This goal evolved (more on this in later chapters), but for the time it was unique and, as a result, warranted considerable dialogue among the members of the research team.

At least twice a month for nearly two academic years, we gathered to discuss curriculum activities. Between these bimonthly meetings, I typically met with each person. During these discussions, revisions from TLC were made and COMPUGIRLS-specific activities emerged. We reasoned that expanding the age requirement from TLC's eighth graders to ages thirteen to eighteen would allow girls who were pushed out of school to participate. We also appreciated the impact of multi-age settings, believing near-peer mentoring could have positive benefits on participants. Collectively, we were quite aware that many in the local urban and rural schools experienced a number of the same constraints that the TLC participants endured. Thus, we decided to recruit from underserved districts. Last, we wanted the participants to know that our home institution was a viable option for postsecondary work. We believed that every participant could attend college, no matter their current situation. It was our job to convey this sentiment. Hosting COMPUGIRLS on our university's campus seemed like an important step to convey the message that every COMPUGIRLS participant had a right to postsecondary education.

COMPUGIRLS' curriculum was empirically based. Individual lessons incorporated activities that reflected culturally responsive theory and its focus on asset building, connectedness, and reflection. COMPUGIRLS also owes its existence to intersectionality. Power, relationality and context, and critical praxis and critical inquiry serve as the guideposts to intersectionality and shape the contours of COMPUGIRLS as the subject of this book and as an approach.

Power

COMPUGIRLS applies intersectionality as a framework that encourages participants to critically analyze the interrelatedness of structural, disciplinary, cultural, and interpersonal power.[9] For this reason, COMPUGIRLS is not simply a coding program. Like any other language, coding does not endow girls of color with infinite power. It should be noted that coding programs in and of themselves are far from useless initiatives. Without other abilities, however, this skill alone furthers "technological ghettoization."[10] There is much more to becoming a successful person in society than acquiring technical acuity. This lesson is particularly true for African American, Native American, and Latina girls, who must consistently confront biases about their competencies, no matter how many computer languages they know.[11]

COMPUGIRLS does not aim to intervene in the girls' lives because their communities are supposedly harmful. Such a deficit approach does little other than reinforce stereotypes about lack of capacity and interest. If we continue fixating on these shortages, we waste our efforts as well as position the people we aim to "help" in problematic terms. What is missing from most girl-centered initiatives are the questions that inspire COMPUGIRLS: Should programs targeting girls who are clearly underrepresented gauge their success exclusively on how well the participants acquire technical skills, take the test, and enter the computing workforce? What place do the "power skills"—namely, the ability to think critically, to articulate one's ideas, to create a coalition, and to engage one's community in prosocial ways—play in this digital age? Rather than measure girls' achievements on how far and fast they move away from their communities with skills the larger society believes will save them, what other barometers are available? Answers to these questions ground COMPUGIRLS and its attention to intersectionality.

For COMPUGIRLS and its participants, power involves recognizing one's circumstances and activating one's skills to critically assess situations and cause change. Power concerns identifying community assets using the communication styles that will cause the most action. Power involves girls of color assuming both technical (coding) skills and social behaviors so that they can become what I call techno-social change agents, individuals who possess technology competencies, a deep understanding of society, and methods to critically analyze and change inequality using digital media. In this sense, COMPUGIRLS' approach to power challenges the notion that all girls can do anything at any time.

The can-do attitude is not an option, at least not for many girls of color.[12] To craft a program that declares that girls can do anything if they put their minds to it dismisses the institutional constraints and sociohistorical background that has created limitations for many and liberty for a few and absolves the social structures that perniciously wrap their tentacles around girls of color in an attempt to extinguish their dignity and hope. A case in point: In 2018 I attended a conference focused on women, diversity, and technology. One of the presenters, a thirty-something African American woman, spoke about the microaggressions she confronted while pursuing her engineering degree.[13] She recounted how fellow students called her a "Black bitch" and refused to sit with her or share resources and information, although they belonged to the same engineering program. A White female panelist at this same conference said that if women find themselves in hostile environments, such as the one described by the younger speaker, they should change settings.

But moving isn't so easy for all women. Girls, including girls of color, who have access to unlimited opportunities, official or unofficial peer mentors, experiences that stretch their understanding of possibilities, and constant reinforcement that they belong anywhere they want can probably do exactly what the second speaker recommended. However, changing locations to situate oneself in a more hospitable context not only is a privilege that only some possess but is a troubling individualist approach. COMPUGIRLS does not dismiss the significance of agency held by girls of color. Indeed, we spend considerable time engaging participants in activities in which they recognize their potential. But we spend as much effort guiding girls to critically recognize the limitations of their capacity that prevent them from doing certain activities, both as a girl and as a woman of color.

For some participants, their stories indicate how naming their impediments is the first and final stage of their empowerment. For others, the critical analysis initiates their journey toward greater activism. In all COMPUGIRLS instances, girls of color find their power by understanding how institutional constructs affect the formation and sustainability of coalitions. Digital media is one of many items used in this endeavor. As participants consider how they can collaborate with others to incite change, they uncover a critical lesson—that girlhoods of color do not occur in a vacuum.

COMPUGIRLS provides a context in which acceptance and activism assume different meanings from those commonly held. Acceptance does not necessarily mean agreement or compliance. Ideas of activism brought forth through a critical pedagogical approach by the adults in COMPUGIRLS may not be corroborated by the girls' views but provide critical information about ourselves as adults. How do girls of color react to our efforts? What is the process by which they reveal their reactions? What do their reactions tell us about their self-perceptions along the lines of race, ethnicity, tribal status, and other markers of their identities? What happens when they speak back to our efforts, for better or for worse? Documenting COMPUGIRLS participants' stories presents a unique opportunity to witness a complicated dance. Girls are both the choreographers and dancers on the COMPUGIRLS stage. Adults and the programs they create and implement need to be pliable, responding to the girls' contextualized movements. Their performances are not generalizable or necessarily representative of any one group. Context plays a critical role that attends to the often ignored point that there are a multitude of girlhoods of color. In this sense, COMPUGIRLS stands in direct opposition to the either/or binary.

Connectedness: Relationality and Context

Relationality within the COMPUGIRLS intersectional framework concerns connectedness and rejecting binaries. The either/or dichotomy has given program developers license to pigeonhole girls, whether as victim or antagonist. For victims, program developers can create a curriculum to move girls toward claiming a victor identity. For aggressors, program developers can focus their attention on fostering girls' ally-self. In neither case is there consideration of the multitude of other narratives girls of color construct. This book illustrates what happens within the space between the either/or. As a result, the COMPUGIRLS curriculum and its activities are not modeled around the idea of putting round pegs—namely the program participants—into a square hole. If we must use this metaphor, we recognize that the peg is more like a rhombicosidodecahedron—a shape with a multitude of faces, vertices, edges, and angles. Contextual variables, such as time, geography, skin complexion, tribal affiliation, and social class, to name a few, are what makes it impossible to create any one program for any one group. Even though this book contains complex stories from 2008 to 2010, COMPUGIRLS continues to challenge generalized efforts even today.

How an African American girl living in the Southwest navigates an after-school program might be far different from how her Native American counterpart in a nearby tribal community experiences the same curriculum. These two individuals may even travel through adolescence at the same rate, sharing the same age. Belonging to an economically stressed school may be an additional common point. They may both be categorized as coming from socioeconomically troubled families. Yet, how the girls come to understand their selves, their girlhoods, and each other will not necessarily be the same. COMPUGIRLS considers and celebrates these contextual elements of girlhoods of color while incorporating girls' standpoints.[14] This approach to context shapes and distinguishes our program's context in subtle ways.

Most coding programs focus on changing girls, not on altering the oppressive systems. For example, many programs that target minoritized youth emphasize the development of what Duckworth describes as grit (2016). Such efforts focus on nurturing the participants' abilities to endure a flawed system. In this sense, there is little push to facilitate girls' abilities to change the forthcoming hostile contexts shaping the cultures of technology companies, in particular.[15] Like astronauts, girls in such programs are taught how to put on a particular suit, navigate in that apparel, and endure conditions in which they were not meant to enter, survive, or thrive—namely technology companies, which continue to be anything but inclusive. COMPUGIRLS does not expect participants to become nimble in an inauthentic astronaut suit and endure harsh environments. We do not expect girls to resolve issues by removing themselves reluctantly and finding other jobs. Girls' stories are not about becoming members in the technology pipeline but about what it looks like being in the here and now of a social justice project-based program that emphasizes more than technical skills and self-awareness. The participants are the stars of COMPUGIRLS and of this book. The featured stories reveal the contours of girls' lives filled with production and reproduction of possibilities.

I include the narratives authored by the girls themselves for several reasons. First, all readers, including the girls who participated, can measure success. Second, the narratives provided snapshots of what the participants surmised about COMPUGIRLS at various points, variations in their outlook, and in some cases triggers that transported them into the new world that adults and participants were attempting to create. Third, narratives such as those contained here were reviewed by the girls and in the voice of the girls. This process helps researchers maintain openness and modesty: there is little wiggle room to inflate what has been accomplished by the girls themselves.

To Do and to Think: Critical Praxis
with Critical Inquiry

COMPUGIRLS demonstrates my attempt to merge knowing, referred to as critical inquiry within the intersectional frame, with doing—critical praxis. This is no easy task. It would have been far easier to develop a program that focused only on critical inquiry and encouraged participating girls of color to deconstruct community issues. This would be significant work and lead to broadening their knowledge of power and structural constraints. Specifically, they could understand how digital media is far from neutral and reflects the biases of its creators, who continue to be predominantly culturally insensitive White men. Alternately, COMPUGIRLS could simply encourage participants to become social justice warriors, using technology to challenge the status quo in radical ways. Again, this would result in more girls of color becoming change agents, actively driving social action. However, COMPUGIRLS weds the two constructs—knowing and doing—recognizing that they are critical principles of intersectionality.

This volume is about the standpoints or points of view of girls of color who are "crafting a synergy between critical inquiry and critical praxis" (Collins and Bilge 2016, 35). It reveals how COMPUGIRLS participants understand their praxes as critical endeavors and how their inquiries into social and community issues inform their praxis. Much like Ruth Nicole Brown's influential research in which she expands girlhood studies by deconstructing Black girlhood, this book explores girlhoods of color by illustrating the happenings at the nexus of doing and knowing. The difference between the works is that I focus on the implications of technology in a particular way.

COMPUGIRLS nurtures a space in which girls' everyday experiences are positioned as assets from which they can solve problems. This praxis perspective places technology and the general ideas of resistance work in the background. To this end, the stories shaping the forthcoming chapters are more than simple tales of resistance; they serve as exemplars of tensions and triumphs of self-discovery and actualization within this digital age. Concurrently, I maintain a heightened sensitivity to the assertion by Gonick and colleagues (2009) that some girlhood projects "expect/demand" girls to be fully self-actualized. How participants use digital media while creating themselves and claiming their girl-centered spaces assumes greater priority than the ultimate results of these practices. External knowledge of social inequality does not belittle the girls' communal understanding. We commemorate the girls' insider knowledge and illustrate how community members, particularly participants on the "rez," rely on others to further their curious minds and practical work. Hence, this book uses girls' stories to illustrate different forms of their engagement in community commitment and resistance.

What Exactly Is It?

COMPUGIRLS primarily relies on critical pedagogical theory, such as culturally responsive and relevant theory (Gay 2010; Ladson-Billings 2014) and resistance theory (Fine with Tuck and Yang 2013; Giroux 2012; Noguera, Ginwright, and Cammarota 2006; Tuck and Yang 2013), to create a distinctive context for participants. Offered as an out-of-school program, COMPUGIRLS hosts cohorts of forty adolescent girls (ages thirteen to eighteen) from economically challenged school districts to engage in six culturally responsive computing courses.[16] Each cohort begins in a six-week summer experience, frequenting a university's campus five days a week for a total of forty hours each week. Depending upon the context, after completing the summer program, girls have the opportunity to return to a twice-a-week fall and spring COMPUGIRLS program. The second year of the program follows the same rhythm as the first, with a summer through spring schedule. At the end of the second year, girls can apply to work in summer internships at local technology industries, nonprofits, or on-campus programs.[17] Bridging what the girls are learning to real-world events begins well before internships. Field trips to local technology industries and guest speakers from such organizations complement their experiences.

Girls learn an array of technical skills. On laptops, girls create video documentaries using GarageBand, Photoshop, and other digital platforms; games; simulations; and virtual worlds. Basic coding and computational thinking skills appear throughout the curriculum. For instance, during one session after the girls created video documentaries, a guest speaker conducted a half-day workshop on HTML so they could develop websites. Many uploaded their digital stories to the sites to publicize their projects. However, COMPUGIRLS makes clear that such tools are simply a means to an end. Learning how to identify, analyze, and present solutions to a community issue is the heart of the program. Technology is the platform on which to demonstrate girls' journeys through the process. Girls learn how to identify a community issue; pose a research question to explore the self-selected topic; read peer-reviewed and popular press articles; synthesize information from such sources; design a research project that may or may not include interviews, observations, and/or surveys; and analyze gathered data to suggest specific recommendations based on their results. Carefully selected and supported in-service teachers and graduate students serve as mentor teachers.

These adults are responsible for implementing the curriculum. Along the way, curricular activities include girls engaged in and reflecting on self.

When girls research a self-identified community issue, mentor teachers call attention to the ways they are becoming culturally responsive. While offering specific suggestions to resolve the topic of inquiry, we encourage them to problem-solve as change agents, individuals who can affect their communities. At the conclusion of each course, we empower girls to organize a closing ceremony so they can practice how to verbalize their community advancement proposals. Importantly, the curriculum requires group work at each meeting so girls can observe and experience the coalition that makes up COMPUGIRLS. In short, COMPUGIRLS is more than a girl-centered technology program.

As a program, COMPUGIRLS highlights contextualized girlhoods of color. Hence, neither the book nor the program focuses on where and when girls of color "arrive" as grown women. Rather, our efforts are more concentrated on what occurs along the way to womanhood. What elements, such as peer relationships and associations between adults and youth, influence the pathways during the navigation process? This is not a step-by-step recipe to create a girls-only program. This is not a description of a context without boys. Rather, this project centers on the stories of what occurs with and among girls of color at a particular time in their lives. By honing in on their lived realities, we see the way their girlhoods push back against the conventional myths of girls of color, and there are several falsehoods outlined throughout. The girl-centered stories that appear in this book illustrate the peer-generated process some girls of color cocreate while navigating a unique space.

Without careful attention to the complexities inherent in girls of color from economically stressed settings, their stories become either flat representations that appear on brochures or websites touting the success of a diversity program, or tales of girls who need to be saved because of some intrinsic deficiency. This book and the program attempt to display the tenuous balance between both of the above notions, shattering their universality with girls' voices. Authoring themselves, telling their stories and interpretations on their terms, as loudly or quietly as they like, does not follow a neat sequential process. The narratives that follow represent only a handful of the thousands of girls who engaged in some part of the program since its beginning.

Integral to this story is how a particular group of girls challenged and developed ideas of power, inequality, and contextualized selves as girls of color. This collection of inspiring narratives contains examples of success and failure, tension and ease, stereotypes and complex identities. Girls' lives may inspire some readers to reconsider how we see, research, and understand girls of color and their girlhoods in this age of technological inclusion efforts; they might frustrate other readers. Whatever the response, this is a story about love.

For those connected to COMPUGIRLS, and for the readers of this book, love shines as what bell hooks calls the "will to extend one's self for the purpose of nurturing one's own or another's spiritual growth." In the COMPUGIRLS context, love does not promote incremental change. Treating participants as a uniform group destined to obligingly assimilate into a flawed system is not an act of love. Instead, COMPUGIRLS and the subsequent pages represent the type of radical love requiring immediate and systemic transformation. Steps to love boldly begin with recognizing girlhoods of color as rich and robust experiences. To love any less powerfully—to ignore their voices, lives, interactions, and perceptions—stymies the growth of our daughters and limits our own schematic progress in this digital age.

CHAPTER ONE

COMPUGIRLS' Development

SOCIAL INEQUALITY, POWER, and social justice have served as guideposts in understanding (critical inquiry) and actively addressing (critical praxis) what was called the digital divide. In 2000, when discussions of how to provide access to technology for students from underserved communities dominated, COMPUGIRLS was not a concrete idea. Yet, the seeds that grew into the program were sown while I conducted a research study.

Driven to understand how the African American girls in one of the nation's most politicized districts were making sense of their lives, I designed a one-year research agenda that has become a lifelong program. The participating girls' standpoints, peer cultures, and understandings of self, others, and the world informed the initial program, called TLC (for Teaching, Learning, and Community), and its later incarnation as COMPUGIRLS.[1] Through it all, the girls who appear in the subsequent sections moved from being research participants to program developers. Their journeys manifest an understudied counter-story to images of disinterested, unaware adolescents. I honor their will and hopefulness. The majority of this chapter features the most notable characters from TLC. I begin with Candice, who, like the other stars in this section, illuminates her impact on COMPUGIRLS' development.

Candice

If we didn't meet in their classroom, I found space at my university for the ten to twelve eighth-grade girls, all African Americans, whose parents agreed they could participate in my research study. When the girls arrived, the university's drab room automatically transformed into a place of possibilities. Candice, tall and thin, was one of the first to light up the blue and gray setting. Her almost-black wavy hair was arranged, as always, in a tight bun at the back of her neck. With large brown eyes set upon an angular dark brown face and a neck resembling a swan's, elegant and long, Candice exuded such grace it would be fair to say she glided into a room rather than walked. Her typical brilliant smile, revealing perfectly placed white teeth, shone luminously. Quick to giggle, even when discussing serious topics, Candice was hungry for new ideas.

Throughout the two years we met together, she never raised her voice but made sure she punctuated each word, articulating the syllables to ensure her speech was clear. Candice loathed unanswered questions or any type of ambiguity. As I asked her and her peers to describe their experiences in their school district—the only one in this northeastern state that no longer was controlled locally but by the state education department—she served as my translator. All of her eighth-grade classmates appreciated her role and looked to her for guidance. I followed their lead. As a result, Candice and I cocreated a unique context in which girls tapped into their agency in unprecedented ways.

During the countless focus group discussions, when I posed complex questions, Candice was regularly the one to reword my queries and say, "She means how do we feel about this stuff." Her words served as a signal, causing the various shades of brown faces to look to me for unspoken confirmation that they could and should speak. "Well? Speak up!" Candice would say, and the free-flowing conversation would take off with very few pauses. Several weeks expired before girls ceased looking to me for permission to speak. At first, there was angst. "Ain't you gonna tell us to be quiet? You just gonna let us talk?!" exclaimed Candice's classmate Moesha. Candice would explain before I could, "As long as you don't talk over each other and answer, sure we can talk! She's not a teacher!"

In actuality, I had been an elementary school teacher. Girls met this fact with incredulity: "You can't be a real teacher, like the rest. You are a different kind of teacher." Perhaps realizing that I was "different" allowed me to pursue questions as to how the girls were making sense of the national attention paid to their district. Or perhaps my inability to fit their preconceived images could be attributed to my contextualized identities.

Even though the university was no more than a fifteen-minute car ride from their neighborhood, I was the first African American female researcher most had met. As a young assistant professor, untenured, I learned about the politics surrounding the areas through the girls and their parents. Granted, the media was rife with stories about the district and its inhabitants, but lessons learned from my recently completed dissertation remained in the forefront of my mind (Scott 1999). After spending years listening to six-year-old African American girls and then describing and analyzing their play patterns, I preferred establishing rapport with participants, gathering firsthand accounts, and working collaboratively on interpretations, no matter what their perceived capabilities. If a first-grade Black girl from an economically challenged district could articulately describe how she and her peers created a collaborative peer culture, I had confidence that the TLC adolescents could also speak their truths. I aspired to gain the necessary trust of Candice and her classmates to tell me about their experiences. And, like my dissertation work, I wanted to center the stories of the participants, as doing so reflected my commitment to accessing their standpoints.

Our interactions took place during a time when I was regularly mistaken as a college student. Although I was in my early thirties, I typically wore my hair in a ponytail and used minimal makeup. I preferred business casual clothes; pants and a top with flat shoes made up my general uniform. This attire was in direct opposition to most of the college students I observed. Never did I wear my sweatpants and sweatshirts or don a baseball cap while collecting data or interacting with participants. However, the young girls saw that I did not wear a business suit, apparel that to them symbolized maturity. Indeed, many of the school administrators questioned my age and ability due to my perceived youth.[2] My apparent youth, though, may have contributed to my ability to connect with Candice and her peers. Additionally, as the girls had already experienced a long history of institutionalized racism, low test scores, and increasing gang violence, they were accustomed to being the subjects of research studies. Our relationship, however, was not the typical dynamic often experienced between researcher and participant. The interactions between Candice and me symbolized an interpersonal connection that the girls lacked in most of their adult-student associations.

Candice did not look to me for affirmation or consent; moreover, her girlfriends came to understand that I relinquished my power to Candice, encouraging her to codirect our focus group discussions. I was the facilitator, taking notes and posing a few questions while providing girls the space to answer on their terms and in their way. What Candice and her peers accomplished was to own the space once they accepted adult (my) regulations. For them, ownership resulted in girls leading other girls, even if they did not demonstrate leadership qualities in other contexts. The emergent research project and its later offspring shaping this book—namely, COMPUGIRLS—encouraged the generation of a space in which girls govern themselves irrespective of their perceived abilities.

In the end, Candice embraced her leadership role, and girls willingly and happily attended our after-school meetings. "We don't mind stayin' after school with you. It's kinda like fun. I like helping you too," I heard. Even though we met at their school in an unoccupied first-floor classroom, girls did not code our gatherings as school-related. The physical space held little significance. Girls did not recognize the Formica desks, plastic chairs placed in rows, nearly bare walls, chalkboards, and the few examples of students' work scattered around the room as school-related artifacts. They blocked out where we met, preferring to focus on what occurred during our meetings. No longer was "staying after" seen as the consequence of inappropriate behavior. Meeting with "the doctor" who belonged to the same racial and gender category as the girls became a club rather than a research project. And the Saturday morning event in my university's room was the pivotal point during which we institutionalized our meetings for decades to come.

Donetta

For many reasons, Donetta would be considered the polar opposite of Candice. Much shorter than Candice, Donetta contained her tightly curled dark brown hair in large braids rooted close to her scalp. She typically adorned her broad frame in sweatpants and hoodies that did not necessarily match in color or texture. Small gold earrings rarely left her pierced ears and represented the only visible jewelry against her dark brown skin. During the two years Donetta attended our sessions, her physique filled out, causing her to look at least three to four years older than her chronological age. Not one to pay careful attention to her speech or its volume, her voice often boomed, causing others to believe she was angry.

In school, teachers labeled Donetta a "problem." Often caught in physical fights with girls and boys alike, teachers described her as "angry, always mouthing off to someone. She's fast." When asked to explain "fast," the adult perception of Donetta revealed an all-too-pervasive image used to describe many Black girls:[3] "You know, she's just too grown. Always getting into trouble. She just knows too much about too many things like boys and stuff." Donetta's comments during our multiple exchanges did not reveal a great sense of maturity. In fact, she resented growing up and led a discussion of "I don't want to be grown. I'm still a girl." During her after-school time with me, she, too, became a peer leader. Unlike Candice, however, Donetta's tactics tended to reveal unspoken "truths" that led girls to strengthen their bonds with each other.

"I'm just sayin' teachers in this school need to be better. They are stupid and don't teach us nothing," Donetta explained. Her angry voice entered the room before her physical body; she had spent the better part of our club time sitting with a teacher because "she said I got up in her face!"

Candice accepted Donetta's complaint but met it with an interesting challenge. "Yeah, but you're always getting into trouble. If you didn't act up, you could learn, and we wouldn't be disturbed and could learn without the teacher yelling at you," Candice countered.

"I want to learn too! They just don't know how to teach! And I'm not stopping you or nobody from learning. You can do what you want!" came Donetta's exasperated response.

Candice continued to push Donetta, asking her to explain her actions, as they seemed counterproductive. "But, why do you act up like that? I mean, it's like you purposely act up, talkin' back to the teacher. Why don't you just ask one of us for help?" Candice looked at the other five girls sitting around the table watching this scene unfold.

Bethany, who was uncharacteristically silent, chimed in. "You know we would help you, Donetta. All you gotta do is ask us. Ain't no shame in getting help. We're all trying to get to the same place."

At this Donetta seemed to quiet down, bowing her head to hide the tears welling in her eyes. Donetta's usual bravado lessened; her voice lowered. "But y'all make fun of me when I read. I mean I can't read." This was interrupted with "We do not! Anyone here make fun of Donetta? NO! And we won't. You can come to any one of us, even in this space, and we can work with you! We will work with you! We can do stuff together or maybe sit next to you and help with the answer. Right?" This encourager looked at her peers for affirmation, and the girls agreed to serve as Donetta's support unit and to help her with her reading. And from that point forward, they began to recognize and value Donetta's assets: "Girl, you are good at math! You explain things to us that the teacher cannot! You need to show us how you got that answer." As a result, Donetta gained assistance in her reading while maintaining her position as math expert. One of the many results was that Donetta became a peer advocate.

About a month after the above incident, I noticed that Donetta was less concerned with herself, feeling that the world—at least her peer world—was not against her. Instead, she took an active interest in how other girls were doing, asking, "You good?" and listening intently to the answer. And if the response to her question was no, she would rally the other girls' attention: "Hey, Shaundra has a problem, yo. Listen up." At this, Donetta would become the facilitator and guide the group to solve Shaundra's issue. In the classroom setting, however, Donetta did not possess that same power.

Inspired by the shift in her after-school behavior, I entered Mrs. Bard's class another month after the noted change in Donetta. I felt hesitant standing at the door of thirty-two eighth graders. My reluctance was due to the evident frustration and fatigue on Mrs. Bard's face. Having been a classroom teacher, I understood how outsiders blamed teachers for students' performance. A visitor, no matter how seemingly kind, reminded the instructor of the severe scrutiny they were under. No Child Left Behind was gaining traction at the time, and with this initiative, high-stakes testing became the supposed best barometer for gauging student success. Teachers were the individuals believed to be fully responsible for student achievement. Family,[4] community members, and peers were rarely considered positive influencers. Thus, I did not take offense to Mrs. Bard's nonverbal expression but wanted to respect her obvious battle-weary response while also exploring how Donetta navigated a context in which adults held a much different opinion of her.

"I was hoping to observe, but if it is a bad time . . .," I said, and Mrs. Bard graciously insisted, with a great degree of listlessness in her voice, "Oh, come on in. I haven't gotten a chance to get you a chair, but come on." Donetta was sitting at her desk with a nail polish bottle prominently displayed. At least twice within five minutes she took out a hairbrush, though her braided hair did not require this tool. The room was completely quiet as the other students were presumably reading the assigned text.

Donetta caught my eye, but before she could acknowledge me Mrs. Bard broke the silence: "Is there a reason why you are doing nothing, Donetta?"

Seemingly annoyed at this accusation, Donetta explained, "I did my homework."

This response did not assuage Mrs. Bard. "Clear off your desk. Put everything away. Your Winnie-the-Pooh diary, the blue book, perfume, nail polish, notebook. Everything!" Donetta did not move. Her inertia caused Mrs. Bard to lay out the consequences: "If you can't clear off your desk, then I'll take everything and put it on my desk." This matter-of-fact statement encouraged Donetta to make some movement. Unfortunately, her efforts were insufficient for Mrs. Bard. "Not on your lap. Put it in your desk."

"But that's my homework!" Donetta exclaimed. At the same time, she moved a crumpled piece of paper and her math book, which had been on her lap, to her desk. The nail polish remained in its place.

That afternoon Donetta skipped into our club, beaming like never before. A bit surprised by her happiness, I asked if she saw me in her class that day. "Oh, yes. I did seen you. Did you see how she treats me? Glad we got our club!" Then she sat next to Bethany to join in the conversation of the day.

Observing Donetta's classroom experience inspired me to create a program in which girls could establish a counter-narrative that need not align with what happened a few hours earlier. Donetta's two performances—one as an angry, disobedient Black girl who could be controlled only through harsh words,[5] and one as a peer advocate willing to support her classmates at her own expense—reflected the complexities of these girls' lives. Equally important, the multifaceted nature of navigating a context in which they were stripped of power and voice inspired me to create COMPUGIRLS as a safe space—a setting where girls could be something other than the identities performed during the day, at home, or with non-school peers. Girls like Donetta and Candice are many different types of girls, depending upon the context. To assume that these youngsters' performances in any one space encapsulate their entire selves limits adults' understanding of the depths of their lives. Henceforth, describing girls such as Donetta as "under-anticipated" makes sense. However, many classroom teachers are unable to create the type of settings girls need to develop their various present or future identities.

Bethany

Bethany, mentioned above, was the most future-oriented of all the girls in the initial TLC program. Her glossy, dark brown hair was always straightened into a perfect bob. Honey brown in color, she loved to smile, exposing a mouthful of braces. Comfortably dressed in jeans and various T-shirts, she carried herself like an "old soul," demonstrating wisdom far beyond her years. Bethany did not move quickly or gracefully but with purpose, as if she had several meetings to attend but was too proud to run toward any of them. At times, she provided thoughtful commentary and encouraged girls to "think about what you gonna do in the future. Don't think only about today because we got to answer to the future. I'm going to Howard University and become a doctor." And when her friends demanded that she explain how Howard is a historically Black university, their eyes lit up, learning this new information.

Candice queried, "You mean it's like our district? All Black?"

Bethany slightly smiled but gently corrected Candice: "Sorta, but it's better. You got to be accepted to go there. Really famous people from our race went there. The teachers want you to do good."

Donetta was not entirely convinced. "Who do you know who went?"

A bit shocked at Donetta's skepticism, Bethany responded, "What do you think?! People in my family went!" at which both girls giggled.

For the next few minutes, girls peppered Bethany with other questions about life at Howard, why she thought she wanted to attend, and how they too could get accepted. Patiently, Bethany answered all of their questions and admitted when she did not know the answer. "I don't know how you get in, but good grades probably." Over and over, Bethany suggested to the girls that the university was a place where they belonged and would be accepted: "They want us to come." Given the political turmoil of this district, Bethany's insistence that there was indeed a welcoming system for herself and her peers convinced the girls that there was at least one institution where they could belong.

A year after I met this group, discussions of their school district disbanding took place in the community. Girls held clear opinions about the tentative plan of them attending nearby, more affluent schools: they had no interest in leaving their current district.[6] The lack of "good teachers" and critical learning activities at their current school were secondary to the sense of belonging they felt. Academic success, in the traditional sense, assumed a backseat position to the social space that would allow them to narrate their assets, value their developing consciousness, and connect so all could move forward toward a future of success. Our club represented the potential of what could emerge once the opportunity presented itself.

Elected to Continue the Conversation

After nearly an entire academic year of club meetings, I wanted to present my findings and interpretations in order to gain feedback from the participating girls and their parents. I sent an invitation to the girls' school district administrators and teachers, yet none of these individuals attended. Instead, for twenty minutes on a Saturday morning, I presented my interpretations of observations and informal interviews to the girls and their mothers. After my monologue, I requested the female-only audience to divide into groups. Each was charged to discuss my presentation. At the end of the group discussions, speakers from each collective reported on points with which they agreed or not. Once all the group representatives spoke, Bethany's mother stood up.

Without hesitation, she said, "We think this was great! We have never before gotten together like this. I mean to really talk about things. And what was also great is we got to talk with our girls and hear what they are thinking and what their friends are thinking. We want to do more of this, and we want you to organize us." It was at that moment that we as Black girls and women decided to create a program that foregrounded elements of standpoint theory. This was more than me merging their experiences on an individual level into an academic outlet, such as a peer-reviewed paper. This was when we as women of color accepted and sought to foster our power as creators of knowledge. Personally, I felt a moral obligation to continue my service as a convener. Although new to my junior professor position, the geographic area, and the institutional requirements that would determine whether I earned tenure and promotion years later, I, like many women of color researchers, could not walk away from the girls, their community, or the families. They were more than research objects.

A few years after this meeting, Eve Tuck published an important essay, "Suspending Damage: A Letter to Communities," that articulates why I chose to accept the challenge put forth to me during that Saturday morning meeting with the girls and their mothers. Although I did not have the language Tuck so beautifully uses to describe what most researchers do when working with communities of color, my soul ached to avoid what she calls "damaged-centered research," described as "research that operates, even benevolently, from a theory of change that establishes harm or injury in order to achieve reparation" (2009, 413). I shared the community's desire to avoid pathologizing the girls' experiences in order to improve the school system. We all wanted the schools to do better and to be better for the students but not at the expense of furthering the image that the youngsters were damaged beings. Instead, and unbeknownst to me, I chose to accept the challenge with the intent of implementing a "desire-based research project." As heads nodded in agreement with the recommendation of future gatherings, a program began to form as well as my research agenda to document "not only the painful elements of social realities but also the wisdom and hope" (416).

The initial response to the request included me drawing on my university resources and developing a three-pronged initiative titled Teaching, Learning, and Community: TLC. Parents attended workshops about their rights in a state-operated district, their daughters learned how to make a digital magazine called an "e-zine," and undergraduate female students of color hosted mentoring events for the girls to discuss college life. Woven throughout the three strands was an emphasis on dialogue and building the type of coalition Gloria Anzaldúa describes as work that "attempts to balance power relations and undermine and subvert the system of domination-subordination that affects even our most unconscious thoughts" (1990, 224–25).[7]

Lessons Learned from TLC

Both the TLC girls and I learned valuable lessons that many teachers and researchers continue to miss when interacting and studying girls of color in high conflict areas. Though the setting was highly politicized, the girls possessed the power to support each other. Over time, they accepted the right to direct and hold each other accountable. It was a relief to many of them that their community contained peers who wanted them to succeed, even when their public performance suggested a desire to fail. The narratives of disaster and discontent occupying the popular media about this district did not define the girls' agency. From these early observations, the significance of documenting the girls' capacity revealed "the character of relations that are sustained by girls' identity practices while affirming the possibilities these practices embody for social change" (Currie, Kelly, and Pomerantz 2009, 182). Our club demonstrated that agency involves how girls negotiate various discourses such as activism, femininity, engagement, and (re)creating their selves.

For weeks to come after the watershed Saturday meeting, our once-a-week TLC conversations created a context that was facilitated by me as the researcher but led by the girls. All of the girls learned to respect each other's contributions, recognizing others' situated knowledge.[8] Space was made by the girls for their subjectivities, as this was a context in which the criteria for being heard greatly differed from typical classroom environments.[9] Moments emerged in which the girls felt comfortable, indeed encouraged, to present what they knew. Sharing information with the group, such as the existence of a historically Black university, became a regular occurrence and was seen as a way to inspire each person to tap into her reservoir of knowledge. Knowledge became a shared construct, not meant to be hidden or kept for an individual's self-aggrandizement. To this end, all girls, no matter what they did or did not do in the traditional classroom space, were perceived as possessing assets.

The girls believed that other settings did not exclusively define who they were or would become. They could be ostracized by a teacher, might struggle with reading, or could be coded as "fast" but knew our club provided new ground for self-definition. It was through their connectedness that one could become a cultural translator like Candice, a math expert like Donetta, or a futurist like Bethany. This did not mean that they were unaware of constraints. But being conscious of the deficiencies in their classrooms and schools did not persuade them to leave these spaces. The girls identified issues as part of the system rather than as their fault. Unlike so many approaches and ideologies, these girls did not see their peers, families, or selves inherently lacking anything except a system to provide them opportunities or the necessary resources for success. Our afternoon gatherings reminded the participants that once given the space, they were more than able to command it in positive ways.

Providing girls a context to foster a peer culture in which recognizing their assets; cultivating a connectedness built on reflection, accountability, and a willingness to share their situated knowledge; and activating one's agency is not typical of most classrooms. The absence of such settings does not mean they should not and could not exist. Thus, five years after that Saturday morning meeting, thousands of miles from that particular university space, and hundreds of hours of watching the TLC program unfold, the first COMPUGIRLS program took place.

From TLC to COMPUGIRLS

One year before our nation elected its first African American president—who also was the first person in this role to write a line of code—COMPUGIRLS' inaugural cohort convened. It was the summer of 2007. As temperatures rose to 120 degrees Fahrenheit, the initial forty COMPUGIRLS participants gathered at my new university's downtown campus, located in Arizona. Brochures and e-mails sent to potential surrounding districts created a buzz that resulted in a host of questions: Is this a coding program? Social justice initiative? Technology camp? Do we allow only non-Whites to participate, discriminating against White girls? Aren't we setting the participants up for failure by offering a single-sex environment, which is a far cry from reality?

COMPUGIRLS stories provide answers to some of these questions but also demonstrate the need to challenge such interrogatives. Why shouldn't girls from underrepresented areas have access to programs that are more than just coding? Why are social justice and coding typically divorced concepts? Isn't White a color? And, most importantly, is it enough to provide girls from under-resourced areas technical skills—namely coding—that research has demonstrated will do little other than place them in low-level careers?

Girls like Candice and Bethany do not need motivation to excel because they already possess it. And the Donettas in the world require more opportunities to recognize and access their assets and build upon them. In short, girls marginalized by contexts underserved by the educational, political, and social systems have the right to the resources and opportunities to acquire the competencies for success. Importantly, aptitudes can be nurtured through intentional strategies carried forth by a multitude of adults willing and able to see girls' potential in ways that cannot always be measured by numbers. And skills entail much more than writing a line of code or even solving one problem.

COMPUGIRLS' First Cohort

During the summer of 2007, I met Montserrat, one of the first COMPUGIRLS participants. A small, light-skinned Latina with long brown hair and an incredibly quiet demeanor, Montserrat barely talked after joining COMPUGIRLS. Painfully shy, she avoided public speaking as much as she could. Years later, after completing COMPUGIRLS' two-year program and working with me as an undergraduate research assistant, she explained during an on-camera interview how she came to the program:

One day in my school, I had to get up and give a presentation, and I cried. I was physically shaken. I could not say anything. I had my paper in my hand, but I could not do it. When I sat back in my seat after that horrible experience, I vowed never to do that again. I heard about this computer program for girls and thought, "Why not?" It sounded cool. . . . When we got here and [I] met everyone, I was transformed. The words "techno-social change agent" don't roll off my lips very easy, but . . . that is what the program is trying to get us to be. Girls who know the technology but more importantly want to know how to make change.[10] We know how to study a problem and make a difference in our community. That is what we learned in COMPUGIRLS, how to work together. The program teaches you how to think, to speak up, and use technology in ways our schools cannot. . . . I know how to program, debug, and build in a virtual world. But I also know how to teach other girls to speak up, to not be afraid, to help each other, and fix a problem. Those are really important skills.

When asked to create a diagram reflecting her retrospective analysis of the six-course program, Montserrat submitted the following figure:

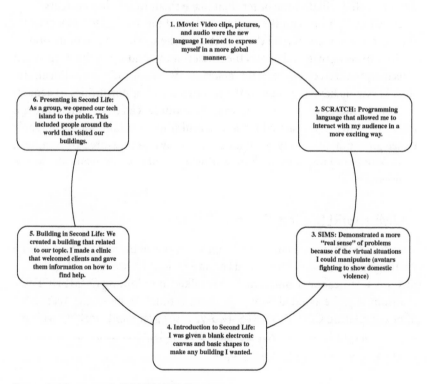

Figure 1. Montserrat's COMPUGIRLS courses

Although she was not privy to the table we later used for marketing purposes, her visual adeptly captures COMPUGIRLS' soul and assisted us in crafting the following:

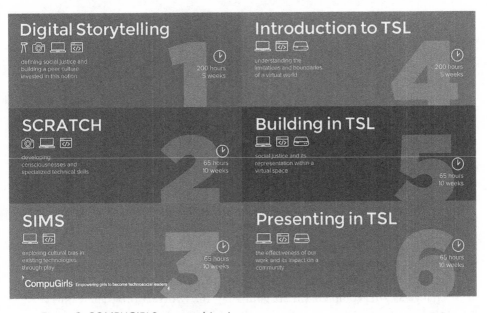

Figure 2. COMPUGIRLS course objectives

The individual lessons for each course follow a similar pattern. A sample lesson from Course IV appears in an article in which Patricia Garcia and I point out that COMPUGIRLS lessons do not chart the path of traditional school classrooms and are far less focused on girls getting the "correct" answer. Our intent is to provide activities that encourage participants to challenge the existing avenues for virtual representation. By the end of the lesson, the participants are able to (1) view technologies as changeable and socially shaped artifacts developed by designers, (2) question the limited representations available in virtual worlds through a discussion of how they view themselves versus how they are represented in online spaces, and (3) disrupt the status quo perception of themselves by working together to redesign the existing modes of avatar creation in virtual worlds through a technology mockup (2016, 74).[11]

Candice, Donetta, Bethany, Montserrat—even though they navigated vastly different spaces, their experiences provided the groundwork that co-constructed COMPUGIRLS.

CHAPTER TWO

COMPUGIRLS' Emergence

HONOR SOCIETY MEMBERS, truants, athletes, and pregnant teens: these are some of the labels affixed to COMPUGIRLS participants. At times, the girls embrace these identities as if they are the only possibilities for them; at other moments, they challenge them and construct more complex descriptors. These decisions about claiming their identities are not static but change as girls complete the six courses of the two-year program. Context plays an integral role as well. COMPUGIRLS participants on the "rez"—meaning those Native American[1] girls who identify as a member of a local Indigenous community—see themselves as different from the Latina and African American girls navigating the nearby urban districts. Differences within groups present another layer of complexity, such as when Ana and Angelica both self-identified as Latina, attended the same high-needs school, and frequented the COMPUGIRLS university-based campus, but Ana was a self-proclaimed activist while Angelica was a budding engineer seeking to cause community change by designing solutions.

Labels are limiting and promote stereotypic views of girls, inhibiting examination of how girls in some of the most under-resourced areas are not defined by their contexts. High-need schools are not exclusively populated with disaffected, uninterested students. There is no doubt that the structural barriers often caused by economically stressed systems present students with challenges that, all too often, lead to truancy, teen pregnancy, and other behaviors that can dampen their ultimate achievements. And certainly, economic challenges can cause undue stress on students: "Nationwide, the typical black student is now in a school where almost two out of every three classmates (64%) are low-income, nearly double the level in schools of the typical white or Asian student (37% and 39%, respectively). The typical Latino student in the region attends a school where less than a quarter of their classmates are white; nearly two-thirds are other Latinos; and two-thirds are poor" (Orfield, Kucsera, and Siegel-Hawley 2012, 7). However, we do not assume that such settings are bereft of students who want opportunities and access to resources that can lead to success. It is within such spaces that many students simply lack experiences that encourage the necessary technical and power skills[2] required for success in the twenty-first century. Hence, the COMPUGIRLS program strategically attends to both the technical skills (such as coding, digital storytelling, creating a virtual world) and power skills (such as critical thinking, persuasive argumentation, team building, presentation) in an attempt to build girls' capacities to become techno-social change agents.

This chapter illustrates how various COMPUGIRLS participants created their programmatic lives within our curriculum. Importantly, not all participants bought into our focus on the technical and power skills. How COMPUGIRLS themselves dealt with those who did not follow the primary co-constructed rules will be revealed. In the end, this chapter outlines the significant pieces of the program that emphasize how important, or not, issues of reflection, connectedness, and asset building appear in certain girlhoods over time.

Why Join COMPUGIRLS?

During the spring of 2007, I stood before more than forty high school sophomores to recruit for COMPUGIRLS' first cohort. Girls representing various races, ethnicities, skin colors, and hair textures turned their gaze to me. "Why are we here again?" one light-skinned African American girl with long curly hair whispered loudly to her even lighter-skinned neighbor. The White girl on her other side watched and waited to hear a response. "Girls—and we are all girls in here, right?" the female teacher asked. Without waiting for an answer, she continued, "We have Dr. Scott here who wants to talk to us about a program at her university for girls like you, COMPUGIRLS. She is talking to all the girls in this school because she wants to know if you would be interested in attending. Dr. Scott?"

Over the next ten minutes, I explained how I was the founder but worked with a bunch of really smart professors to create this program based on what I had learned at my other academic job. Rather than repeat the programmatic goals verbatim, I paraphrased to the group how we specifically constructed COMPUGIRLS to ensure that girls from areas that have fewer resources get an opportunity to develop their ability to become innovators, to think more deeply and critically, to solve a community problem, and to have fun with other girls while learning amazing new skills.

Although I admitted to having been a classroom teacher, I impressed upon the avid listeners that the program would not be like school; there would not be any grades or tests. And even though there was an application, acceptance was not based on grades. "Wait, you mean anyone can apply? Even if you don't do good in school?" asked the lighter-skinned girl. I explained that we were not interested in grades and would not request a transcript but were looking for girls who really wanted to be challenged and to learn something new. The program was free, it would begin in the summer and last for five weeks, and it would go on for two years. Participants would be given bus passes if needed and lunch and would get to borrow a laptop. At the end of the program, they would obtain gift cards based on attendance and completion of their projects. "Are we making robots or something? Do we keep the laptops?" These inquiries, which I answered with a quick no, were far less interesting to the girls than learning that the program was only for girls. This revelation caused the listeners to begin murmuring to each other and wiggle with excitement about the prospect of attending. This realization also resulted in a barrage of inquiries regarding the boundaries of this program and which girls were invited to occupy this space.

"So, no boys, right? They're going to be mad!" "I like it, no boys! We can do what we want?" As I explained that a girls-only space did not mean an unstructured context, that we had a curriculum to follow, I learned that this description was too foreign for them to grasp or fully believe. This particular school, like many in which I conducted these recruitment sessions, was typical of a high-needs high school—predominantly occupied by African American and Latinx kids whose parents believed the education system would set them up for success.

Success, as Montserrat from chapter 1 explained, was "finishing high school, getting a job, and helping my parents. I mean, they were immigrants—my father did not even finish middle school—but we had a house and one car. They were doing fine, so I thought that was all I needed to do." Granted, she did not make this statement until years later while working on the COMPUGIRLS project as a researcher and becoming a first-generation college student, but for her, a program housed on a local university campus challenged girls to think beyond high school and their immediate communities. What was most intriguing to the earlier cohorts was what a girls-only space could become. Little did the participants know that it was their job to cocreate the space with each other and us facilitators.

After a few weeks post-admittance, participants cherished the girl-centered space, believing that the inclusion of boys would change the rhythm drastically. Years after that first recruitment session, we began asking participants, after completing at least one course, to describe their concern if COMPUGIRLS became Compukids.[3] One girl explained: "They [boys] would yell out things like 'girls don't work hard enough,' [and] I don't think they'd agree with what we were saying. If boys were here, the conversations would be very different; they want to focus on why men catcall and stuff like that. I think the topics we are doing would be different; they would be offended; they might make offensive comments about our videos, etc. I think it would be hard for boys to come in; the issues we talk about would be different." Another respondent indicated, "We're with a group of girls; boys would not be uncomfortable, only disruptive. This is really about girls being very able to learn from each other. I think it would be very different; they would talk against us and they don't respect our opinions. Engineering is mostly boys, so they couldn't understand feeling left out." At the same time, a few girls from the identical cohort expressed a different opinion, believing boys' inclusion would certainly make the experience "different" but "it would be fun; there would be a competitive edge."

The out-of-school space provides an opportunity to maintain a girls-only context and explore its impact without many of the inherent constraints of schools. In the main, COMPUGIRLS protected the girls' space against any perceived threat that would make it "unsafe." Participants cherished being with all girls—a theme that will be explored in greater detail in subsequent chapters—because they could define themselves without fear of exclusion or recrimination. This does not mean that the peer system that COMPUGIRLS created was flat, devoid of certain skills being valued more than others. There was discord among the girls and hurt feelings. They corrected each other, called attention to issues, and ceased following the curriculum if social issues emerged. They would disrupt the flow of instruction and peer activities if they believed an individual was not positively contributing to the girl-centered norms. It was believed that boys would, perhaps unknowingly, not allow girls to be themselves or to define their selves, peer rules, and regulations on their terms.

In the girls' minds, the absence of boys allowed participants to lead, be quiet, talk, fail, bond, and empower each other without worrying about what boys would do or think. The average COMPUGIRLS participant is an adolescent of fourteen years old, and such concerns are typical of most girls in this age group. Occupying a girls-only space was powerful; occupying one that was populated by African American, Native American, and/or Latina girls afforded them, and some members of the higher education community, unanticipated lessons that opposed taken-for-granted narratives about race, gender, ethnicity, and social class. I dare say that my own positionality, as the Black female founder, may have contributed to the cultural norms. Although I never discussed with the girls their perceptions of my Black femaleness and its influence on their setting, they did reveal their delight with me being in charge, expressed verbally (as with, "We like it when you come in") or nonverbally through grins or waves. The more acquainted I became with my new geographic context, the more I realized my anomalous position.

Between 2005 and 2007, the American Community Survey reported that Arizona's African American population hovered around 3 percent. And since fewer Black women live in Arizona than Black men,[4] many students, as well as adults, had limited encounters with women who looked like me. Coming from an area and a family where Black women worked multiple jobs, I found this perplexing. This made my COMPUGIRLS work more valuable. I wanted the participants and their parents to broaden their understanding of the complex lives Black women lead. I wanted them to see that Black women could work and concurrently engage in community advancement. I wanted to model desire-centered research and give myself to the girls as a subject of inquiry. In this unique context and within this framework, I wanted to make myself open to COMPUGIRLS participants as a complex being, filled with contradiction and self-determination that exceeded unidimensional notions of Black femaleness.

As that initial recruitment session continued, the White girl who had been silent up until that point raised her hand to ask, "Can White girls attend?" I did not hesitate in stating that all girls in the room had the opportunity to join COMPUGIRLS. Her question, however, made sense, given the earlier marketing material we used.

Our website, brochures, and flyers all stated that this was a program for "girls of color." In most people's minds, those words equated to African Americans, Latinas, and Native Americans with little to no attention to Asian Americans, Native Hawaiians, or Pacific Islanders. Periodically, I would receive an e-mail about "reverse discrimination" when the correspondent assumed White girls could not attend. Consequently, the student's question was not a surprise. What was more alarming was the way interested or critical individuals understood—or thought they understood—why we used this language. Much later on, when the program received a sizable grant, lawyers representing the funding agency also asked, "What will you do if White girls want to join? Will you not allow this?" My response did not assuage this concern: "Of course not. We will not disallow any girl to attend, but White is a color, so when we say girls of color we mean all girls." Interestingly, parents never expressed these worries.

At the same time, no one questioned whether nonbinary students could join. Granted, the absence of this consideration may have been due, in fact, to the times. In the United States, there was no legal recognition of "nonbinary" as part of the gender spectrum until almost a decade after the first COMPUGIRLS cohort.[5] References to being cisgender were far from ubiquitous in the year 2007 when I was recruiting. Nevertheless, concerns as to whom COMPUGIRLS accepted or did not accept tended to come from teachers, all of whom identified as male, or from adults wanting to ensure a particular law was not broken. In fact, the parents of the White girls who did attend never seemed uncomfortable with our collateral or the fact that their daughters were in a predominantly non-White context. Whether in agreement or not with our using the term "girls of color," some administrators eagerly sought to partner with us.

A number of school administrators agreed to collaborate with the program quite readily because they had been in my graduate level courses as students. These individuals understood that equity and equality are not the same, meaning disenfranchised communities may need greater access to opportunities than more affluent ones in order for both groups to have equal chances at success. As a professor of school administrators, I also pushed the adult students to expand their definition of success. High-stakes test scores may dupe us into believing that they are the best indicators of student knowledge and teachers' abilities to teach, but I regularly challenged this notion. Although it took several weeks of class discussions, including considerations of the biased history of standardized testing, stereotype threat, and how other contexts (such as those informed by the Reggio Emilia approach) formed innovative systems to assess student progress, most graduate students came to understand my theories-in-use. These claimed that the experiences of girls of color were different from those of White girls and could not be essentialized with static meanings or definitions representative of all girls, regardless of their identity group, and free from any temporal or spatial context.[6] Both time and place make a difference, as does how a particular setting values certain features while considering others with disfavor.

For the most part, the negative e-mails came at a time when labeling a program based on race or gender was far from popular. There was no Black Girls Code or Girls Who Code. Society was still suffering from the misconception that all the diversity efforts from the 1980s were successful. Affirmative action had worked, correct? Weren't there more African American and

Latina women going to and graduating from college than ever before?[7] These presumptions of progress have conflated the ideas of diversity and inclusion while ignoring how power works, particularly for girls of color. An intersectional analysis reminds us that power is about relationships.[8] Race and gender are only two features that constitute our experiences and our selves. How a social context uses these and other elements depends on a multitude of factors, not the least of which includes social class, skin complexion, and ethnicity.

There should be no shame in calling out one's race and gender, even though these two categories alone do not represent any individual's entire existence, achievements, failures, or relationships. In the abstract, girls should be proud of themselves. Yet, African American, Latina, and Native American girls learn very quickly that their race and ethnicities should be hidden, as they are markers of perceived inferiority. COMPUGIRLS teaches that it is not one's features alone—one's race, gender, or ethnicity—but how structures such as digital media render these and other characteristics as signals that warrants subjugation. COMPUGIRLS participants learn that it is not their belonging to a particular racial or gender category that makes them not achieve but how a power structure uses race or gender to institutionalize practices that position some individuals as less-than. This program provides girls a series of opportunities to recognize this distinction and enhance their abilities to engage in intersectionality as critical praxis. To collectively be engaged in this process builds a coalition among girls who refuse to allow a single unit of analysis, such as race or gender, to impede their progress or define who they want to and can become.

Belonging to a program that highlights some features that others thought should be ignored caused many participants to feel connected. Ironically, the categories the e-mail senders believed would lead to exclusion actually encouraged girls to cross boundaries to develop relationships with each other. Joining COMPUGIRLS was not a recognized political move made by the girls to protest any one concept or an attempt to build a disruptive group of Black and Brown bodies (although it was threatening to some observers to see girls assemble in one space). Girls saw the program as a unique opportunity to establish innovative alliances while learning skills the school administrators knew were important but lacked the resources to provide. Girls knew computers were "cool" but were more intrigued by the possibility of being in a space so unlike that which school afforded. A space that was off-campus, was girls-only, provided computers, and unapologetically called attention to characteristics some educators willed invisible made for an attractive mix of ingredients, even for White girls like Kelly.

Light brown freckles peppered her long face; her straight brown hair fell to her shoulders. Kelly entered COMPUGIRLS because Montserrat convinced her that they should do it together: "I said to Kelly when the teacher announced the flyer in our class that we should do it. We had been friends for a long time, it was our freshman year, and we thought, Why not." Yet, once in the program, Kelly and Montserrat barely interacted. The following dynamic between the two became the norm.

During the initial small group work in which five girls sat with their mentor teacher discussing what they had accomplished since their last meeting, what they hoped to do that day, and who should present to the whole group of forty the answers to these reflective questions, Kelly's group remained in the front of the class while Montserrat's occupied the highest level of the room's stadium seating. Kelly always listened pensively during these exchanges with a placid look that would trick an adult into thinking she was bored. Never interrupting any of the speakers, she was one to summarize their words, checking on her own understanding: "So, are you saying that you looked up the peer-reviewed articles on our topic and found three we could use?" Efforts girls made to identify supportive research material were of particular interest to Kelly.

Each group was obliged to pinpoint an agreed-upon social or community topic and propose ways to research the subject. Kelly took delight in thinking and sharing with her group mates "cool ways we can look into sexual harassment. I mean, we should look at statistics and do our own survey—not, like, a lot of people would admit to being harassed, but if we word it right, maybe stand somewhere in school and ask people anonymously, we could get some important information." For Kelly, accessing information from people was incredibly important, as she, like other participants, came to see individuals' perspectives, their standpoints, as more reliable than studies conducted by others who came from outside the community under investigation. Quick surveys or longer interviews with individuals became her preferred means of delving into a subject. These potential interviewees possessed assets—valuable inside information—and Kelly saw it as her responsibility to build a relationship with them and with fellow COMPUGIRLS participants to gain access to their perspectives.

For Kelly, identifying solutions to the topic was not only a curriculum requirement but an obligation to reveal the truth of a subject. Success hinged on engaging in this practice with others. And within the two years she participated in the program, she never revealed any discomfort engaging in this work as the only White girl in her cohort. It was more important to complete the project well, coauthoring their work and lifting each one up, than to focus on her Whiteness. In fact, the only time Kelly talked about her racial identity was when she agreed to work with the girls on the reservation, which will be discussed in chapter 5. In fact, working across racial lines was more of a new phenomenon for the Latina and African American girls.

Around the second week of the program, after eighty hours of interaction, the girls were much more comfortable with each other. As they looked more closely into their topics, mentor teachers—the trained adults responsible for direct instruction—spent considerable time balancing the technical lessons with discussions of equity and equality. For instance, when girls learned how technology could be used to darken models' skin tones and began experimenting with this technique, the adults led a conversation as to who would benefit from these acts and who would be placed at a disadvantage.

Malia, one of the few African Americans in her cohort, spoke first: "I mean, why wouldn't someone want to be the color they are? What's wrong with that?"

Ariel, incredibly shy, interjected, "We as Latinas, or at least the girls I know, are taught that being light is beautiful. Dark skin is not beautiful, so those who are not light-skinned are thought of as not beautiful and miss out on things. Like, miss out on maybe having friends, getting asked out, teachers being nice to them."

And before Ariel could finish, Malia's excitement caused her to hop out of her seat and sit back down with a big grin of recognition. "Oooh, I know what you're talking about! I know exactly what you are talking about! I go to a store with my little sister who is a little lighter than me, but we look alike, and everyone comments on how pretty she is. I mean, I may be in basketball shorts and all, but so is she, and no one tell me how pretty I am or come up to me to help me. And that junk be happening at school as well."

More girls dialogued, sharing stories of how lighter-skinned girls tended to receive "better" treatment and attention, even from other girls. Before moving on to their laptops to "play" with iPhoto and see how they, too, could modify their complexions, they shared countless stories of how their families, friends, and various adults preferred lighter-skinned girls. The speakers' interpretations were all the same, regardless of their own skin tones.

Realizing their commonalities and differences caused Malia to confide in me many sessions later, "I have never talked with any of the Latina girls in my school, never, and I've been there for like two years. Now, I am talking to them in COMPUGIRLS and we see a lot alike. We would not be able to do this in school." Having the freedom to talk about colorism[9]—that is, how the color of one's skin shapes an individual's experience, regardless of that person's race or ethnicity—and how technology reinforces the script that "lighter is better" served as the catalyst for girls to see across lines of difference. Manipulating the technology to recognize that it was a tool in this system, one that they too could master, served as the glue bonding them. Lines of difference became porous. Inclusion in the group relied on more than the racial categories in which they belonged or even the sexes of its members. Instead, "true" COMPUGIRLS participants were those who demonstrated they bought in to the curriculum.

You Cannot Come

Akilah was relatively tall for her fifteen years. She had a slender build and curly jet-black hair, and her brown skin had a distinct red color that made some question whether she was African American or from India. Akilah was quick to disabuse anyone from thinking her racial identity was anything but Black: "I may have curly-straight hair, but I'm Black, and so are a lot of my family." Akilah arrived at the orientation, a two-hour event at my university where newly accepted COMPUGIRLS participants and their siblings, parents, and/or caregivers gathered before the start of the actual program. Many girls attended with signed permission slips, consent forms, and photo release documents without adult accompaniment. Akilah was one of these appearing without an adult but seemingly eager to participate.

Once she began attending the daily course, Akilah made clear that she enjoyed arguing. No matter the situation, she provided an oppositional view, intent on making her point: "That doesn't make any sense! I don't agree." Even though fellow participants asked Akilah, "Then what do you propose? What are your ideas?" she did not provide them. Instead, Akilah could be relied upon to disrupt the flow of a conversation. Whether it be while girls identified who was going to present their daily accomplishments to the whole group at the conclusion of the day or when they deliberated on interviewing the police or the victims of domestic abuse, Akilah disagreed with every suggestion. I never heard her make one specific recommendation during the year of her periodic attendance.

After the first few days of the summer experience, Akilah loudly commented, "Where are the computers? I thought this was a computer camp?" Girls and mentor teachers reminded her that they would not gain access to a laptop, emphasizing again that it was a loan, until they presented their topic to the group. The girls created a rubric as to how groups should be assessed. Had they put in sufficient thought for each person to take a laptop home for the remainder of the session? Mentor teachers guided girls to enumerate negative and positive issues on the first day of the program: "If the ideas don't make sense. If they are not organized and have a clear research question. If the presenter isn't clear, like, we can't hear her. They need to have a plan, like, who they will interview or give a survey to and why these people, if they are stakeholders or not. It needs to make sense." The participants determined the "rules of engagement"—namely, how they would listen to each other ("No interrupting and junk"), how they would provide feedback (such as the sandwich approach, which begins and ends with a positive comment and contains some critical feedback in between), and how they would hold each other accountable ("If you are going to represent us you need to come correct")—and built their expectations for each other and themselves. Therefore, when Akilah ceased coming after the third week, girls were quick to raise their concerns: "She was supposed to do the research and we haven't seen her. No one lives near her so we don't know. Do you know, Miss?"

Any day a girl is absent we immediately call the parent or guardian. Rather than imply that her absence could lead to a punitive action, we choose to express worry and attempt to reengage the missing individual and her family. So, each day, we left messages for Akilah's parents, which varied between "Hi, Mrs. Lyles. This is Robin, Akilah's mentor teacher from COMPUGIRLS. We really miss Akilah coming to the camp and want to make sure everything is OK. Please call us back when you can so we can talk about it" and "Hi, Mrs. Lyles. This is Dr. Scott, COMPUGIRLS executive director, and we haven't seen Akilah in a while. Let me give you my personal cell phone and office phone to talk about getting Akilah back." This approach harkens back to my days as a classroom teacher. I remember all too well teachers contacting parents only to report some negative occurrence in the classroom. Implicit messages were regularly sent during these phone calls that the child was the problem and, as a result, did not belong in the setting the teacher tried to control/maintain. The idea of calling a parent, particularly a parent of color, with a positive statement was far from the norm. I wanted the COMPUGIRLS' parent connections to be an oppositional tales to this tradition. I yearned to create an environment in which parents knew that not only were their daughters welcome, but we would actively remind them of their belongingness in the space. Even with my intent, though, none of our attempts resulted in a response from Akilah or her family. However, on the last day of the program, while girls prepared for the closing ceremony—final presentations to parents, school officials, community leaders, and university administrators—Akilah reappeared with the laptop. She did not demonstrate any concern, acting as if she had not been missing the past several weeks.

The girls did not include or exclude her once she returned. She sat quietly next to her group, unusually silent as they worked feverishly to ensure the flow of their presentation made sense. Akilah was seemingly undeterred that none of her group mates asked her opinion, and unlike her initial bravado she did not offer any comments. She sat next to her group mates with her closed laptop while they busied themselves so they could "come correct" in front of the next-day's audience. It was not until Akilah engaged in these same laissez-faire behaviors during the second course did the girls demand she be treated differently.

Before the conclusion of Course I, during which girls created their digital stories around their social or community issue, we previewed Course II: Scratch.[10] The idea of creating their own games or simulations using the coding language Scratch excited some girls, while others looked on, perplexed as to what this meant exactly. Although Akilah was not present during these conversations, she received the phone call and mailing sent to all participants from Course I. Great effort was made by mentor teachers to let girls and their parents know that we wanted the youngsters to participate and that they privileged us with their presence.

Telling young girls who were quite aware of the social scripts outlining their perceived deficits that both they and their families belonged at the university-based program was one tactic that COMPUGIRLS used to demonstrate their belongingness. We extended this approach to indicate that we—the program staff—were the fortunate ones, as the girls gave us their time and the parents provided us the opportunity to get to know their daughters. As a result, the relationship between the program staff and participants was built on recognized reciprocity. The girls and their families benefited from the program, just as the program and its staff benefited from the girls. Recognizing that the girls and their communities possessed assets that were as valuable as the experience we aimed to facilitate, if not more so, created a unique dynamic that most girls learned to enjoy. But more important issues occupied Akilah.

For the first few weeks of Course II, Akilah attended up to the point that she gained access to the laptop. Afterward, she again disappeared until the last day of this fall session. Again, the girls said nothing to her while she observed final preparations for the second closing ceremony.

By the third course, focusing on the life simulation game The Sims,[11] Akilah again arrived at the orientation. This time, however, her boyfriend escorted her. Although all her paperwork was signed as before, her confidence seemed shaken. The two stood in the back, whispering loud enough for me to catch a few phrases: "When do you get the laptop? I thought they were here." "No, I need to go to class for a few." The boyfriend, whose name she did not share, although the mentor teachers made a point to welcome her back and ask his identity, remained silent with everyone except Akilah. It was clear that he was annoyed at our procedures and unwilling to remain the entire time for the orientation. Before we presented to the audience of girls, their parents, and caregivers examples of Course III, he abruptly left the room. Akilah was not far behind, refusing to stay before we divided girls and parents into groups to engage in an activity.

As usual, Akilah returned the first day of the third course. Before any of the adults could talk with her, Ana greeted Akilah with a decision that was made without adult knowledge: "Akilah, you can't come in here and take the laptop and not participate. This isn't a library. You can't check it out. We need the laptop to get our work done, so if you don't want to do the work and be a COMPUGIRL, then you don't get the laptop." At this, Akilah assumed the same frustrated look her boyfriend had painted on his face during the orientation. Her uncharacteristic silence emerged and settled on her countenance like a mask that had become all too familiar. Unlike her past self, she did not oppose the statements or attempt to dissuade the speaker or others that their perception was incorrect. Akilah sat quietly through that one day, never to return to COMPUGIRLS.

Akilah's refusal to play by the girl-created norms, even though she had the opportunity to cocreate them, does not dismiss a striking institutional issue. Clearly, she understood that access to a computer was important. Repeatedly, she entered our space to gain what no other institution could provide her. That her school lacked enough computers for each student to have regular interaction defined what was initially called the digital divide.[12] However, Akilah, like many other skeptics both then and now, did not understand that access alone to hardware is not enough.

Again, Akilah's story occurred at a time when programs providing individual laptops in schools were just beginning. During this period, access to hardware was the "silver bullet" for closing the technology gap, or at least this was what was believed. What kids did with the technology, however, was far less important. Eventually, scholars and practitioners realized that students in the more economically advantaged schools had access not only to more complicated technologies but also to a host of other resources that maintained the schism between the technological haves and have-nots.[13] Teachers who were regularly receiving professional development on how to use and guide students in technology innovation; exposure to curriculum that focused more on innovating than merely on using technologies; and fast internet speeds were some of the advantages certain communities enjoyed. Equally important to these affordances was the belief that certain individuals were inherently technologically talented while others required interventions in order to build on their gifts.[14]

Why shouldn't COMPUGIRLS participants have the same resources as their counterparts in affluent spaces? Too often, well-meaning program developers implement efforts that are believed to work with kids of color while there is no evidence that it works with any students. Learning how to debate, negotiate with others, and collaborate, among other power skills, are taken-for-granted talents regularly infused in elite, liberal arts settings.[15] And there are a host of social actors, including youngsters, guiding students in the learning process. Our program draws on empirically based constructs proven to increase students' achievements in a multitude of settings and, as one participant explained, "COMPUGIRLify" these approaches. However, as Akilah demonstrated, our efforts are not successful with all girls of color from disenfranchised communities.

Akilah's story reminds us that no one approach could work for every member belonging to a particular race or social class group or navigating a unique context. Akilah did not see herself as a part of COMPUGIRLS, and this image was reinforced in her relentless commitment to argue with the others and not follow one of the primary rules—support each other. Certainly, constant agreement was not the norm in the program, and debate was welcomed as long as the speaker could present the reasoning behind her words. Contestation that would enhance the project or approach or would strengthen the community was acceptable, but arguing for the sake of disruption was not. Ultimately ostracized by the group, Akilah did not express any remorse. When contacted about returning, she said, "No, it's not for me." Other girls with whom she did attend school revealed, "Yeah, she just wanted the laptop because she didn't have one at home. She wasn't about the program." They took offense at her unwillingness to buy into the program and protected their space against this effort to move them away from their goals.

Being a COMPUGIRLS participant meant more than manipulating a laptop for individual gain. The importance of belonging to a group that created the rules and procedures for administrating consequences was part of the experience. Losing an individual to an unnamed boyfriend who cared little for the program, its participants, or guiding adults was a small price to pay for guarding the program from within. As will be discussed in later chapters, girls were always mindful of how others, particularly adults not affiliated with COMPUGIRLS, made sense of their potential and achievements along race, gender, and social class divides. They would not risk incorporating anyone who would contribute to the stereotype of them being nothing more than disaffected females of color.

Participants dramatized their space, determining rules of acceptability that would criticize others in gentle—and at times not so gentle—ways. The structure of the program allowed girls to ignite their agency with mentor teachers, who asked girls on day one what rules they would like to see implemented. Adults followed participants' lead when girls issued reminders of the rules. This was not a natural process, however.

Throughout the first few weeks of the summer program, adults reminded the participants about their positions in this space: "Girls, don't you remember you said no group can get the laptop unless they persuade you that they have put forward a sound proposal for a project?" Even with the rules written and displayed on the wall in front of the room, girls did not automatically believe they were both the authors and the adjudicators of the norms. Participants would quickly giggle and say, "Oh, yeah. We said that," and determine the next steps. These constant reminders from the adults were administered less and less often as the weeks continued and the girls claimed the space as their own. Inevitably, some mentor teachers were less comfortable with relinquishing their control than others. But for the most part, girls came to learn that not only could they innovate with technology, they could create their own social system that required adult abidance rather than direction. At times, their agency emboldened some to push back on curriculum requirements, ultimately causing us to revise our standards. What was most intriguing, however, was that their agency inside the classroom was far more pronounced than when they physically moved beyond our four walls.

During the summer programs, girls met for eight hours a day, five days a week. Each morning, after small groups presented to the larger cohort, they worked for the remainder of the day on specific activities among their five-person small groups. Mentor teachers would sit close to the groups but as the weeks progressed would do little to interrupt the flow of conversation. Girls determined each individual's roles based on stated interests or perceived skills. Angelica, who demonstrated a great aptitude and willingness to debug (find, identify, and remove errors in programming) during Course II, became the "technician" for her small group but would help any other girl in the program. Ana was the "program director," galvanizing her peers to stay on task and always be mindful of who and how they represented themselves; Zaire's desire to ensure counter-narratives of what is normal made her the "researcher" who was responsible for gathering peer-reviewed articles and presenting to her team her interpretations as to whether the written words accurately reflected the perspectives of the marginalized. Adults first provided the groups with these titles, although by Course III, girls did not use them. Labels were no longer needed as girls knew who possessed which skill and felt comfortable acting on this insider knowledge. What took considerably more time for girls to know and internalize was their overall place and sense of belonging in our physical space.

The Issue of Space

We intentionally held most COMPUGIRLS courses on the campus of the university where I taught. The campus was nestled among high-rises and cultural buildings, without a house or apartment complex nearby. A few houses built in the 1930s had been renovated as coffee shops or boutiques, but the number of these buildings diminished as the years progressed, with far more of the old domiciles torn down to make space for modern university buildings. At the time of the first COMPUGIRLS cohort, the school occupied seven four-story buildings arranged in a rectangle. Each building stood alone, forcing visitors to exit outside to get to the interior of another. A wrought-iron gate at the entrance of the campus stood approximately fifteen feet high with the name of the university crowning the arch. During off-hours—when there was no activity sponsored by the school—the gate was locked, and the buildings became impenetrable to those without a key.

In the center of campus was a large water fountain, which was a favorite spot to visit before summer temperatures reached triple digits. A small café sat in the corner of the building facing our space, but its prices were too high for us to use their catering services. Instead, we contracted with local restaurants and had lunches delivered during the daily summer sessions. Snacks were also provided throughout the day, many of which mentor teachers purchased out of their own pockets, but lunch was the focal point. Pizza, Chinese takeout, sandwiches, burritos, and other items girls stated were "cool" arrived on the first floor of the building we typically occupied. Girls could help themselves, taking as much as they liked, and choose to eat in the makeshift lunchroom or outside near the fountain, if weather allowed, with their small groups and mentor teachers.

Program staffers who were not mentor teachers took over while the instructors took their lunch breaks as well. Without much program funding, graduate students served many roles: checking out laptops, digital cameras, camcorders, and tripods; managing attendance; ordering food; and relieving mentor teachers from classroom duty. Girls tended to sit apart from the grad students, though, and talk quietly about various issues. Periodically, they would pose questions to the graduate students, asking, "What's it like being in graduate school?" "What do you do in graduate school?" "Why would you go to school so long?" For the vast majority of participants, having access to another set of adults beyond the classroom allowed them to ask questions they would not normally have the opportunity to ask.

Graduate students enjoyed talking with the girls, as many of them lacked that opportunity as well. Most were pursuing advanced degrees in education but rarely interacted or spoke with youngsters beyond a research study. It was refreshing to be in a space free from academic constraints or method-ological obligations. Adults and girls could talk about a host of topics, all of which were kid-driven. Boys, academic standards, school life, issues with non-COMPUGIRLS peers, conversations and arguments with parents—these and other subjects shaped the interactions. Program staffers became integral parts of the participants' support system. When one member left to visit her native Southeast Asian country, girls lamented her absence, accosting me at every turn: "Where is Lily? When is she coming back? We miss her."

The girls could direct the research topics they explored, how they would hold each other accountable, and the contours of their relationships with surrounding adults. In addition to having this form of power, we encour-aged them to physically move their bodies. Going outside for lunch and congregating in the courtyard allowed girls to take control of their physical selves. In the classroom, the only rule affecting movement was that no food or drink was permitted near the laptops. Otherwise, girls could sit, stand, move around, or even work in the hall as long as they did so with another participant, informed a mentor teacher, and did not disrupt the classrooms occupied by college-age students or offices populated with university staff. They did not abuse this privilege or exploit it. In fact, adults themselves could be found sitting on the floor, standing at the back of the room, or lying down outside with girls while they worked on their projects. All members of the community knew when to subscribe to more conventional methods.

When girls visited local industry sites for our end-of-session field trips, they were quick to follow the rules of engagement. Rather than waiting for a pause to share their thoughts with a peer presenter, they would raise their hands while visiting an industry's laboratory. Sometimes facility tours limited the physical liberties the girls were used to having; for instance, occasionally they would be expected to sit erect in chairs while listening to an industry host. However, they still maintained their critical gaze, taking note of how adults approached them.

After one Latina engineer visited the classroom a week before the girls went to the adult's place of work, Ana explained, "She just talked at us, didn't ask any real questions. It was boring." The girls' verbal expressiveness and agency did not dissipate, regardless of the physical spaces or contexts. Put simply, girls learned to shapeshift, to move their bodies according to the contextual expectations while maintaining their voices. They learned to control the volumes of their narratives, always mindful of expectations that opposed the bound spaces of the program. In a later chapter, I discuss how this ability did not mean they ceased worrying about the larger community's beliefs that they belonged, or not, in certain places. As program developers, we wanted girls to believe they too fit in on the university campus. We made an intentional decision to meet there. We wanted them to become habituated in the space and to allow their bodies to both bring and gain energy in the facility. We purposely hosted COMPUGIRLS at the university in hopes that over time participants would not skirt around the building like shadows. Rather, we trusted that being in the university during adolescence would convince their bodies and souls that they deserved to be at such an institution of higher education in later years. Unfortunately, we did not take into account the long-standing history the institution maintained.

University buildings and programs may be in a community but not of the community. How these girls and their families understood the university and their places as future students were troubled by the lack of sustained interactions between the two environments. The school was an unattainable space that did not enter the minds of most girls or their parents until invited to the COMPUGIRLS orientation. Nevertheless, the implication of ultimately owning the space within the concrete walls reflects the significance of facilities on girls' understanding of self in both present and future terms. Over time, and with regular attendance, the girls enrolled at the university site came to own the space, establishing and maintaining norms and moving their bodies more freely. They delighted in giving their families a tour when they attended the closing ceremony. Yet, as is discussed below, these sentiments of belonging were not shared by the Native American girls who navigated our curriculum on the "rez" and in their community center's facilities.

Candy

"Candy!" exclaimed Vonda, a member of a local Indigenous community. Set within the windowless space of the Boys and Girls Clubhouse, part of the community center, six Native American girls ranging in age from thirteen to fifteen formed a circle. After Vonda said the word, others chimed in with "Yea, candy!" Although I was completely confused, the one fifteen-year-old who did not follow suit understood the peer-generated rule—that is, when a girl did not speak clearly or loudly, the listeners reminded her to speak up by yelling, "Candy!"

With a smile on her face, Laurie restarted her monologue. "Fine, I'll do it again. My plan is to research graffiti in our community. Everyone thinks it's bad and stuff, but I know a lot of graffiti artists, and there is, like, another side to this, and I think if people understand it, hear from them, you know, it won't make them always look so bad and people can stop arresting them for art."

The girls-only audience members nodded their heads, affirming Laurie's goals, but each provided comments or questions: "How will you tell their story without getting them in trouble?" "You should interview the police to hear what they have to say." "How does this relate to equity and equality?" Laurie deferred to the mentor-teacher, an adult member of the same community, who explained that the technology they would soon learn would allow Laurie to maintain the confidentiality of the artists, interview folks in the community no matter where they were, and include music that supported the forthcoming story.

Excitement tinted the girls' eyes as more faces broke into smiles. This was an incredible change from the first program week, when the girls maintained their fixed gazes on the floor. Silence had been the norm. Even Vonda, who attended that first week clearly "under the influence," had refused to respond to anyone or anything. One week later, however, Laurie reacted effectively and wrote the others' inquiries in her notebook; Vonda led her peers in actualizing their rule; and girls were eager to create their digital stories.

The girls in this community space claimed their norms with the same conviction as their COMPUGIRLS counterparts in the university setting. Typically, however, their voices were much more subdued than those heard thirty miles north on the downtown campus. Nevertheless, there was no doubt that they set the rules. As a smaller group, most work was conducted individually with the mentor teacher sitting with each participant every day for at least thirty minutes. Guest speakers for this cohort were not individuals from industries but elders from the tribal community. The mentor teacher explained, "This is a good opportunity for them to hear about our culture. They never get together like this, and a lot of them are interested. We should ask some of the leaders who are part of the senior group to come and talk with them." In addition to leaders from the Tribal Council who welcomed the girls and their parents during orientation, almost every week some adults visited the program. More often than not, I was not invited to these talks. We agreed on my absence, since I was not a tribal member. Far from feeling insulted by the request for my removal, I appreciated the honesty from which it was given. I had not had many occasions to collaborate with non-Black communities before my professional move. Nevertheless, I was acutely aware of the long and deplorable history of many researchers disrespecting Native communities for their own purposes. Seeking to create a respectful relationship between me and the Native community began with my own self-awareness.[16]

I understood that Native communities did not automatically see me as an ally. My Black femaleness did not give me a pass. I was an outsider, a role I played for quite some time. Understanding my positionality caused me to feel a great sense of honor once partnerships were established. To this day, I often begin conversations with Native American partners stating my gratitude for being an "honored guest" in their lands. These words are important to both think, say, and perform. Particularly for COMPUGIRLS on the reservation, my resolve was to collaborate with the community in order to facilitate the building of its own capacity. In short, my understanding that sacred conversations should be honored and willingness to remove myself from them reflected my own critical inquiry and critical praxis.

After community member visits, girls like Sabrina seemed somewhat relieved and also a bit more driven. Nervous energy became more prominent after the talks, as if the words from the elders inspired girls to be more focused and responsible.

"I'm going to talk with the girls about what it means to be a girl from our community. And I need to thank you for getting them together. I didn't think they were interested. But I'm going to talk with them about the things they need to know and probably don't. I need about ninety minutes," Elaine, a small tribal elder with salt-and-pepper short hair, told me the week before her scheduled visit. Her eyes sparkled with delight, although she relied on a cane to assist her movements.

Mimi, an exceptionally quiet fifteen-year-old community participant, was so motivated by Elaine's talk that she did not move her eyes from her screen the day after Elaine's visit. Even conversation with her neighbor failed to break her focused gaze. Other pairs of girls followed a similar communication pattern, sitting on the hard plastic chairs and barely moving. Girls would not take a lunch break but leave their cameras or digital devices periodically and go into the adjoining room to make a plate of fruit, pick at a sandwich, or grab a piece of pizza. They stood alone in the room, slowly chewing while looking through the glass window as others continued to work.

Sitting on the floor or moving into a hall was not a possibility for this group. The remaining rooms of the Boys and Girls Clubhouse were always occupied by another program. Outside, an ocean of sand teemed with prairie dogs. Although the virtual world course allowed the girls to move into the main building of the community center, this new space did not encourage them to communicate any differently with each other. In hopes that the internet connection would be better in the primary corridor, the girls moved into that quieter space with their laptops. They did not interact or talk much, despite being crowded in a much more limited physical context.

Still, COMPUGIRLS provided an opportunity to remind the girls of their connectedness to a culture. Visiting adults were excited to serve as cultural facilitators. Buy-in for these participants relied on how well individuals expressed interest in and concern for becoming a community member. Commitment to their traditions became a public act manifested through the topics, which ranged from graffiti in the community, multiple myeloma in the community, or language and cultural loss in the community. All subjects pertained to the community. Technology was a platform but not the focal point. And as the years progressed and some participants ceased their drug use while others became pregnant, the rez site became an incredible display that challenged the taken-for-granted notion that Native Americans are technophobic.[17] COMPUGIRLS participants on the reservation demonstrated a core principle of the program—that is, technology should serve the purposes of the community. And it is the connection among community members that will foster girls' potential to become change agents.

Adult Roles

Tribal leaders, elders, Alani (the rez mentor teacher), and I were the primary adults interacting with the COMPUGIRLS participants. Our responsibilities were distinct and tended not to overlap. The leaders and elders, unasked, assumed the role as cultural guides, instructing girls in traditions they erroneously believed the young cared little about. Alani, as well as the one male Native American mentor teacher who worked with us for one semester, ensured that the girls not only completed their projects but felt supported. Living in the community, Alani made a point to visit their homes, call on weekends, and give them rides to and from the community center. She spent countless hours serving as mentor, teacher, and sister. Even though she never completed her college degree ("I took some classes at the community college"), she regularly explained to the girls that "this is a university program! You may not get college credit, but you learn stuff you will need in college." She never specifically stated what exactly that "stuff" was, but the girls listened carefully to her. Alani served an integral role in the program. As a cultural liaison, she regularly explained to COMPUGIRLS research team members and me, during the countless hours of curriculum development, preferred methods to present to the rez participants, given technology's limitations and affordances. Importantly, Alani never described girls' potential as part of the limitations. Challenges were found in the COMPUGIRLS program itself or in how we structured the curriculum.

If a girl completed all six courses, she was eligible for a paid summer internship. Most placements lasted for four weeks at approximately twenty hours per week. A graduate student from my university's higher education program became the internship coordinator as part of her practicum. Girls and their parents met with this individual approximately one month before placement. The purpose of the hour-long conversation was to describe responsibilities to both the girls and their parents: "An intern must arrive at least fifteen minutes before she starts work, so you need to be on time. We can help with transportation, you know, like give bus passes, but if you cannot be there you need to call me immediately. Parents, please call me if there are any problems. Also, we will help with clothing. We are going to go on a field trip to a place that will loan us, the girls, business clothes for their internships. You can even get bags. Again, this is a loan, like the laptops." At this, the girls sat up straighter in their chairs, excited about the impending shopping trip: "Can we pick anything to wear?" "Do they have shoes?" "Do I have to only wear a skirt?" This dialogue set expectations for the girls and their parents and also demonstrated how to apply their COMPUGIRLS skills to the workforce.

Internship sites submitted descriptions of proposed work after receiving invitations to participate in this portion of the program. Our material emphasized the candidates' technology and critical thinking skills and their ability to write, to conduct basic research, and to work independently and interdependently. A combination of nonprofit organizations, university departments, industries, and small start-ups were intrigued that girls acquired these skills in the course of our program. That participants had constructed their own abstracts, identified a research question, articulated methods to answer the question, and wrote a paper with a reference list impressed many sites.

Girls were aware that they were exceeding expectations but did not express this recognition to outsiders. They deconstructed people's surprise while in our program space, asking, "Why wouldn't [we] be able to write an abstract?" to which another participant would remind the interrogator, "Because they don't think we can do anything." "Well, shoot, we can!" Some sites refused to trust the girls' abilities, and as Kelly explained while she worked at a local think-tank, "All they give us is photocopying and collating. We know they saw that we can research because we showed them our paper during the interview, but they won't give us anything to research. It's kinda boring, but I guess we are getting some skills. We get to sit in on some meetings, although we don't get to talk or participate. We take notes, and we read them over and give to whomever."

Unfortunately, some of the internship sites encouraged girls to silence themselves, believing that they could not contribute to their organization in a substantive way. Girls muted themselves but used our space to dialogue and make sense of the experience and how to capitalize on it. For instance, in response to Kelly's complaint, the coordinator said, "Well, read over the notes you are copying. Read everything you copy. You can learn that way." Adult coordinators helped guard girls' agency and burgeoning ability to critically inquire about differential treatment. As girls interacted more and more with adults in the workforce, the internship coordinator became the touchstone, reminding girls during their Friday meetings that they were far more than what may have been expected of them in their sites. This became incredibly important for Deirdre.

All girls from the university-based program attended their summer internship sites in pairs. Due to transportation issues, both the girls and Alani from the rez site decided to elect only one girl from their cohort to be the intern. Deirdre became the representative. Like many of her peers, she was quiet while talking with me, although Alani made it clear that she was very interested in pursuing her associate's degree in graphic design. Therefore, Deirdre was to travel the thirty-five minutes to the local technology company and intern in its graphic design department. Unfortunately, her unexpected pregnancy caused her to be late several occasions over a two-week period.

Upon learning that Deirdre was having issues arriving at her internship, the coordinator and Alani crafted a transportation plan in which Alani would take her to the industry site. This meant that Alani would pick Deirdre up from her home, drive her to the industry site, return to serve as the mentor teacher to the new crop of girls, and leave them early to pick Deirdre up, who would then assist with mentoring alongside Alani. For the most part, this system worked. On days when Alani could not take Deirdre, the industry allowed Deirdre to telecommute. On these occasions, Deirdre would accompany Alani to the community center, where the internet connection was faster than at her home.[18] This allowed Deirdre to be in the company of other COMPUGIRLS participants while continuing her work miles away.

Deirdre gave birth to her child a few weeks before the final closing ceremony, during which we celebrated interns. She beamed as we called her name to receive her certificate. While her mother held her daughter, all clapped as she strolled to the stage. No one exuded more pride than Alani, who hooted upon hearing Deirdre's name. Sitting next to the baby, she whispered as the little one kicked her legs in delight, "You see your mother up there? She did it!"

Ultimate Intent

COMPUGIRLS is invested in a present and future where women and girls of color have agentic relationships with technology, and not as a result of digital media. Although COMPUGIRLS is often labeled a technology program, its core principles emphasize sociocultural elements such as identity (for example, race, gender, and ethnicity), interpersonal associations, and community advancement. I argue that through engagement and careful analysis of these constructs, girls will come to understand their selves (critical inquiry) and develop a way of being in the world (critical praxis). The process provides them the additional benefit of seeing themselves as part of a "collective struggle," as described by bell hooks. Importantly, and over time, girls create "homeplaces."[19] Hence, we extend Gibson's findings on whom students characterize as a technologist—most youngsters "consider 'technologists' to be 'scientists,' the type of person who undertakes 'difficult things'" (2017, 20). Those "things" involve innovating with "high-tech" tools, in their minds. We acculturate this definition while the COMPUGIRLS technologist also embarks on a difficult task—namely, identifying a social issue and searching for a solution carefully analyzed through firsthand data—and then attempts to translate the information in a way that will move her community. The "high-tech" tools available to COMPUGIRLS participants serve as the platform on which they can learn which, how, and to what extent structures and systems contribute to their success in this digital age as well as discover the constraints preventing their liberation and participation in technological innovation. This knowledge allows them to further inquire and challenge the various structural domains of power.

As the following chapters show, the front-stage story of COMPUGIRLS demonstrates far more than simply how well the girls own the technology and find themselves and each other. How culturally responsive computing practices,[20] such as those the COMPUGIRLS program fostered and implemented, can broaden girls' knowledge, assert a different vision of digital equity, and reflect a new form of girlhood studies, re-centers resistance work and what is commonly perceived as activism.

CHAPTER THREE

This Isn't Like School

HER SKIN WAS SLIGHTLY DARKER than café au lait, and her shoulder-length, wavy brown hair framed a cherubic face. She entered a room with authority, pausing slightly to survey her surroundings as if assessing who may be allies and who may prove to be her foes. At sixteen years old, she was quite aware of her physical and cultural positions. With a measured voice that moved quickly over words in a rhythm much like rapid drums, she proudly self-identified as Latina. She also was quick to recognize that Indigenous blood ran through her veins. She understood her cultural background just as well as the consequences of its meaning in the digital age. Knowing she lacked the opportunity to learn any substantive technological lessons beyond the tiresome PowerPoint and word processing her economically distressed school allowed, she came to COMPUGIRLS through a circuitous route. Slow to smile but quick to laugh at the irony of a situation, Yvette knew her truancy from school did not endear her to most school personnel. Yet regardless of her reputation, Yvette not only joined the first COMPUGIRLS cohort but illustrated to many what a girl can do when provided opportunities to focus on becoming rather than on being.

This chapter showcases how the traditional barometers for success poorly reflect a girl's developing consciousness. Equally important, Yvette's story demonstrates in no small way the position digital media can play while girls express their agentic selves. In observing how Yvette found and operational-ized her agency, we see the sometimes painful but important journey young women craft in building coalitions.

Not for You

The one-hour presentation was the first time the girls and their parents/caregivers met the COMPUGIRLS staff. For most, it was also the first time they had visited a university campus. During this occasion, we ate breakfast, introduced the mentor teachers responsible for direct instruction, showcased digital products, and attempted to excite the girls about their participation. Typically, girls enter this space timidly; parents who seem unaccustomed and uncomfortable navigating formal institutional settings are also usually silent. On this day, only a few quietly greeted the program team with a quick "Hola."

Their performances were not surprising, since many parents from low-income environments are often accused of being "uninvolved." In actuality, many are simply silenced due to their own bad school experiences. Labeling them as "uncaring" or "disinterested" misses how the silence of some parents is representative of generational distrust of institutions that have made them feel they do not belong.[1] Like the experiences of too many of their daughters, the distress of navigating school-like places is far from enjoyable. Like their daughters, they, too, are under-anticipated. Yvette, on the other hand, entered COMPUGIRLS not showing any of the "normal" signs of a disinvited guest.

Yvette eyed a chair with a group of Latina and African American girls who, like her, were seemingly not accompanied by an adult. The table seated all five of these girls; Yvette was the oldest and Gennifer the youngest, at age thirteen. The gray rectangular tables, located in one of the university's newest classrooms, created a U-shape; most seated individuals could easily watch the drop-down screen. The few adults in attendance were mothers or older sisters, who occupied seats as far away from the front as possible. A few fathers sat next to their daughters or stood nearby, leaning against the wall. In this room filled with close to sixty persons, talking was at a minimum. Yvette looked around and down at the paper, which contained the day's agenda.

Unlike some of the other girls present, her gaze was not furtive. She directly glanced in the faces of the girls and the program staff, seemingly assessing each individual on her personal mental scale. Even when a girl or adult returned her look, she completed her internal evaluation without rancor until she found herself ready to examine the next countenance. Her movements were deliberate yet cautious, seeking neither approval nor confrontation.

Throughout the morning's presentation, Yvette did not pose any questions or make any comments. She listened to me as the executive director and program coordinator silently, collecting all the paperwork requiring a parent or guardian signature. When placed into her small group, she met her mentor teacher and group mates with little more than a nod and a few words. However, those words did reveal an important fact about her life—like many girls of color attending economically challenged urban schools, she shared the same distrusting sentiments as those of their parents.

Beyond stating her name and age, Yvette's placid demeanor unfurled when she stated the name of her school—Gomez High School. Although her facial expression did not drastically change, her attitude toward this institution was clear through her elocution of its name. There were many reasons Yvette disliked her school. As an urban setting in which the vast majority of its Mexican American and Black students qualify for free and reduced lunch, Gomez has had its fair share of struggles. Known in the community for frequent student-led fights, large classes, high teen pregnancy and drug use rates, and an abysmal graduation rate, Gomez High School is not a school students wish to attend. Although there is open enrollment allowing youngsters to register in any high school in the district, most Gomez students do not know or possess the grade point average to explore any other alternative.[2] Gomez High School is a place Yvette attended only sporadically. Her decision for self-imposed exile was not too surprising, although it came at a price: she was originally discouraged from applying to COMPUGIRLS because of her consistent truancy. She came thanks to a social studies teacher who happened to see Yvette one day in the neighborhood; we would never have received her application through the usual channels.

On one of the few days Yvette did attend school, she stood outside her guidance counselor's office overhearing talk about COMPUGIRLS and became intrigued: "As soon as I heard about social justice I was interested." However, seconds later, once Yvette was in front of her counselor, there was no mention of the program. As Yvette explained, "I guess she didn't think I would be interested since I barely come to school." Without further information, she quickly dismissed COMPUGIRLS from her mind until Mrs. C approached her: "Mrs. C told me it was about social justice and I should apply. She told me she knew the director and that she was really into social justice issues. Unlike anything I learn in school, that interested me. And we also got to learn something about technology. That sounded cool too, but I was more interested in the social justice stuff." Mrs. C, a graduate student enrolled in my class on urban education and social justice, supplied Yvette with the application her guidance counselor had withheld. The teacher hoped that such an experience would "motivate Yvette," since she believed her to be "such a bright kid with lots of potential."

Some may label Yvette's acts of truancy as markers of oppositional identity. That is, some would explain Yvette's school absences as an act that signified her "antagonism toward the dominant group by resisting school goals" (Ainsworth-Darnell and Downey 1998, 536). But a more complicated framework to describe her self-removal is needed. More and more stigmatized youth fail to assume their disenfranchisement unquestioningly. Rather, we see more youth nurturing a personhood that allows them to retain a sense of autonomy and ownership against the repeated oppressions played out by their schools.[3] Yvette's refusal to attend school was not indicative of her low self-esteem or inability to succeed, as is often believed when using the oppositional framework. Instead, Yvette absented herself from the setting she perceived as defiling her dignity. In part, this self-preservation tactic is one that far too many urban youth use to obtain what Tuck calls "dangerous dignity," a "stance of informed defiance. Wise comeuppance. It is in response to an anticipation of humiliating ironies . . . [and] encompasses strategies employed by youth to re-vision who they are because of and in spite of their schooling" (2012, 85). Yvette escaped on her own terms.

She took control of her time, though not realizing the effects a prolonged absence could have on her academic standing and future aspirations. She was decidedly not performing the intended script: attending substandard classes and quietly listening to teachers who actively voiced their mistrust and low expectations of students. Her self-removal from school, however, did render her temporarily invisible, since, in one example, the guidance counselor failed to offer her information about COMPUGIRLS. How many other prospective girls without the intervention of a Mrs. C could have applied and been unmuted? Thanks to Mrs. C, who saw that Yvette and probably many of her female peers were "willfully lost in fearful power struggles that position them as mute" (Brown 2013, 184), Yvette seized the opportunity to produce a counter-normative performance to maintain her self-respect.

In general, students forced to navigate urban schools know they are missing opportunities and resources that their more affluent counterparts possess. And for many, they seize occasions to learn what those others know. More often than not, school officials encourage their "A" students to engage in enrichment experiences—those activities that the school cannot regularly offer but officials know will enhance students' learning. Those youth who demonstrate promise tend to be the ones provided with enrichment programs. Indeed, one middle school gave COMPUGIRLS applications only to those girls who had a 3.0 or higher grade point average, regularly submitted their homework, and had no disciplinary incidents on their records and whose parents were believed to be the most responsive. Unfortunately, this exclusionary design prevented the vast majority of the female student body from ever experiencing COMPUGIRLS. More importantly, it reinforced to the students the same belief that Yvette had upon exiting her guidance counselor's office—that only a select few are worthy of supplemental support.

Programs need to collaborate with schools in accessing unselected students. It is insufficient to simply state to schools, as I mistakenly did, that we want to recruit ALL girls. There have been too many programs that have made this same request but actually mean they want only the A students. More work needs to be done by us academic folk and program developers to clearly articulate to school officials our intent—to develop a program with a holistic view of girls from under-resourced communities that extends beyond traditional markers of success (such as grades and attendance). These conversations need to be transparent and include all school personnel. It is not enough to simply get buy-in from the principal or assistant principal. Girls interact with teachers and guidance counselors far more than with the school leaders. When we say "all," we need to pay careful attention to inclusionary practices.

When I used the word "all," I thought my intention was clear. Given my previous classroom experience, I avoid exclusionary strategies at all costs. I philosophized that all students should be afforded high potential activities, even if their performance in one setting does not suggest success in another. What I failed to recognize is that even districts and school officials willing to support COMPUGIRLS may not fully support our philosophy. Consequently, for programs that receive an overabundance of applications, more nuanced ways of selection must be implemented.

GPA Does Not Reflect Me

The year Yvette applied to COMPUGIRLS, we received over two hundred applications for forty slots. Since the number of COMPUGIRLS-like programs in the nation was much lower at this time, we anticipated this response and preemptively devised an admission plan. Our intent was to accommodate a diverse group of girls. Clearly, we wanted racial and ethnic diversity but created an application that requested girls to also indicate their technology experience, home language, and GPA and to write an essay. During in-person recruitment sessions, we made it clear to applicants that we planned on weighing the essay's content more than anything else. An essay could be short and would not be exclusively evaluated based on grammar, syntax, and spelling. An advisory board including a school official, a high school student from the school, and an industry supporter assessed the essay on a ten-point scale: content was worth seven points and mechanics worth three points.

Most applicants responded to the question "Do you believe your current GPA reflects your abilities?" by simply checking the "No" box without further explanation. Yvette, however, took this opportunity to scribble within the confines of the space a more complete answer:

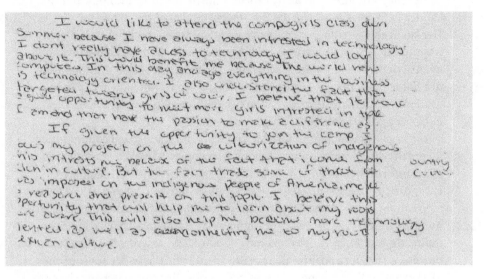

Figure 3. Yvette's response on GPA

Yvette's handwritten response indicated that even though she did not know a lot about technology, the lack of opportunity had not dampened her interest. In fact, she expressed her understanding that technology was instrumental for future job success. Recognizing what was missing in her life signaled an important moment in her development. Without exposure to the COMPUGIRLS curriculum, Yvette manifested what hooks calls an "important initial stage of transformation—that historical moment when one begins to think critically about the self and identity in relation to one's political circumstance" (1994a, 47). Her relatively young age did not blind her to the digital landscape shaping the world, nor did it discourage her from creating a new one. In those few words, she articulated her identity as technologically marginalized, yet this realization did not automatically lead to the appropriation of defeat or inaction.

Upon reading her essay and having not yet met her, the advisory board was moved by her words. That she realized her dispossession was disturbing enough, but to unabashedly seek methods to cease its continuation—that is what should be at the forefront of program developers' minds. For this self-expression should not be confused with her simply assuming an identity as a "technological have-not" or "know-not," terms Tapscott (1998) uses to describe communities and their inhabitants who lack access to technology. Yvette may not have had an advanced knowledge of technology, but dissimilar to "know-nots," she did possess the potential to narrow the divide. Her latent ability to do so stemmed from her resisting this label and willingly positioning herself to increase both her technical skills and consciousness as an activist. The two were inseparable, as she later revealed. Although she did not express the root causes of her disparate technological experience until much later, Yvette came to the program demonstrating some aspects of Unger's (2000) notion of "positive marginality."

Unger posits that marginalized individuals and stigmatized communities do not necessarily develop simple coping strategies. Instead, many individuals transform their stigmatization into "agentic attempts to reclaim experiences of being marginalized in ways that allow individuals to resist and even thrive in the face of social stigma. Thus, through individual and group-level meaning (re)making processes of stigma-related stressors, social stigma can, indirectly, result in positive outcomes" (2000, 832). Described as a multistep process, assuming a positive marginality identity begins with choosing one's identity rather than having it determined a priori. To that end, change is both a collective and an individual responsibility. Yvette was concerned about not only changing her present life circumstances but doing so as part of a coalition. This was a much different image from that held by those who simply saw her as a truant.

Her essay symbolized a rather nuanced idea of Black girlhood. Brown's 2013 articulation of Black girlhood holds true—as a theoretical construct, it is not only about Black girls but about all girls of color whose perceived racial inferiority gives reason for their subjugated positions. Consequently, Yvette and other COMPUGIRLS participants recognized their positionality and used this growing comprehension to fuel their action. At the same time, Yvette respected the significance of how this awareness provided intriguing "potential of the collective—the entering into relationship—to build and create something beyond a self-serving good time" (Brown 2013, 187–88). She was not simply aiming to be a part of a community for community's sake but sought to be a member of a dynamic sphere of relationships that would actually do something. Her recognition, which evolved as she progressed in the program, resonated well with Ali and colleagues' expression of Black feminism as a "process that is formed through relationships and ideas" (2010,

656). The need for inclusion and alliances rose to the fore of her and other participants' consciousness through our curricular activities.

Although her identity as truant did suggest an alternative lifestyle, girlhood studies correctly note that in these terrains there are multiple examples of resiliency, resistance, agency, and hope (Willis 2009; Kennelly 2009; Taft 2004). Words from her application demonstrated more than the "can-do" attitude that Harris (2004b) critiques; without much schooling, Yvette understood that activism concerns more than imbuing in girls the belief that they can do anything. This individualism was nonexistent in her stance and gave way to her emphasizing the power of collective efforts. Although she had yet to realize the other necessary ingredients for what she sought, her writing challenged the common image of any girl at age sixteen, but particularly one labeled as a truant Latina.

Entire careers would be diminished or at least found to be less impactful if the images of downtrodden, ignorant, angry females of color would disappear. With little demonstrable history of working effectively with communities of color in general and with girls of color in particular, more and more digital programs targeting underrepresented groups have emerged. This is not necessarily negative. Our girls need more access in order to master digital experiences. The troubling point is that this increase of programs has not necessarily inspired more anti-deficit literature on girls of color. Where are the articles documenting the complex thoughts and ways Black and Brown girls come to know each other and their selves? Are White girls the only ones experiencing girlhood and all its complexities? The obvious answer is no. However, without multiple counter-narratives, the simplified notion persists that our daughters remain troubled, "at-risk" youngsters unworthy of study but objects of interventions.

Describing a program as an "intervention" suggests disrupting the perceived dysfunctionality of certain girls with culturally foreign methods. Referring to a program as an "enrichment experience," though, sends a different message. Drawing on an asset-building approach, it suggests that the strategies will build on the girls' lives, not because they require fixing but because they warrant additional richness that may not be readily available due to a host of structural constraints. For our purposes, an asset-building approach required us to provide multiple lessons and activities in which girls drew on their strengths as a collective. Our thinking resonates with Green and Haines, who state, "Institutional obstacles . . . are difficult to overcome through individual action but instead must be addressed through the activities of collectivities" (2015, 17). If presented to the girls in this way, demonstrating that efforts will capitalize on their burgeoning knowledge while providing sustained opportunities to claim their voices in all their complexity, then more girls and adults might understand that there is no one narrative, no one label that represents the totality of girls of color. To assume anything else not only is a disservice to our daughters but limits our approaches to dismantle deficit thinking.

More Than Digital Products

Yvette tended to listen intently to most adults, whether she agreed with them or not. For her, she quickly found the COMPUGIRLS space to be one in which her opinion mattered. She swiftly understood and learned to accept the constructs of culturally responsive computing, mentioned in the introduction. Most importantly, and without being told the various theoretical tenets of culturally responsive computing, Yvette came to expect that the mentor teachers would encourage girls to reflect upon what they and others were saying; serve as guides in the process of leading the girls to locate their voices and become change agents; and push them to recognize what they knew as assets while always seeking to know more in order to make a sustained impact that would provide greater equity for all disenfranchised communities. The degree to which her mentor teachers engaged in this process varied. Within the variance, we can see how some mentor teachers have difficulty with relinquishing their need to "save the girls"—a move that Gonick (2001) describes was commonplace in initial "girl power" efforts. Nevertheless, and as will be illustrated below, how Yvette responded to the adults' acceptance of what the program attempted to normalize revealed much about her ability to negotiate and claim her and others' positions as change agents.

For most girls, arriving at the university site was an issue. Although we provided bus passes, many did not know the route or their parents did not trust the bus. After the first few days of the program, we realized the problem and began providing bus schedules. We also developed a system where mentor teachers were stationed on city corners close to the bus stops but still on university grounds. These individuals greeted the girls and walked them back to the appropriate corners after each daily session. At times, this meant waiting with the participants until the bus or the appropriate adult arrived.

Mentor teachers learned who would come to each corner and would walk the entire group to the classroom once all participants were present. If a girl was late, she had to enter the university building by herself. With the room that COMPUGIRLS used located approximately a hundred meters from the entrance, the distance did not present an issue; nevertheless, girls preferred to arrive early to avoid entering on their own. Although the majority of the forty girls lived and attended school no more than two miles from the university, most had never entered any of its buildings until the orientation. The girls explained that the university seemed like a place that would not welcome them: "It's not like we would ever go to school there."

To them, it appeared to be an impenetrable space centered in their community. Thus, the prospect of walking unaccompanied into this space was too foreign for the girls (and by the same token, their parents). "I'd rather arrive early and wait," claimed one participant, which caused mentor teachers to expect some girls at least thirty minutes before the start of our session. If a girl arrived after her group entered the building, she would almost run to the classroom. "What if someone stops me?" Regularly, we informed the one security guard, who tended to be Latino not much older than many of the girls, that our program was in session and asked him to please direct latecomers to the appropriate room. Additionally, signs with arrows were placed on doors directing all to room locations. Still, the fear outweighed our attempts. Being seen and potentially treated as an actual intruder occupied most girls' minds during the first few weeks. Yvette, however, never believed she did not belong in this space.

The first day of the actual program, Yvette was late. Unlike other stragglers, who tended to enter sheepishly and quickly, Yvette simply walked in, paused at the entrance to locate the faces of the girls from the orientation, and casually approached her group. Just as she initially embodied her image of a disaffected teen, she opposed the traditional anti-feminist views of how girls' bodies should move. Rather than follow the traditional feminine gender norms, established by middle-class White culture, such as the expectation that girls' bodies should assume less space, remain confined, and perform less self-assured movements than boys' bodies,[4] Yvette constructed a different script. Without provocation, her nonverbal communication reflected self-confidence, assertion, and an I-do-belong attitude that deliberately managed her body in a space coded as inhospitable. She entered the program having an impressive sense of control over her form and demonstrated to her peers the significance of the specific staging of her physical self (more on this point in the "Conflict and Love" section below).

As Yvette progressed through the program and navigated spaces she never believed she would visit, she maintained this physical assertiveness. This experience opposed what occurs in many formal coeducational spaces. In those facilities, Jackson, Paechter, and Renold explain that girls learn from teachers not only that their learning needs are subordinate to those of their male counterparts but that girls are "excluded from areas within schools which have been taken over by boys, giving them, despite efforts on the part of many schools, less play and social space than is available to boys" (2010, 13).[5] In part, this implicit exclusion encouraged Yvette and her peers to claim the space as their own.

Marking a space as one's own is as important as naming one's self and experiences. Kids in general rarely have the opportunity to claim a space, create and maintain its norms and mores, and re-create it when the system proves to be unsustainable. Yet the absence of opportunity does not mean they lack the acuity to accomplish such tasks. Adults, though, continue to police youth, and particularly youth of color, for fear that left to their own devices, chaos would ensue. This belief is even more pronounced for girls of color. Consequently, being provided with a space to call one's own raises suspicion for some girls.

It is incumbent upon us adults to respect their skepticism, not as a personal indictment but as evidence that the girls understand the system far better than we may think. They understand that their schools do not trust them to control themselves, much less their spaces. At the same time, they may not have access to the words to articulate this wisdom or how to change it. Nevertheless, we need to capitalize on their knowledge, believing that if they can conduct a structural critique, they are more than capable of cocreating their own peer system toward positive ends. Lack of opportunity does not automatically mean that when provided autonomy, the privilege will be abused. It does require additional facilitation and guidance from an adult who recognizes that many girls of color possess untapped understanding and abilities. Such cognitive and practical talents can serve as a conduit to leadership, even if the path may not resemble the one that is adult-constructed.

On day one, Yvette received a writing pad and pen. Like most of her peers, she was surprised not to have immediate access to a computer. "Wasn't this supposed to be a technology program?" many girls thought. Their reactions were not too disturbing, since the majority view of digital media concerns manipulating, using, and, for some privileged groups, creating technology products. Eventually, the girls came to understand that success with technology is not merely about creating more digital products to benefit an already flawed system. With careful consideration, critical analysis, and skill to question how certain digital media supports injustices, mere technical skill acquisition correctly assumes a less significant role.

If we were focused only on skill enhancement, we would begin with the laptops and might see the proverbial technology pipeline populated with more diverse women. However, more African American and Native American female computer scientists or Latina technologists do not guarantee more equitable practices. Our approach approximates Balsamo's (2011) argument that culture needs to be centered squarely in discussions of technological innovations, illustrating that the most significant creations do not necessarily make an economic impact as deep or significant as the cultural consequences born from the innovation.

Emphasizing connections among each other so that girls feel empowered to create their own social system with situated cultural norms is important when providing enrichment opportunities to girls of color. Technology becomes a resource in building the collective, a means to document the creation of associations. We oppose the "technological determinist"[6] belief and emphasize technology as a means toward social justice ends. What is integral is finding one's self in relation to others while building an empowered community.

As the computer slips into the background, exercises on how to actively listen to each other and how to pose questions, requiring peers to unpack statements and understand that they are accountable to each other, dominate our time. In this context, the interpersonal associations do not resemble those that occupy most youngsters' social interactions.[7] Our emphasis on community action requires crossing boundaries that often become lost in technological spaces. If we were to introduce the technology first, girls would focus far more on how it works rather than on how it may contribute to subordinating communities, further biased images of social groups, and suppress empowered plans. Discourse requiring girls to dismantle how technology, schools, and other social systems encourage participants to name the oppression must come first. From this perspective, a need for coalition building can emerge. Matsuda inspires our attempts: "Working in coalition forces us to look for both the obvious and non-obvious relationships of domination, helping us to realize that that no form of subordination ever stands alone" (1991, 1189). Thus, we start with an exercise that on its surface seems to be about rule creation. In reality, this initial activity is more about encouraging girls to listen to one another's voices and become one another's allies.

As the mentor teacher explained, "Okay, we need to have some ground rules, you know, rules so everyone can have a good time and learn. Since the program is for you all, you are going to break into groups and come up with ideas as to what you think the rules should be. Oh, yeah, and someone in the group has to get up and present the suggested rules, and we as a whole group will vote on them." Yvette quickly became the presenter for her group.

Upon receiving the instructions, she quickly turned her chair to face away from the front of the room to look more directly at her group mates. Others followed her lead, and the five girls formed a tight circle with the mentor teacher—Tanya, White and middle-aged—seated slightly outside of it. "So, what do you think?" Tanya asked the group. As the girls looked at their hands and periodically at each other, Yvette was the first to speak. "Where are the computers? Don't we get laptops?"

"Yes, you will, but not until later," Tanya answered.

"But when?"

"How will you know how to take care of the computer if there aren't rules?" Tanya replied, just as evenly as Yvette asked. This nonhostile response satisfied Yvette, allowing her to return to the matter of rule formation.

After the allotted fifteen minutes passed, Yvette raised her hand to be the first to present her group's ideas. She was persuasive in her reasoning, stating, "My group, we, uh, came up with these rules. OK, so we think you have to earn a computer. We think you need to be quiet but should work together and listen to each other. No eating or anything around the computers, because if we mess them up then others won't be able to use them. That's all we discussed."

None of the young listeners requested additional information or posed questions. To her surprise, however, a few mentor teachers did respond to her suggestions by encouraging the silent onlookers to address her points: "What do you like about Yvette's group recommendations?"

As the sound of silence deepened, Celia, another mentor teacher, jumped in. "Girls, I know some of you had the same ideas as Yvette just presented. So, you must have thought it was good. So, what was good about it?"

Without much more provocation, Isabella, a slim fifteen-year-old Latina with long, straight brown hair and glasses she typically had to push back on her nose, raised her hand; her group mates looked at her in awe. "Go ahead and tell us, Isabella. You don't have to raise your hand. Simply talk when no one else is." To this remarkable point, most girls smiled and looked at each other in disbelief. It seemed that their surprise reflected important realizations about the setting and their role in it.

The privileged cultural capital[8] in this space was not participants' technical acuity but their verbal expressiveness and ability to support each other. This does not suggest that those girls who did develop exemplary technological skills were not recognized. On the contrary, both mentor teachers and peers publicly lauded an individual's ability to edit, debug, or build in the virtual world by encouraging her to show how she accomplished a task in front of the group of forty. However, her ability to articulate her steps, explaining how she came to the sought-after result, and to ensure that her audience fully understood why she conducted a particular action was more prized than simply possessing technical ability. Value was placed on sharing one's knowledge, not keeping it to one's self but ensuring others could benefit from it. This is one of the highest acts of love.

Conflict and Love

Describing how love can transcend race and gender, bell hooks writes, "Racial difference meant that we had to struggle to maintain the integrity of that bonding. We had no illusions. We knew there would be obstacles, conflict, and pain. In white supremacist capitalist patriarchy—words we never used then—we knew we would have to pay a price for this friendship, that we would need to possess the courage to stand up for our belief in democracy, in racial justice, in the transformative power of love" (1994a, 25–26). Standing together, celebrating each other's accomplishments as part of loving each other, is not easy or seamless. Internal strife may occur concurrently given perceptions from external observers.

We cannot ignore the fact that when Black and Brown bodies come together, this often incites fear and distrust from the dominant culture—namely non–Black and Brown bodies. Black and Brown *female* bodies congregating in the same space also raises suspicion. Are we planning a revolution? Plotting? Identifying ways to usurp the dominant culture? Or are girls simply preparing to fight? These and other interrogatives plague the minds of many, particularly adults observing girls of color. Too many adult educators seek to defuse the ensuing chaos that such girls' anger may incite.[9] It is of little surprise that this "concern" allows adults to respond in the same way that Lorde describes as the dominant culture's response to Black women's anger—that is, "to turn aside . . . with excuses or the pretexts of intimidation," thereby "preserving racial blindness, the power of unaddressed privilege intact" (2007, 132). Irrespective of all the technological advances, what remains "intact" is the notion that Black and Brown girls lack the intellect to use their voices in ways that, at times, defy biased expectations of what they can accomplish. That the girls can create a collective on their own that leads to Black and Brown girls working as allies to communally combat injustice as an interdependent team is rarely explored, much less documented. Key, here, are the interpersonal associations.

Sacred girl-centered relationships unfold in COMPUGIRLS space. Grounded in reflective response and shaped by active listening, girls willingly nurture positive dealings with each other. This engagement assumes precedence over all other interactions, including time with the computer. Indeed, one of the notable rules that this first cohort created was "PBT"— people before technology. If an individual demonstrated greater interest in a digital item (such as a laptop or camera) or computer program while a fellow participant was talking, it was permissible for any one individual to yell, "Hey, PBT." To this, the rule breaker would quickly cease "disrespecting" the speaker, who had also waited for everyone's full attention. In the beginning weeks, the mentor teachers were typically the only ones to engage in this practice, but as time progressed the adults rarely had to say this, as more girls felt empowered to make the call and fewer needed reminding. They learned to become one another's advocates and allies, a process that began as soon as Yvette awaited feedback to her suggestions.

Yvette was becoming impatient, shifting her weight from one foot to the other as she leaned against the podium in the theater-style room. At the same time, she maintained eye contact with the mentor teacher while also pressing Isabella for a response. "So, what do you think, Isabella? I want to hear," Yvette stated. Hearing the assertion in her voice caused the few girls who were not smiling before to turn the corners of their lips upward, and eyes turned to Isabella, who finally spoke: "I like how you, uh, said we should, uh, support each other but that, like, everyone needs to work hard." Yvette's dark brown hair shook gently as she nodded her head in agreement.

Once silence had recaptured the room, mentor teacher Celia continued, "Now, do we have any suggestions for Yvette or questions about her rules?" The room fell into ten seconds of soundless thought. "Well, I would like to hear you say more about why you think everyone needs to work hard," Celia said, addressing Yvette. "What do you mean exactly?"

Again surprised by such a direct question, Yvette moved her weight back on her heels, causing her body to sway away from the podium. Her answer caused a few girls to nod, but a few looked around in abject guilt. "I know some girls may be here just to have the opportunity to have a laptop and could care less about the program. That is not fair because not everyone got into the program who wanted to go. We who are here, we need to work hard because we don't need to be here and others could be. You know?"

No one responded to her rhetorical question. No one needed to. Again silence blanketed the room, but this time the girls' looks were seemingly more reflective. Followed by a quick affirmative response from Celia, who again asked girls to provide a positive statement to Yvette, the next speaker approached the podium while Yvette's applause subsided.

"Boy, that was a little scary! Everyone looking at me, but that was cool too!" she said in a loud whisper to her group mates, who patted her shoulder or smiled broadly. It was her mentor teacher who verbalized the others' appreciation: "Great job. You did our group proud." And the joy on Yvette's face shone beneath the beads of sweat that had begun forming on her forehead. Over time, Yvette found equal enjoyment in presenting to large groups and participating in teacher-facilitated discussions.

Critical pedagogy must include activities in which members of a collective create their cultural norms that will include affirming one another's voices yet motivating all to do more, be more, and demand more of themselves and their communities. In our context, groupness is devoid of competition and what hooks calls a "privileged voice of authority" (1994a, 84). Many STEM activities utilize competitive framings to motivate participants, such as in robotics competitions (Rusk et al. 2008), but this often excludes girls and children who are from cultures that strongly value consensus and coopera- tion. Still, this does not mean there is no lead voice rallying the troops.

Reminders of being in a space that they can call their own becomes im- portant to inspire the girls. At the same time, this strategy does not support an us-versus-them dynamic. Instead, these and other activities encourage girls to engage in the coalition-building process rarely discussed with such young participants. Rather than focus on how individual girls build their selective technical skills and work singularly on a technology project, our method aims to heighten girls' sensitivity to the threats that could dismantle their work. Naming those barriers and engaging in the cocreation of a safe, multi-mediated space with a heightened sensitivity to participants' subjec- tivities require more than the usual critical pedagogical approaches.

In concert with Crabtree, Sapp, and Licona's description of feminist peda- gogy, we too recognize intersubjective complexities, such as questioning the notion of a coherent social subject or essential identity, articulating the multifaceted and shifting nature of identities and oppressions, viewing the history and value of feminist consciousness-raising as distinct from Freirean methods, and focusing as much on the interrogation of the teacher's con- sciousness and social location as the student's (2009, 1–3). Our work extends this conceptualization to consider how digital media can and should play a role in the process of learning and teaching about one's self and each other as social actors able to make change.

The girls come to learn that questioning each other is not an offensive move. Requiring girls to consider the potential implications of their actions on individuals other than themselves allows them to build the necessary re- lationships to make change. We are attempting to create an activist habitus[10] predicated on relationships in which girls from various cultural backgrounds listen and learn from each other while, simultaneously, cultivating a sense of urgency to change the conditions of their communities, however they define them. Introduction to this process and its ultimate success requires time and a "cultural guide"—a girl who leads her peers in cocreating and maintaining the cultural norms shaping the COMPUGIRLS context.

Yvette assumed this role although she, too, was new to the expectations. Indeed, there was no formal process, no declared statement saying, "Yvette is now the guide." Like in most instances when a norm emerges, it was an organic process that did not always lead to anticipated results. As will be discussed below, she was not always successful in her pursuits. Her failures at persuasion, however, did not lead to a dissolution or even a weakening of the group; her standing was never threatened to the extent of her losing potency. Conflicts seemed to strengthen the peer bond while also heightening sensitivities to injustice.

Selecting a Topic as Critical Pedagogy

Drawing on her COMPUGIRLS application, Yvette attempted to convince her group to pursue the topic of Indigenous communities and education for their first project, the creation of a movie: "I think we should look at how Native Americans were colonized. You know, the boarding schools and how they were almost decimated. And I'm not only talking about Native people here but also in Mexico. Maybe we can do a comparison." Although Yvette aimed to engage in the very work Giroux (2012) emphasizes as the necessary charge for disenfranchised youth—that is, to take her "personal woes" and make them into a collective problem—her group mates did not reflect much enthusiasm about the topic.

Tanya, the mentor teacher, responded to Yvette before any other girl. "I think that could be very interesting. Here in A-Z we have a lot to learn about the Native cultures. I know I don't know much, and I have lived here forever," she said laughingly. "But what exactly do you want to learn? And why is it important? To whom?"

"I don't know, Miss, but I think we should talk about Native Americans, because if we are talking about social justice, they are one of the most wronged groups in America."

Tanya continued while the others shifted in their seats, watching their conversation like a tennis match. "A lot of horrible things have been done to Native peoples, yes. But are there other groups anyone can name who have also endured hardships in this country?"

At this point, the other girls begin to participate in the conversation, answering Tanya's question: "African Americans." "Mexicans." "Chinese," offered Gennifer.

However, Yvette pursued her original point. "Yes, I know, Gennifer, that the Chinese who built the railroads were mistreated and Blacks were slaves, but Natives were slaves too. Why can't we study them?"

Tanya responded, "Yvette, think about the questions we ultimately need to answer. I'm not saying we shouldn't study something about Native Americans, but how will we study them and advance their community? Do you know anyone on one of the local reservations who could work with us?"

Yvette admitted, "Well, no, yeah, no."

Tanya continued, "I'm not saying we shouldn't do this, but let's think about the how. We need to also think about methods. How we will collect data? And without access, do you think there is anything wrong with only relying on books or articles?"

"Yeah, there is a lot of made-up stuff in books. I wouldn't want to rely on that by itself anyway. But what about the boarding schools?"

"What about them?" And this back-and-forth continued for another sixty seconds, with Tanya posing questions to Yvette and others. By the end of the hour, Yvette was visibly excited.

"I learned that my ideas weren't stupid, but that I have a lot to learn! I thought it would make absolute sense to study Native Americans, but once we talked about it, it was more like me wanting to just study something without making a difference. I want to make a difference and be an activist, not just research stuff." After an additional thirty minutes her group mates decided to leave the room in order to hash out their ideas, "because we are getting real close, Miss, but we cannot concentrate in here. We are going to make the best movie ever."

Ultimately, the group did not research Indigenous communities. "That wouldn't make sense. None of us are Native, and how would we get real information?" one girl explained. This change of mind did not deter Yvette. She became just as enthusiastic about the new topic.

To someone unfamiliar with the curriculum, the exchanges between Yvette and Tanya may appear problematic. And for Yvette, who could rarely contain her passion about a topic, her speech could be coded as hostile. Tanya, however, did not interpret Yvette's remarks in negative terms. Tanya admitted after the first five weeks that she enjoyed conversing with Yvette, because "I don't have time in my regular classroom to do any of this talk; and to hear what she is thinking about social justice is really great. I mean, I never knew any of the things she says, or at least I didn't realize them, even though I work a lot with kids who look like Yvette." Later she added, as she pondered Yvette's stance and impact on the group, "I am learning so much that it inspires me to go home after being here and find resources for Yvette and the group." Tanya not only looked for peer-reviewed articles and newspaper articles on the group's topic but also played around with the technology so she could "come back the next day or the next and build off what they said and show them how to express it using technology."

A critical pedagogue is never a bored pedagogue. There is always work to be done. Facilitating a lesson does not cease when the lesson is completed. To be a critical pedagogue requires educators to do extracurricular work that probes into cultural and personal identities and where these are situated. Only reluctantly do the girls disclose information about themselves and relationships. Mentors must listen carefully and gently extract data that bridges where students are coming from and where they are going. Lesson preparation is ongoing. Mentors must be adroit, ready to shift directions and help the group shuttle in a different, preferred direction. This does not suggest the critical pedagogue should not be prepared prior to interacting with girls. The point is, teaching in a context that values students' whole selves obliges the educator to engage in an iterative process emerging from dialogue with the girls. This needs to occur even when an agreement is not present.

The mentor teacher shares gatekeeping responsibilities with students. In COMPUGIRLS, gatekeepers are not to sit in judgment but are meant to ensure movement and facilitate openness and participation while helping target the discourse. As much as possible, no participant should view it as her duty to inform another individual or her group mates that they are "right" or "wrong." To be sure, the adult mentors may be more concerned that the group does not waste time or digress and lose important perspective; but there is value when the girls find and correct themselves, discover essential and nonessential elements of discourse, agree to parse the issue in slightly different terms, and seek to align the process with good research, considering what will change the world they live in for the good of the greatest number. Adult action in COMPUGIRLS may be interpreted as reintroducing the deficit model. On the surface, Tanya's interjection could display her investing superior knowledge and wisdom and divesting students of ownership. To inform students that they are duped, misled, or viewing an issue without the same information available to the teacher-expert removes responsibility from the group. Tanya, like most COMPUGIRLS mentor teachers, did not assume a role as a cultural missionary.[11]

Graham Greene[12] and James Michener[13] had deep distrust of those who were cultural missionaries. Although both used different literary devices to showcase the dangers of such individuals, they were rightly skeptical of reformers who, for the sake of redemption, tolerated colonialism and hijacking of cultural privilege. Those who promote COMPUGIRLS must maintain intensity and commitment but guard against deprecating other selves while sharing their perspective. We are not cultural missionaries proselytizing our beliefs and downplaying any perspective that does not line up with ours. We do not have a monopoly on truth. Our work is unfinished and depends in large measure on what we learn as we interact with students. Adults must guard against unwittingly silencing students. At times, however, when adults encourage youth to speak, it results in the promotion of silence.

Everything I Say Is Wrong

When the girls began their second course, on The Sims, during the fall semester, Tanya continued. But juggling COMPUGIRLS' twice-a-week schedule, which included Saturday mornings, became taxing. By the time the girls began their third course, on Scratch, Tanya ceased working in our program. "I hate leaving them, but I really don't have the time. It wouldn't be fair to them," she said. Not only was she being governed by her own busy schedule, but she also was thinking about the welfare of the group.

There were many flashpoints during the program. Interaction with a strong girl, such as Yvette, and a new mentor teacher, Laura, ignited tensions and controversy. Laura was a middle-aged White woman with over ten years of experience teaching. As she and Yvette interacted, their relations were strained. Yvette's perspective: "She doesn't listen to me. Everything I say is wrong, and we end up doing what she wants to do and not what we want to do." Laura's interpersonal skills, especially sensitivity in recognizing and acknowledging Yvette's leadership, were at issue. She spent little time conversing with Yvette and did not recognize she spoke for the group. This neglect was grievous and dangerous, from Yvette's point of view. Quite likely, the source of antagonism was Laura's confidence that as facilitator she controlled the clock and movement with regard to problem solving. As the below incident demonstrates, because she failed to consult Yvette or seek input from the group, friction was generated.

Yvette's self-selected Scratch project focused on the negative effects of gentrification in urban schools. She didn't verbalize any new or compelling reasons for selecting a different topic from her original interest in Native American culture. She did open a window when she explained, "I just think it is important to know why some people want to keep us [low-income African American and Latina youth] ignorant. You would think they would understand it hurts the entire economy and society as a whole, but I guess not." Yvette had growing interest in structural barriers that hinder children's educational experiences. Perhaps her passion to determine how systemic challenges affect education impelled her to examine the new theme.

Charged to create a game or simulation using the programming language Scratch, Yvette was particularly excited to design an animated story about her topic. Her enthusiasm waned a bit when she realized the importance of debugging. Far from her favorite COMPUGIRLS activity, she drew on her peer relationships for assistance. Unfortunately, she found her new mentor teacher less supportive than the girls: "And when I asked Miss Laura for help, she just did it herself. She didn't show me how to do anything." This type of assistance annoyed Yvette. "I ended up going to Gennifer [her thirteen-year-old best programmatic friend], who showed me how to do it and I did it. Maybe I didn't do it as well [as she], but I did do it." This peer support occurred outside of program hours over the phone. The relationship between mentor Laura and Yvette deteriorated, exacerbated by this incident.

As the date for the closing ceremony approached, Laura attempted to guide her group to think about how they wanted to present their Scratch projects. "Okay, girls. What makes the most sense to you?"

As usual, Yvette spoke up first: "I think we should do something really different and cool! Like, I don't know."

Without recognizing Yvette's comments or her passion, Laura turned to another group mate and asked, "What do you think, Zaire?"

Yvette managed her anger, but her body language conveyed resentment at being ignored. Zaire, however, repeated Yvette's point. "Well, I agree with Yvette. We already did the boring-like presentations with girls standing up there talking. Let's do something really fun."

Yvette returned to her original suggestion after Zaire's endorsement. "Yeah, maybe we can have a guest speaker come in and talk to us about our work or something like that."

Before another girl could respond, Laura provided her view of this idea. "But that doesn't answer the question, and we don't have a lot of time to plan. Girls, we need some specific ideas." Yvette clammed up and refused to share any of her thoughts.

COMPUGIRLS provides support and guidance for teachers unaccustomed to or uneasy when utilizing a program that solicits untrammeled participation. Sometimes teachers are stymied and do not know where to turn. Their teacher education programs have not prepared them for the openness of our efforts.

At least, that was the case when I was instructing preservice teachers and the focus was on classroom management and ensuring the greatest number of kids knew the material to pass the standardized test. There was little to no time dedicated to the ideals grounding COMPUGIRLS. Although culturally responsive teaching practices were well articulated by this point in many teacher education programs, those pillars of asset building, reflection, and connectedness were not universally learned. I had hoped that the semester-long, weekly three-hour mentor teacher training I had devised would provide a sufficient foundation emphasizing these elements. Little did I realize the need for sustained engagement and what Paris and Alim (2014) call "culturally sustaining pedagogy." Preparing educators to focus less on achievement and more on how to engage students to sustain their valuable cultural knowledge in the face of a society that devalues their significance is complicated work. Orientation for our program, while multifaceted, cannot anticipate how or when girls will hurl new, provocative challenges at the group. Monitoring and supervising activities of the group is important, but no more so than relinquishing much of that power so that the girls can engage in some self-directed activities and discussions.

When I asked Laura about how she felt it was going, she admitted, "I never learned any of this in my degree program, and I specialized in multicultural education!" The radically new exposure led the adult mentor, a professional, to step aside and permit the girls to create a world according to their specifications. Many multicultural programs are interventionist, include adult supervision, and are still oppressive.[14] Our program relied on the girls to develop their world with minimum adult guidance.

Laura did not accept this approach; philosophically and in terms of economy, she preferred to be directive rather than allow the girls to pursue their line of inquiry. This did not negate her good work. Like so many teachers, Laura genuinely cared about the girls and wanted them to succeed. Care, however, is not enough to truly engage COMPUGIRLS participants to become techno-social change agents. To some extent, Laura's reluctance to entrust important aspects of the project to the girls was residual, a reflection of her cultural bias. All teachers bring bias to their work; professional training may paper over some of these biases, but nothing eradicates them. One task of COMPUGIRLS is to examine conflict and extract what girls of color, from underrepresented communities, can teach us. When professionals realize they can learn during the process of teaching, the total experience is more satisfying for both the adults and students. Our teacher training navigates culture—how to challenge girls to honor their own backgrounds and situated identities while setting high expectations that enable them to compete and effect change in the larger world. Our professional development may not be enough, but it is a start.

Teachers must be prepared for the challenge; indeed, they should cultivate it. And teachers should be equipped to recognize differential abilities. For example, Yvette might not have been able to debug, but she had other admirable talents. Likewise, Gennifer, who was fairly sophisticated at debugging and shared her knowledge with Yvette, deserved recognition and praise. It is not necessary for the teacher to do everything or be at the center of every activity. The diminished role of the teacher accompanies the group's rising significance. But teacher approbation fosters acceptance of the community's agency and its confidence that what is being done really matters.

During the remaining three meetings, Yvette was quiet, busying herself with debugging or talking with her group mates. She did not participate in small or whole group discussions at the same level as when Tanya was her mentor teacher. Notwithstanding this decreased level of activity, Yvette continued to attend and was never tardy. "I really love working with the girls more than anything," she confided to me.

Even though Yvette's more taciturn self did not result in embracing her school identity, COMPUGIRLS was a safe space for Yvette, thanks to her peers. She continued to participate but was more subdued. She was engrossed by technical aspects of the program and retreated from highly visible leadership. She managed the conflict with Laura by withdrawing from more conspicuous group activities, deferring to the mentor, and reducing prospects of antagonistic behavior. Yvette may have acquired greater technical skills, but it came at a price.

How They See Us

From day one, Yvette's peers respectfully listened to her. Her direct manner and occasional admonishments enlarged her authority. When Yvette spoke, her peers took notice and typically followed her directions. As the closing ceremony drew near, mentor teachers spoke far less to the girls. Even Laura became less directive and focused her energies on uploading projects rather than on providing verbal feedback.

With only three days left before the culminating event, girls made final edits to their projects. While mentor teachers circulated among the individuals and pairs to assess their progress, girls rarely lifted their eyes from their laptops. One day after almost thirty minutes of class time, mentor teacher Nellie disrupted the room's silence with, "It's time to show everyone what you have. Even if you haven't finished, you will have time. But we need to give you feedback now." Slowly, girls lifted their eyes toward Nellie. In most of the groups, the girls' faces were twisted with anxiety, and they glanced anxiously at group mates. Whispers of "We aren't even close to done" and "I have so much to do" were heard. At the same time, the girls were eager to present their work, because "then we can go back to working!"

After all the groups presented, the mentor teachers realized that time was short and the girls had far more to complete than the scheduled classroom hours would allow. The closing ceremony was a celebration. Similar to the "priming activities" in Reggio Emilia schools, it was a routine to document "shared collective activities."[15] COMPUGIRLS participants were the primary organizers and problem solvers. Thus, rather than offer them a solution, mentor teacher Lilly posed a significant question: "Now that you have seen everyone present [their projects], what do you think as a whole?" For the first time since week one, there was silence. With laptops closed, girls looked down at their hands or gazed at corners of the room, hoping to avert the eyes of their peers. Yvette responded first, repeating some of her earlier critiques but now with a racialized twist. Although not requested to do so, she stood to speak:

> I want to say something. I know some of you have put in a lot of work. Gennifer, she stays up late at night editing. Claudette, I see you online asking Gennifer questions late at night. But I know some of you aren't putting in half as much. You only come to take the laptops home and, like, play. In a few days, we will be getting up in front of people to show them what we have done. And you know some people are expecting us not to succeed. They think a bunch of Black and Brown girls from, you know, our city, can't do. But we have this program where we can show them what we can do and a chance to do it at the closing ceremony! Some of you need to really get it together, because you can.

Yvette resumed her seat while girls shifted their eyes. In an almost synchronized motion, they quietly and quickly opened their laptops and continued working.

Yvette galvanized the group. Through a bit of shame, she goaded the girls to action by confirming their agency and reminding them that "others" expected them to fail. She played the race card and reminded them they could do better, but effort was required. No adult, especially an "outsider," could have made such a speech without offending the group. Yvette utilized her leadership to rally a demoralized and flagging cohort to unite and finish a job they had started.

Groups require attention just as a garden requires weeding. Yvette didn't belittle the group; instead, she drew attention to the girls' potential, what had been accomplished, and what remained to be done. She confirmed their strength and acknowledged the forces that would mute and minimize them. She called them to do what they knew they could do, and to do it for themselves. Hidden, of course, was her agenda for social change, an agenda lost in the shuffle of many other concerns.

With grace, she led the other girls to their primary focus. At a crucial moment, she gave arms and legs to what had become a fleeting prospect. She enlisted others (Gennifer and Claudette), citing their contributions, lifting her talk above the self-serving realm and co-opting members of the group who had shared talent and energy. Her language was spare but also political, opting to strengthen a collective bond and renew commitment to social change. Moving from apparent concern with technology to using technology to achieve higher good, she demonstrated an important aspect of critical analysis. Yvette's words echoed what Penley and Ross had said years earlier: "Cultural technologies are far from neutral, [rather] they are the result of social processes and power relations" (1991, xii–xiii).

Yvette reflected a high level of realism about the potential of the girls' mediated social worlds. She did not assume that their interactions or the program alone would remove the isms (such as racism) from the surrounding society. Her conception of both the problem and possible solutions reflected complexity and thought.

While employing an intersectional lens[16] to articulate their collective struggle, she refused to accede to notions of powerlessness and called the girls to coalesce and bind their multiple identities for social change. Currie, Kelly, and Pomerantz's (2009) description of selfhood mirrors Yvette's assessment and approach: "others," explicitly the anticipated closing ceremony audience, might see the girls in images of deficiency due to their race, gender, and place of origin. Whether these perceptions applied to their technical literacy or some other skill was not clear. Nevertheless, her sense of how others would see them (their selfhood) did not dampen who she believed they could become. In essence, she was providing the girls guidance in how to manage the structural inequalities Crenshaw stated must be recognized in intersectional work. Namely, intersectional analyses must explore how "any particular disadvantage or disability is sometimes compounded by yet another disadvantage emanating from or reflecting the dynamics of a separate system of subordination. An analysis sensitive to structural intersectionality explores the lives of those at the bottom of multiple hierarchies to determine how the dynamics of each hierarchy exacerbates and compounds the consequences of another" (1991, 249).

At a relatively young age, Yvette understood the convergence of the girls' race-gender-social class and how the nexus caused some to automatically believe they could not achieve. Yvette expressed anxiety that the girls' incomplete products would substantiate those claims. In doing so, she failed to question how the perceptions emerged and were maintained but did not deny their existence or potential impact.

Yvette's forceful pleas to her peers ("get it together") reflected a particular cultural perspective about personal control.[17] In trying to unite participants to avoid feeding race-gender-social class stereotypes, she encouraged the girls to recognize and control themselves. Perhaps idealistically, she implied that if they were successful in completing their work to a high standard, the biased images of lazy, unmotivated, incapable girls from their under-resourced areas would be mitigated or possibly eliminated.[18] Their technical completions would serve as the counter-narrative to cultural deficit rhetoric. This suggests a tension in her thinking. Her demand was for the girls to change. By her logic, their individual modifications had to become outcome-oriented, and then there would be a correction in the system's perception of their potential. The irony of this strategy is it places the onus on the girls, just as deficit thought does.

This incident suggests that when guiding girls in this type of critical work, we must also encourage them to question their strategies. Girls and the adults steering them need to realize that girls of color can operationalize the same techniques and engage in the same oppressive acts as the forces they challenge. This does not commend greater adult intervention. What we need are more sustained opportunities for girls, and all underrepresented persons and communities, to reflect on their actions, particularly when engaged in social justice work.[19] Fighting hegemony and its practices does not inoculate one from their influence. At the same time, using a popularized tool from the dominant culture—such as technology—can prove helpful in the struggle. But there are no substitutes for careful review of strategies and inquiry as to whether these are the best, most beneficial measures.

The technology the girls were to present during the closing ceremony and the social networking occurring in the wee morning hours were constructs in this process of empowerment. In this context, the digital media was not the text of analysis but rather the tool that led to reflective action. Our efforts reflect Kahne, Middaugh, and Allen's point that digital media is a tool, an avenue "for political expression and mobilization," and thus it can create "new possibilities for civic and political participation" (2014, 35). Technology's use in this process informed how Yvette defined resistance.

Scholars, like Fine (with Tuck and Yang 2013), conclude that while there is no final victory in resistance work, it can lead to the necessary "dignity" and "hope" due to marginalized youth. Perhaps this view is pessimistic, but it does not suggest the work should cease simply because of injustice's pernicious nature. Yvette used the presence of false images to motivate the girls. Interestingly, she believed that as a group they could exceed expectations. Yvette's imagined girlhood was more about building a coalition within which collective skills could redefine how others saw them. The exact expertise necessary for this movement was not clear, but what was affirmed was the construct of we-ness (togetherness).[20]

The impending deadline and Yvette's speech stimulated the participants to action. For the next hour an air of intentionality dominated, and there was little talking over the sound of computer keys clicking and a few hushed whispers. Everyone seemed conscious of time and hurried to complete tasks. Yvette's group was ahead of schedule, so she roamed the room monitoring other girls' progress. Rather than stand over them, she pulled the nearest chair and sat down to watch or listen to the work-discourse. Periodically, she offered advice, mimicking questions that mentor teachers modeled during week one: "How does this relate to social justice? Is your topic about equity or equality? Who could benefit from your work? More importantly, who wouldn't want you all to present this topic?"

Girls did not respond directly to Yvette, but her presence was acknowledged. The questions she raised prodded the groups to refine unresolved concerns and tackle issues. Yvette did not need verbal affirmation; she was making a difference—she could sense it. Members of groups turned to each other and answered questions they had never raised: "Oh, that's right. We need to talk about that somewhere." Yvette smiled slightly upon hearing these words and moved to another group.

Going to MIT

Urging others to be reflective and action-oriented became a valued characteristic in this particular COMPUGIRLS peer culture. When the girls were charged to elect two spokespeople to present their Scratch projects at a Massachusetts Institute of Technology–hosted conference, Yvette won the free trip based on these qualities and not her technical skills. Gennifer accompanied her best friend.

"The last time I was on a plane was, like, when I was a kid! And look at all the rain. I don't want to wear shoes. Do I have to?" Yvette exclaimed upon arriving in Boston, the first day of the conference. Her beaming smile was not dampened by her soggy clothes, wet feet, or hair. "I really cannot believe I am here. I mean, we are at MIT, Gennifer!" And between sessions, the girls and mother-chaperone visited other sites in the Cambridge area. "I had heard about Harvard but never in a million years thought I would ever see it or be walking around on the campus!"

The initial awe of the setting did not diminish the girls' critical inquiries. Before conducting their session, Yvette asked me to what extent they could include some less auspicious comments: "I don't want them to ask us to leave or anything, but you know when you said at the end of the presentation we should talk about, you know, specific recommendations? Well, can we make recommendations about how they are doing things?" And to a standing-room-only audience of approximately forty conference attendees, Yvette presented her peer-selected project, titled the "Negative Effects of Gentrification on Urban Communities."

"I'm a little nervous, but excited. This is great!" she whispered to me seconds before I introduced the girls and the program. Walking barefoot to the front of the room, Yvette assumed her familiar stance, tilted more toward swagger than deference but with confidence relaxing her body. If she was nervous, it dissipated after a few moments. She looked audience members in the face and, absorbed in the subject, proceeded without faltering.

She discussed the importance of her topic. "Many people think gentrification is a good thing, particularly for poor neighborhoods. I don't think it is, and this is what my Scratch project is about." For the next four minutes, she explained the research she conducted to create her project and how debugging was "not her thing"; she acknowledged and validated Gennifer's technological skills and important role in the project by proclaiming, "Luckily, my friend, Gennifer, helped me, because I completely didn't understand it." The audience of MIT students, Scratch developers, professors, and other conference presenters listened politely, smiling at this revelation. However, Yvette's final words were what caused most people to look up in surprise:

Now, I am about to talk about recommendations, because that is what we are supposed to do in a presentation. Well, I have two things to say. There isn't much diversity in the Sprites.[21] I mean, yeah, you have an African American girl Sprite, but she has an Afro. And there are a whole lot of African American girls who don't have Afros, so there needs to be more diversity there. But also, yesterday, I went to a plenary talk, I think that is what they called it. And they had all these kids, I guess about my age, from all around the world talk about Scratch. They talked about beta testing. They brought kids from all over, and none of them looked like me, or Gennifer, or Dr. Scott. Don't you want us to use your products? I think so. So why not come to where I live and ask kids who look like us to do some beta testing? We have a lot to say.

And with those words, Yvette once again caused a crowded room to hush.

In the End

Yvette took other trips on behalf of COMPUGIRLS. Even though she traveled as far as Alaska, speaking with every middle and high school girl in one district, the MIT trip stood out in her mind. "That was really cool to see everyone listening to me. I mean, even one of the creators was there, and she didn't seem mad at what I said. I hope they do something about it," referring to her Sprite recommendation. Her enthusiasm did not fade once she completed all six COMPUGIRLS courses in two years. Program staff, including me, often invited Yvette to visit and work with the girls as a near-peer mentor. Understanding that she needed a financially compensated position, however, we encouraged her to attend school so that she could be officially hired and paid as a consultant. The hope was that she would apply to university, and I could provide her funding. But for reasons that were never very clear, she missed the deadline. "I just didn't get it in." This was one of the few times Yvette's smile did not appear on her face. "What about community college? Take classes there for much less and then maybe transfer?" the staff encouraged.

Yvette was able to enroll in a few community college classes, none of which were technology related, because "I need to get the basic core out of the way, like English and math." Before the semester ended, however, Yvette needed a full-time job "to help out at home." Again, program staff made introductions, and Yvette acquired a job in a call center located in our office building.

Approximately three months after working in this program, I saw Yvette. When I asked how she liked the job, her description represented one of the rare instances she discussed COMPUGIRLS' impact on her technological literacy: "They promoted me after like a month or so. I can't believe it, but I was troubleshooting a lot of things for them—you know, things with computers and stuff. This is where I think COMPUGIRLS really helped me. I don't know everything there is to know about computers, but because of what I learned in COMPUGIRLS, I know how to figure things out." While her metacognitive examination served as a clear definition of computational thinking, it was more than that.[22]

At times, Yvette's story did not correspond neatly with experiences of other COMPUGIRLS participants. This chapter is not meant to suggest her uniqueness. In fact, the differences between Yvette and others dissipated as time progressed. For instance, after the first course, more and more girls ceased fleeing through the campus halls, fearful that they did not belong. Whether Yvette's initial stance was the reason for this shift cannot be said with any certainty. What is intriguing, however, is the consequence of her self-imposed silence.

One could argue that she was muted by her guidance counselor and, thanks to Mrs. C and the program, she was saved. A better explanation is that Yvette silenced herself in school and, at times, while navigating COMPUGIRLS. As Melissa Harris-Perry explains, choosing to be silent differs from being silenced: "When we are silenced, you have something to say but no one will listen. When you choose to be silent, to quiet it down, to listen, you've actually exercised the other part of voice. The part that makes your voice sound like something."[23]

Yvette's actions led to her joining the program, spurring the respect of her peers, traveling throughout the nation as a COMPUGIRLS activist, and becoming an impressive technologist. It is doubtful Yvette employed tactics for dramatic effect. Most of the time she seemed to be self-aware, cognizant of what she was doing. There were occasions her peers did not heed or recognize her leadership, but she was rarely daunted. She was not reluctant to discuss what she didn't want to do (such as debug) or label what she wanted to do (social activism). In the end, however, she conducted research with her group and produced projects, drawing attention to the girls as a whole and her singular ability. Yvette and so many of her COMPUGIRLS peers developed an awareness and appreciation for research that equipped them to challenge the status quo. Exactly how these girls would shape resistance and their proposals for creating a new order was never certain. But the fact that they undertook a difficult endeavor and stuck with it was a testimony to their immersion in the COMPUGIRLS program.

Our work is far from linear and often presents unanticipated challenges. All of the girls have unique lives, cultures, and experiences. COMPUGIRLS cannot and does not aim to be a fix-all program. To claim such a stance would oversimplify the girls and their communities. We do hope that our efforts will increase girls' understanding of how and when to apply technical skills to social problems plaguing their community. Concurrently, we hope the girls will innovatively identify ways to build coalitions with change agents.

It is easy for participants to miscalculate progress, especially inflating completion of a project and equating it with systemic social change. An important task for mentors is framing what is done in the classroom and then asking the girls to look at what is feasible in the "real" world. An embellished sense of accomplishment will distort views about social change and lead to exaggerated pronouncements about transformation and the value of school efforts. More than anything else, mentor teachers help provide perspective and proportion. This type of work requires careful attention to critiquing systems rather than individuals.

Not only do girls labor to unpack oppression, but they do so methodically and with an aim—to challenge the structures upholding social hierarchies. There are many bumps in the road, including instances where sight is lost and victims are blamed. Nevertheless, their efforts provide a nuanced representation of youth resistance work. Fordham's metaphor of resistance provides an accurate critique of most youth efforts: "If you've got an umbrella and it's raining, you put the umbrella up. The rain doesn't fall on you any more, right? But what does it do for the rain? Resistance is similar in effect. The rain is coming, we can put up an umbrella and resist the rain but it does nothing to stop the rain. It doesn't change the rain, it doesn't keep the rain from falling, it does nothing to the rain" (2014, 102). Girls, programs, and scholars need to aim for the source of the rain in order to know where to place the umbrella.

Creating a girl-empowerment program is popular. Ensuring that the experience is meaningful and disruptive (at least to the status quo) is less appealing and requires a considerable amount of work. There have been and will continue to be countless twelve-hour days of work, six days a week, to effectively implement this program. And the girls and mentor teachers are not the only ones forever affected by COMPUGIRLS. To this day, my now-teenage daughter recalls the many Saturdays we spent at the program. By the time she became school-aged, she was quick to repeat some of the conversations from COMPUGIRLS. I recall several instances when she argued for equal rights to a swing set, questioned other youngsters' and teachers' differential treatment of her and other Black and Brown children, and vociferously represented the interests of bullied peers, even when it jeopardized her own social standing. Her actions also caused me to have several unpleasant conversations with school administrators.[24] In short, the type of critical inquiry and critical praxis engendered by the girls seeped into the lives and souls of more than themselves.

Dislodging hierarchies, for example, is easier to accomplish as an exercise than in the social order. Many adjustments and a good deal of negotiation proceed and take place when the pyramid is challenged. If the benefactors, who are not always united in support, coalesce because of attack, then the job is complex. Any change in power structure or allocations takes time. Moreover, there may be a number of unanticipated, unplanned consequences that cannot be envisioned until the change progress is initiated. It is comparatively easy to talk about girl power in the abstract; when it is directed toward problem-solving and new arrangements of the social order, massive problems ensue.

We are not promoting change or girl power as if it is relatively costless and facile to achieve. The type of girls-of-color power expressed in COMPUGIRLS is slippery and elusive and as volatile as the forces it challenges. It takes on many guises but doesn't present itself as benign. It is situational, taking its character from those who breathe life into it. It is both tough and gentle. It resists the corrosiveness of those who would demean it. It has endurance, because it is embedded in the life of a lively and alert community. Its fluidity rests in constant movement to reexamine its principles and tenets, question moral integrity, and broaden its embrace to include a more diverse and inclusive group. Girls-of-color power maintains the grace to admit its flaws and make concerted efforts to correct them, refuses to flail those who stand outside its circle, and attempts to create a better and more equitable community in spite of past failures. That this is ambitious work can hardly be argued. It calls on girls to undertake a herculean job.

Girls-of-color power is more than simply resisting gender, race, or ethnic discrimination. The girls learn that their cocreated culture takes place only to the extent they create conditions for and birth meaningful changes in the social order. We concur with Taft that efforts to create and sustain girl power should not be limited to "incorporating girls into the social order as it stands, rather than empowering them to make any meaningful changes to it" (2010, 23–24). This becomes unmistakably true for girls of color in COMPUGIRLS.

Through interactions with each other and mentor teachers who understand and exercise their role as critical guides, girls-of-color power becomes possible. Unfortunately, some mentor teachers resist what Jocson describes as a "pedagogy of possibility" and what the girls come to expect: "practices that allow for dynamic constructions of meaning as well as representations of themselves within the environment" (2013, 7). These incidents, however, do not cause disruptions that make our program wobble more than momentarily. Mentor teachers juggle their own principles and sense of moral stamina as they engage in the program and often recalibrate their approach and understanding of what the program is about and of the integrity of its methods. The strength of the newly formed community eventually will be enhanced precisely because neither mentors nor students fail to question the inner workings of what makes a nurturing community.

The conflict between mentor teacher Laura and Yvette was beneficial. Both learned important lessons about their understanding of COMPUGIRLS. They were willing to go on, albeit altering their perspectives and positions, but for the sake of larger goals not rejecting objectives or disparaging the other. And both appeared to recognize the unfinished work was more important than the impasse that pitted them against each other. The mentor admitted shallowness in professional preparation, and this was a first step toward a remedy. Yvette, perhaps because she was younger and less adept at handling failure, didn't abandon the program but retooled and utilized several avoidance mechanisms to stay out of the orbit of the mentor. She sulked and grieved her ineffectiveness. Yvette seemed to concede that the mentor, at least in this case, might have been tougher than she; she certainly appeared to back off and permit Laura larger influence in decision-making.

She learned to renegotiate herself in space, and, although awkwardly, pressed toward the goal she had set forth.

COMPUGIRLS is not owned by mentor teachers or by me as its founder. When creating a program for girls of color, we as developers relinquished a large portion of power and turned it over to participants. The transfer of ownership wasn't seamless, and at times adults claimed that they had "given in" to the girls. So, work with adults who implement and girls who navigate the program is ongoing. This requires providing considerable time for girls to engage in the "critical consciousness" work that Gonick explains should inspire students to explore how "social forces shape subjectivity and how these processes can be challenged through critical reflection and action" (2012, 53). But the assumption that all adults internalize and operate according to tenets of the program is false. A continuous fine-tuning of the program, as well as a careful exposition of the philosophy underlying the lessons, must be carried on.

COMPUGIRLS is taking shape within its own provenance as well as in the classrooms. There are many threads of activity, and both adults and girls must be willing to deal with the unfinished nature of the program and to find better ways to express strategies that energize participants to embrace its goals. This approach is filled with uncertainty and requires adults to listen for the "multiplicities of discourse" rather than impose notions of what counts as real ideas. As a process, girls can create a space in which adults can learn much about their perspectives of justice, alienation, coalitions, and change. What has remained outside the parameters of discourse, what was "off limits" and ritualized to the extent it was unquestionable, now deserves scrutiny. Concurrently, we confront our own awareness of what constitutes girl power by boldly defining girl-of-color power. As will be discussed in the next chapter, many COMPUGIRLS participants find this emphasis on autonomy and the potential to orchestrate their space invigorating. A new girl-culture emerges that does not rest on any of the negative characteristics typically applied to girls of color. COMPUGIRLS' girl-culture rests on mobilizing participants, including adults, to be accountable to individuals other than themselves.

CHAPTER FOUR

Sounds of Silence

DURING THE SUMMER OF 2007, I often found myself teaching the first group of COMPUGIRLS participants. In this role, I carefully considered what was expected of mentor teachers. And I was hyperaware of body movements and language, as critical feminist pedagogy stresses.[1] While I engaged the girls and listened to their concerns, I noticed that they, too, began to pepper their peer-talk with critical inquiries: Shouldn't we care that the media makes us look like we are only about sex and junk? Don't you think this makes boys think we're easy? Doesn't this affect why your mother won't let you go anywhere? After a few weeks, discussions of biases, identity, stereotypes and isms soon became the property of the girls and not the adults. Encouraging girls to do more than facilitate discussions, however, became more complicated. When the girls didn't raise issues or questions, they tended to be detached and not interested.

In this chapter, I include two cases to illustrate how girls talked about connections they built among themselves and mentor teachers.[2] Both instances present a reimagined view of silence and activism. Not far beneath the surface, girls performed a complicated dance creating an alternative cultural space, which they endorsed and encouraged the group to accept, one aware of conventional assumptions about femininity and girl-of-color power. The analysis pays particular attention to how the girls interpreted and reinterpreted critical pedagogical practices.

Charlotte

In the spring of 2008, Charlotte was one of the youngest COMPUGIRLS applicants. Yet despite her chronological age of fourteen, she was wise beyond her years. A reserved African American, she was quite tall, with medium-brown skin, small eyes, and dark brown hair arranged in neat braids. She rarely looked anyone directly in the face; she typically glanced at the floor during interpersonal associations. It was surprising to hear her clear, crisp voice. As she fully punctuated each consonant and enunciated each vowel sound as if individual words mattered more than the complete sentence, listeners took notice of her speech, no matter its low volume. Her application essay indicated why she wanted to join COMPUGIRLS:

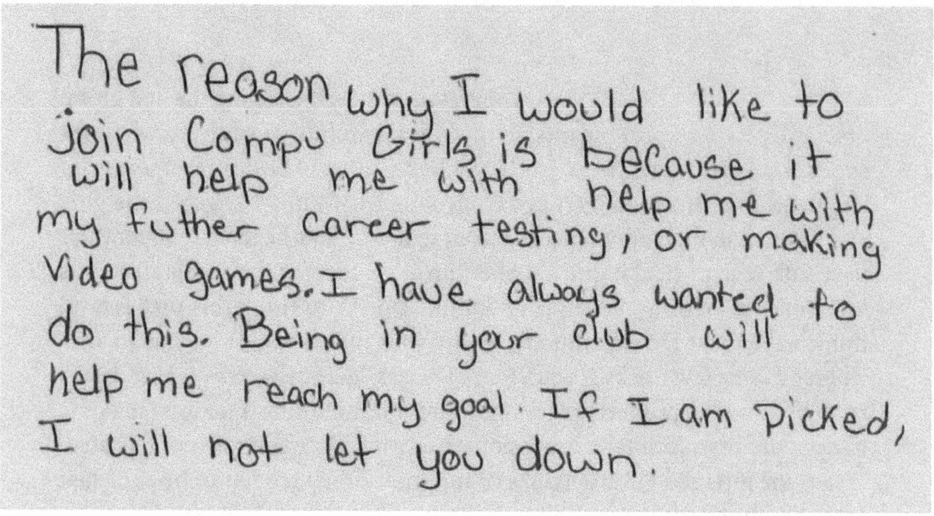

The reason why I would like to join Compu Girls is because it will help me with help me with my futher career testing, or making video games. I have always wanted to do this. Being in your club will help me reach my goal. If I am picked, I will not let you down.

Figure 4. Charlotte's application essay

Concern about not letting me or the program down was not very evident upon first meeting Charlotte. Although her sheepish smile remained on her face when she spoke, she expressed greater concern for the collective than for me or any individual.

During the first COMPUGIRLS course, Charlotte tried to be invisible. Group work did not pose a problem, but neither her peers nor mentor teacher seemed aware of her presence. More often than not, Charlotte would not contribute to the conversation, and no one invited her input. Occasionally she would make mention of the technological capabilities her group mates may not have known but then retreated to the shadows.

For Charlotte, the self-imposed marginalized space she occupied was one of silence—she determined when she would speak. When she decided to break her muteness, her peers listened and willingly followed her suggestions, even when they did not provide verbal assent. For instance, when her group initiated discussions of how the software program GarageBand could be used to make movies, Charlotte quietly but forcefully reminded them of this impossibility. Without lifting her eyes from her laptop screen she said, "No, it won't do that. You need to play with the other thingamajig, the, uh, whole system." Her response may not have been the most pointed, and to someone who could not readily identify the "thingamajig," her advice would seem useless. However, without turning their heads in her direction, the two speakers looked at each other and said, "Oh, that's right. We cannot use it for that. It's for the music. OK, we need Photoshop to import and change around our pictures and use that as part of the movie." A smile crept across Charlotte's face.

Time and again, Charlotte chose this communication style with her fellow COMPUGIRLS participants. In turn, few girls approached Charlotte for assistance. Charlotte, who typically completed technical tasks before all others, would physically position herself next to individuals or groups and in such a way implicitly offer her assistance. Acting as if she was incredibly occupied by her own work, she would not directly intervene or hover over girls, as Yvette chose to do. Close enough to hear discussions but far enough away to seem unconcerned, Charlotte would quietly offer advice or guidance without narrowing the self-imposed physical divide between her and others. Never intrusive or gloating over her superior grasp of skills, she remained on the sidelines. Barely above a whisper, her words sometimes seemed tentative. But they didn't denigrate the girls. Although her recommendations were sometimes oblique, they were transparent enough to be encouraging. Her statements of "No, you can't do that" or "That is wrong" were readily received without hesitation or reproach. Once a group of girls resolved their issue and did not express any other worries or assert a technological impossibility, Charlotte would casually and slowly move within listening range to the next individual or set of girls "in need."

Even when she returned to the program after completing all six courses and volunteered her time as a near-peer mentor, she applied the same strategies. As a result, Charlotte continued to develop her agentic abilities well beyond the program's conclusion. Her commitment to the community spanned time and locale. She used her technical skills to assist the group and claimed no special privileges and sought no recognition.

Different from School

Why do COMPUGIRLS participants, across time, value this type of indirect and at times abrupt guidance? Although I never directly asked participants their preference, I did purposely ask mentor teachers to assume the most facilitative approach possible. How well my suggestion was received varied (see, for example, Laura's struggles in the previous chapter). Nevertheless, when teaching the graduate course that was required for mentor teachers before they could interact with the girls, I spent considerable time explaining that we were not to duplicate school in this space.

This was an important lesson. Always mindful of my own obligation to critical pedagogy, I tried to be reflective in my decisions. Because I believed that schools had already failed far too many of the girls and their families, an anti-school approach inspired my critical praxis. Assuming an anti-school approach meant the girls would take over the lesson, lead all problem-solving activities, and tap the mentor teachers sporadically. For some mentor teachers, this was a dangerous business. Letting go and allowing the girls the freedom to physically move around the space (as Charlotte did), intervene when they wanted, and interact at will caused some adults too much discomfort (a point that will be discussed below). The girls, however, believed in this space, even though it seemed far different from their school environment.

During recruitment sessions, I always made a point to share with prospective students the expectations I set forth with the mentor teachers. Most girls were amused that I would dare pull back the veil and discuss how their potential teachers were treated as students. I did this, in part, to illustrate how the COMPUGIRLS power dynamics were different from those in their school settings. My hope was that explaining the limited agency of the actors (mentor teachers) in this counterspace would encourage them to reflect on and ultimately challenge the matrix of domination shaping their school lives. Knowing the system and its oppressive forces is important; understanding who may be actors fighting against or for the system is the next step. I thought this type of information could assist girls in identifying potential allies to join their efforts.

Too rarely do girls navigating economically stressed communities get the opportunity to see the vulnerability of their teachers. Instead, adults in such settings assume positions of authority, pretending to have the "right" to lord it over these "unsalvageable" girls. Take for example Crenshaw, Ocen, and Nanda's 2015 report, *Black Girls Matter: Pushed Out, Overpoliced and Underprotected*. Based on proceedings from a 2012 conference conversation, the report uniquely and assertively addresses what the authors call "the knowledge desert that exists around the lives and experiences of Black women and girls" (8). The girls understand their maltreatment. Girls from Boston and New York City surmised that teachers impose zero-tolerance in school settings in order to control and police them. The girls reasoned that the adults believed they "can't be trusted or 'they are loud and rowdy, ghetto,' and stuff like that" (31). In such depressing contexts, adults create and sustain biases based on stereotypical representations. And to bolster adult authority, most pretend to be omniscient and omnipresent, free from recrimination, no matter how egregious their actions. In such hostile environments, girls seldom accept what they deem, and rightly so, unreasonable demands. The school classroom may become a battlefield, and quiet moments do not necessarily represent peaceful submission by either the teacher or students.

Just beneath the surface, African American and other Brown girls may be seething, fully aware of what is going on and why they are being treated in such a negative, disdainful manner, and doing what they can, within the constraints of institutional norms, to offset and negate the demands. So when teachers assume a less autocratic role and delegate more autonomy in the classroom to students, youth may wonder if entrusting more independence to them is some kind of contrivance. While seldom overt and almost never violent, many urban classrooms are places of intense contest. Even the proposed surrender of teacher authority is viewed with suspicion. Thus, when we told prospective COMPUGIRLS participants that they would have the liberty to determine their topics, decide on the most appropriate methods to explore their areas of interest, and create their own adjudication system, it raised some girls' suspicions (as with Yvette), while others became excitedly intrigued.

Charlotte's space, the one in which she physically removed herself from individuals while remaining tuned in to their technological needs, provided her latitude to ultimately become an activist. Unlike so many generic images of Black girls (for example, the seductive Jezebel, the emasculating Sapphire, or the docile Mammy) resulting in stereotypes that Harris-Perry (2011) describes as creating a "tilted room" for which Black girls and women constantly have to correct, Charlotte developed her own script. Her quiet fortitude was neither controlled nor disdained. Without coercion from her group mates or mentor teachers, Charlotte played out an antithetical image of Black girl activism. Neither loud nor needing immediate control, she was afforded multiple and sustained opportunities to quietly challenge her fellow participants to become more technologically knowledgeable. Opposing the myth Barbara Monroe (2004) claims the dominant culture both maintains and perpetuates—that communities of color are technophobic and simply care little about technological innovation—Charlotte created an interesting counter-narrative to technological activism.

For Charlotte, her subtle interventions included indirect associations, which was also the case for many other COMPUGIRLS participants. Ensuring that the other girls understood the technical skills and encouraging them to expand their knowledge beyond what we taught became her personal practice. Charlotte's strategies solidified membership in the group and earned her grudging respect for her unique modus operandi. But her pedagogy was set in opposition to some mentor teachers and was not always acceptable to them. Charlotte created her space to resist.

Let Them Do What They Do

Once Charlotte progressed to the COMPUGIRLS course involving The Sims, she used the same quiet approach to resist our curricular objectives, deciding that they were not adequate. In her mind, our expectations did not do a good enough job of allowing the girls to research their topics and use the technology of The Sims to describe and analyze their findings. For this reason, she ignored our expectations and created a much more complicated project.

Interested in the correlation between socioeconomic status and child abuse, Charlotte first researched which strata of society (lower-, middle-, or upper-income) had the highest reported cases of child abuse. She examined child abuse in families living in poverty and those classified as middle-income. With these parameters, she researched what a "typical" household of each family would look like. She focused on the type of furniture, or lack thereof; physical facilities; neighborhoods; proximity to neighbors, grocery stores, and restaurants; number of individuals in a household, and number of digital devices in the home, such as television and computers. Once she obtained the information, she built two different Sims worlds based on her research findings. Although both families in her created worlds had a baby, she purposely programmed the parents to have markedly different demeanors.

Within the lower-income Sims family, she built a few sparsely furnished rooms. Charlotte pointed out to me that she purposely did not put a desk in the home because "the parents don't have money for something like that. Kids do their homework on the floor or on the bed." A television was the only digital device. Multiple siblings made their way in and out of the space, and the nearest school was quite a distance in this digital landscape. Importantly, she programmed the parents to be very impatient. In contrast, the middle-income family's home contained more furniture and had large windows, there were fewer siblings, the family was closer to the simulated school, and the home was surrounded by a large plot of land. The parents in this scenario possessed more books, a home computer, and the basic equipment for a child—that is, toys, a crib, a high chair, and so forth. The building of these worlds served as the platform for her project.

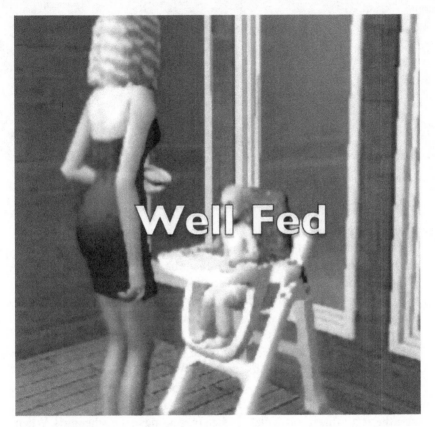

Figure 5. Charlotte's Sims family (1)

Once Charlotte was satisfied with her two home settings, she commented, "Now I let the Sims[3] do what they do." She attentively watched, took notes, and recorded how the parents interacted with the baby. As a digital ethnographer, she documented how various stressors in the low-income household kept parents from paying careful attention to their youngest child. Coded more like neglect than explicit abuse, Charlotte concluded that life in economically challenging settings often prevents parents from providing proper care for their babies.

Figure 6. Charlotte's Sims family (2)

Charlotte presented her project to the whole group explaining, "It's not like they want to abuse the baby or nothing, but like in this image here, you know, like the mother has to travel far to get the other kids to school and then to her job and doesn't have time to pick up fresh milk at any store. There is no store really in the neighborhood anyway. And then no one is really watching the baby except an older sister, who isn't really watching so the baby drinks the spoiled milk and throws up."

Unhappy with how her recorded voice sounded narrating her project, Charlotte used the computer to change it. A masculinized computer voice presented her research question, the method for obtaining information, findings, and subsequent analysis and recommendations. The actual comments were the very same she articulated when presenting to the other girls. When asked why she did not simply use her voice, she explained, "I don't think it sounds—I don't like how it sounds." No further explanation was given, and none was demanded. In the end, the girls voted Charlotte's creation to be one of the most innovative and requested it be showcased at the closing ceremony. Charlotte agreed to this honor, as it did not require her to talk. Her projected male voice told the story.

When engaging in critical pedagogical work, curriculum designers need to leave room for revisions. This inevitably means providing participants space to push back on our well-intentioned objectives. Their resistance may create a much more nuanced end than our adult minds could imagine. Resistance in this context challenges the status quo or some other external force. A critical space must include one in which students can oppose the very efforts we construct in searching for a social justice end. Undoubtedly, this approach is scary. Without building a high level of trust and respect as well as a peer system in which girls feel a sense of belonging, chaos could ensue.

For girls like Charlotte, the sense of belonging emerges from the possibility of simply being in a space that values who she is rather than what we expect her to become. This requires adults to let go. Charlotte reveled in her almost-silent space and gained validation for this identity by watching her brief words increase girls' technological savvy. Neither encouraged to speak up nor criticized for being too interfering, she could be the digital sage for multiple cohorts. This does not suggest that critical practices should not maintain high expectations and challenge students in unprecedented ways.

Gay makes it clear that culturally responsive practices as a critical pedagogical strategy must be rigorous and present regular and consistent opportunities that "replace pathological and deficient perceptions of students and communities of color with more positive ones" (2010, 54). Gay accurately describes what Charlotte actualized through her self-directed peer associations, promoting excellence by creating "community among individuals from different cultural, social, and ethnic backgrounds; and develop[ing] students' agency, efficacy, and empowerment" (49).

Charlotte had never played with The Sims program prior to participating in COMPUGIRLS. Her objections did not signal a fight against the power dynamic. We did not code her opposition to the curriculum as a form of disrespect. On the contrary, it was her incredible drive to seek ways to fully explore a social issue that caused her to stretch the boundaries of our efforts. Critical pedagogical practices must allow students, including girls of color, to construct different performances of their subjectivities, even when such acts seem to reproduce particularized ideals of silence and subjugation. Closer inspection of these behaviors may reveal that the almost silence of girls of color is not synonymous with insensitivity or passivity. Charlotte's silence was more than a coping mechanism; it was a studied response to a classroom culture she was determined to challenge. And Charlotte's apparent withdrawal in no way signaled either defeat or tacit acceptance of adult norms. In fact, Charlotte challenged all goals; those her peers had established were as vulnerable as those set forth by mentor teachers.

Silence should be reinterpreted and not automatically perceived as a sign of weakness or defeat. Claiming one's silence assumes a different but equally agentic performance of subjectivity. This embrace of silence counters the dominant belief that it symbolizes failure; it also extends how space can be used to allow for the presence of silence as an asset. Our efforts do not concern interventions but providing the context for girls to reinvent themselves and encourage others to do so on their terms.

Allowing Charlotte to physically position herself where needed,[4] as well as redefine the power dynamics wherein adults were not the bearers of knowledge, granted the girls a different vision of critical learning. It was also incredibly time consuming for Charlotte to engage in her strategies. A formal educational space in which most adolescent girls have no more than fifty-minute blocks of time with a given subject would hardly allow for such movement. Nevertheless, she built an interesting coalition around technological acuity through multiple short but powerful interactions. Although Charlotte navigated the room by herself, her movements were in concert with the needs of her peers. She built a coalition around technological resistance.

Charlotte perceived impediments for her peers. And not only did she recognize these potential roadblocks, but she advocated procedures or pathways to deal with them. The visioning process was in the hands of Charlotte. Both students and mentor teachers knew this, and the concession was not easy for either. Charlotte could be an irritant as far as her peers were concerned and not only disruptive but a show-off from the vantage point of teachers. This young woman was in uncharted waters but pulled off her offers of technical assistance as well as challenges to the curricular goals largely because of timing and a manner that didn't disparage her peers or frustrate the mentors too much.

Small group activity made it easier for Charlotte. One of the advantages of this dynamic is that it provides a broader platform for individual differences and more space for design and creation of innovation. Charlotte never asked her peers to endorse her behavior. The way she took charge in her newly created space suggested she did not care what adults thought about her; she simply wanted to act on what she concluded to be vital.

Charlotte possessed valuable capital and made sure it was available to her peers. Her peers accepted and integrated Charlotte's knowledge. The exchange required no currency: Charlotte was self-assured and willing to share, even when not invited; her peers received her offerings without celebration, and groups continued moving toward their goals. It should be recognized that Charlotte was more concerned with method—except in the illustration about The Sims and child abuse—than with substance. This may account for why she did not clash more with adults. She got what she wanted without creating a climate of loss for mentor teachers. The COMPUGIRLS experience with Charlotte may lead to the program revising success or celebration. Does unspoken assent and integration of knowledge indicate a new nonverbal mode of reward? One thing is certain: Charlotte sought no praise, and her peers lavished little or none on her.

COMPUGIRLS resists the stock stories depicting girls of color devaluing individual achievements. Commemorating what an individual knows becomes commonplace in this peer culture, particularly when it benefits the collective. To this end, the Black and Brown girls in this informal education space have room to engage in self-definition practices. As a result, the girls learn not to define themselves, as Collins describes, "in opposition to others" but through the context of the COMPUGIRLS community (2000, 113). This is a powerful, peer-directed act. According to our model, girls no longer expect adults to assume the primary role of guide; mentor teachers are co-learners.

In the COMPUGIRLS program, the development of resistance and creation of alternative space is not complete. For instance, Charlotte disliked her voice and chose a masculinized one to convey her ideas. She needed growth in the domain of accepting herself. She was still influenced by patriarchal views, since she believed a male voice was superior to a female's. This cultural residue may damage future development, not only muting her voice but limiting how far she projects to rise.

Charlotte's resistance was commendable, but how far will it take her? She was decisive and skilled at moving onto the main stage but not taking too big a swath that would disturb all actors in the space. What kind of response will Charlotte's resistance generate? Critical feminist scholars, like Lorde, articulate activism as a "transformation of silence into language and action [which] is an act of self-revelation, and that always seems fraught with danger" (2007, 42). As Charlotte's story illustrates, however, using one's language—speaking out—does not always mean speaking loudly.

Silence

Like so many other images in our society, a raced-gendered-classed lens of silence affects perceptions and actions of both the silenced actor and hegemonic silencer. Take for example Fordham's (1993) seminal work describing how school personnel label Black adolescent girls' talk as "loud." Such a characterization is dismissive and pejorative, designed to assign a "place" jailing girls' actions. There is no accommodation made for enthusiasm or exasperation; teachers lambaste Black girls without knowing (or caring) what they are talking about. If girls of color accept these markers, it is easier to pigeonhole and ignore the silenced girl. The dominant culture and, in this case, its accessories—teachers—steal the voices of Black girls. They are unable to articulate their view of the world, and their perspective may be different from that of the teacher, their male counterparts, or most White students. Silencing is not accidental, and its effects are seldom benign.

When girls of color are silenced, anyone may claim to speak for them. There are few attempts to determine authenticity. In fact, silencing displaces any need to check for validity. The value of the person is diminished to such an extent that nothing that is spoken is as worthwhile as outsiders, "others," who speak for the silenced. The views of the silenced are not important. They don't shape policy or govern the allocations of human capital or other resources. What matters is that the institution and its space function according to the desires and norms of the dominant group.

If individuals are unheard, objectified things can represent them and the totality of their experience. Peer-directed activity can be branded as deviant, if noted at all. Indeed, in the first year of COMPUGIRLS, there was minimal research about girls of color and their digital production, innovation, or experiences. Granted, there was a host of data illustrating how girls of color were the technological have-nots,[5] but many of the conclusions were based on judgments of investigators who accepted without question the belief that silenced girls could hardly be counted on to provide credible information about their souls and experiences in schools.

My colleagues and I discussed this troubling and pernicious identity of the technological have-nots and how our programs' critical pedagogical practices seek to dismantle and reconstruct it (see Scott, Sheridan, and Clark [2014]). We explored the differences between our programs' nomenclatures and that of technological should-nots. In short, and quite similar to Reed's assertion, I imagined the have-nots as populations whose language and traditions are absent or unfairly represented on the web, who lack access to "culturally relevant education in using digital devices and resources," and whose opportunities are limited by government or corporate forces (2014, 7). I added to this description one other item—that is, populations who are denied opportunities to engage in technological innovation that may lead to high-level positions.

There is considerable agreement that education should provide leadership for an emerging, more sophisticated and interlocking society. But a tacit policy utilized against the have-nots is to provide education and training that ensures servility, not leadership. The gap between leaders and have-nots widens and with each successive generation is harder to bridge. Society denies investments to have-nots and allocates just enough resources to shore up the position of those who are dominant. Many computer programs fall into this rubric, preparing have-nots for positions that will never shake the foundations and promote social change. Education for innovation, in the technological arena, isn't available to have-nots. "Catch-up" programs promising technical literacy may be limited to the acquisition of non-innovative skills such as the assembly or disassembly of computers and the rudiments of coding.

Society has made two mutually important judgments: first, have-nots cannot learn innovative skills and become leaders; and, second, the social value of technology will be well served if a two-tier system is fostered. Warschauer (2000) describes how this system works and is justified by sharply differentiating "technological workers" and "technological leaders"; have-nots are prepared for the former, and the more privileged for the latter. This system is not "separate but equal" and reinforces differences.

Not all students navigating under-resourced schools automatically fall into the have-not category. More and more, the have-nots resemble the White male students whom Margolis (2008) describes in *Stuck in the Shallow End*. Allowed to police the have-not space so only certain (other White male) students can enter and gain knowledge, the have-nots control accessibility and stymie change as they exclude others.

This is not an American-specific phenomenon; it surfaces in other societies. Freeman's (2000) fieldwork documenting the experiences of women in Barbados illustrates how these individuals are encouraged to complete computer-based clerical work, such as entering data for airlines. The low-level pay does not allow them to play out their sought-after identities as professional workers. Membership in the information and communication technology (ICT) sector as "pink collar" workers does not provide the rewards and freedom expected as a result of ICT employment. The rise of low-skilled and low-paid females in ICT jobs who have little or no access for upward mobility opposes a central tenet of American educational philosophy—that, as Horace Mann, the first Massachusetts education secretary, argued in 1848, "education, then, beyond all other divides of human origin, is a great equalizer of conditions of men—the balance wheel of the social machinery."[6]

The lack of empirical data documenting how girls of color make sense of their position appears to buttress why girls of color are not interested in higher-end and more lucrative STEM disciplines—that is, digital media, information technology, or computer science. The link between silence, invisibility, and disinterest remains unquestioned. Data, such as the Girl Scout 2012 report titled *Generation STEM* (Modi, Schoenberg, and Salmond 2012), discloses that African American and Latina girls are, indeed, quite interested in STEM, in some cases more than their White counterparts. Additionally, that report and other research present the factors that positively encourage some girls to continue in this field while others are detoured.[7] These works provide important nuances of girls' digital experiences but do not take into account the agentic nature many girls of color develop in certain culturally responsive contexts. Just as Yvette's physical removal from school did not suggest a loss of faith in education writ large, a girl's silence should not be automatically equated with disinterest or self-imposed dispossession. The opposite of silence is not always loud talk or easily recognizable action.

For many girls of color, silence is a weapon. It can serve as a means to control successfully navigated space and create an alternative culture with its own norms. Silence can, simultaneously, be a key to one's emancipatory identity, a vehicle toward self-discovery and transformation. It can also be a waiting device in hopes the "enemy" will give up and retreat, allowing individuals to do the work they know needs to be done. Silence can be a way for girls to remove distractions from their line of vision so they can create coalitions.

The "danger" many girls experience emerges from the very individuals who believe they are "giving them voice." Too many well-meaning teachers, program developers, and community activists working in communities marginalized by race, gender, social class, and other variables ardently believe their duty is to "give voice" to the "voiceless." Assuming their intervention is, in part, a political move to "free" the marginalized from their silence, this form of supposed activism diminishes the activity of the disenfranchised. The danger of "giving voice" not only jeopardizes the activists' possibilities for making a change but limits scope and vision of what that change should be, the context fostering movement, and who is entitled to lead it.

Recognizable representations of girl activists, although limited, tend to follow the adult perception of girls engaged in extraordinary feats. Girl activists appear as youth creating exceptional spaces that adults admire, in part, as a fascinating, nonthreatening subculture. Such descriptors, however, tend to be more appropriately affixed to White, middle-class girls' activism. Kwon correctly reminds us that "while white youth are imagined as the nation's future and thus need guidance, the youth of color are not often imagined as future agents of democracy but as objects already under suspicion and state surveillance and regulation" (2013, 7). And girl activists of color require management and control—at least, this is what is commonly believed. As the following case illustrates, control does not necessarily mean silencing the girls. Without allowing girls to define their agentic selves, on their terms, dominant scripts of girl activism will remain narrow.

Leave Us Silent

"We're not sure what we need to do, Miss," Angel informed me with a down-cast look. None of the other three group mates appeared particularly happy; their countenances were located somewhere between frustration and disappointment. This was a considerable difference from when they joined the summer program. As part of the second COMPUGIRLS cohort, they began during the sweltering summer months. Unlike the other five small groups of girls seated in the college classroom, this group rarely discussed anything, at least not in front of their mentor teacher, Miguel. When he was present, there were long silences between his questions and the girls' answers. Often they did not answer his inquiries at all.

"So, how exactly are you going to do this movie?" Miguel asked his group. With great patience, he allowed silence to envelop the girls for more than thirty seconds. Only one participant, Diana, maintained eye contact with Miguel. With her long, straight, dark brown hair framing her light brown face, she appeared older than her fourteen years. Typically dressed in jeans and a short-sleeved T-shirt, her evenly cut bangs swung as she moved her head. In a soothing voice that rarely increased its volume, Diana provided thoughtful answers to any question. She was invariably polite regardless of the group's unease or how harried the interrogator seemed. Fluent in Spanish, she never spoke of her Mexican heritage until much later in the program. Not a recognized leader among her group or the entire thirty-eight-girl cohort, Diana was very observant. With an expressionless face, she carefully and silently watched all adults and their behaviors. She enlisted the surveying power of Rachel in this important endeavor.

Rachel was the only African American participant in her group. One year older than Diana, Rachel was slightly taller, with dark brown skin. Depending on the day, her hair appeared in Afro-puffs or braids, and she normally wore bright or white clothing. Like Diana, Rachel was not particularly loquacious. Her voice was deeper than the voices of most other girls in her group, carrying a certain gravitas that caused others to take notice. When posed a question, her responses were assertive and clear. She often made explicit references to research she had found but maintained a critical eye, reflecting one of the key lessons the program aimed to teach—intragroup variance.

Regularly, Rachel would answer a question with something like, "In this article I found in [the digital library system] it said women are not in technology, but, uh, what women, you know? There isn't anything in there that says anything about women who look like me or someone else. So, how can

I know if the suggestions are for me or not?" Rachel did not use this strategy until the conclusion of the summer session's second week. However, by the end of the third week, she consistently used this technique when Miguel, her group's mentor teacher, was frequenting the bathroom or getting water or for some other reason had temporarily left the group. During these events, the other mentor teachers located in the same room would keep an eye on the group. Direct interaction was almost nonexistent.

Miguel's brief absences caused the girls' energy levels to increase slightly. Few talked above a whisper, preferring to huddle close while one served as the lookout, periodically glancing up to see if he was coming back. At the moment of Miguel's return, the long periods of silence resumed. "So, what did you all decide while I was gone?" Miguel would ask. Downcast eyes to avoid any contact with him became the norm. Even with Diana's direct gaze, he did not call on her. "Nothing was decided, then?" he would continue, to which girls would mute themselves—assuming a silent persona. This vexed Miguel. Questions hung in the air, blanketing the girls with a sort of heaviness too often detected in poorly run urban schools.

Adair used her experience to elaborate on how silence and limited activity in the classroom were used to discriminate and negatively label poor kids: "When we sat glued to our seats, afraid to stand in front of the class in ragged and ill-fitting hand-me-downs, we were held up as examples of unprepared and uncooperative children. And when our grades reflected our otherness, they were used to justify even more elaborate punishment that exacerbated the effects of our growing anomie" (2002, 457). Although Adair talks from the position of a White female who successfully completed her version of girlhood, the experience she describes is one reflected in Miguel's group. Although these COMPUGIRLS participants belonged to a different race or ethnic category than Adair and her classmates, Miguel learned to perceive them as "uncooperative." Equally disturbing, these girls' "anomie" grew as Miguel attempted to understand and control the situation.

"OK, then, well I don't know how we're going to do anything so, go ahead," Miguel would decide. Without any other direction, the girls would open up their laptops and work individually until the next time Miguel excused himself. This routine became the way in which the girls worked on their video documentary project. As Miguel's absences became longer and more frequent, the girls moved through the daily lessons without much adult intervention.

In creating COMPUGIRLS, I envisioned it as a counterspace, a context that was not like school and its conventional forms of teaching and learning. I had hoped the learning context would be ripe with occasions during which girls could safely interrogate themselves, each other, and the mentor teachers.

I believed that through this type of learning, girls could create coalitions that would gird them against the social injustices they researched. At the same time, I was well aware of Davis's (1994) point that coalition building is more complex than simply stating the need for social change. To allow coalition building to occur in a form that may not resemble one's own preconceived notions and to encourage mutable paradigms for developing and maintaining alliances across racial categories—that is the spirit I had hoped to take hold of the space. To these ends, I believed that success in this digital age required more than simply being technologically literate.

Taft argues that youth activists tend to draw on their identity as "youth" more often than on their other subjectivities as "an especially significant aspect of their collective political identities and therefore the identity around which they most often focus their claims to political authority and legitimacy" (2010, 49). She states that this does not exclude youth activists from exclusively focusing on these types of experiences: "Girl activists are concerned about many of the same issues as adults from similar social context" (57). Taft elaborates on how social positioning of group members increases the significance of their activist work: "For groups who are marginal to, or excluded from, politics and social movements, authoring their presence and agency is a vital aspect of their identity work" (48). For the Latina and African American COMPUGIRLS participants who are forced to endure formal educational spaces in which they themselves are often treated as technological have-nots, finding a space in which they can capitalize on their marginality is liberating.

In COMPUGIRLS, we actively talk about one's positionality not as a limiting factor but as an element to contest and redefine.[8] The girls find ways to engage in this process with or without the assistance of the mentor teachers. They discover their own means to create a supportive culture that ensures no girl is left behind, even if it means excluding the adult. As a political endeavor, COMPUGIRLS creates a unique space resting on important notions of coalition building and resistance. Like many educational endeavors, however, the vision of what could be is not always accepted or operationalized by those who have direct contact with youngsters.

Sitting in my office one late morning, I noticed Miguel passing by. There were several hours left in our COMPUGIRLS day. Therefore, I wondered why he was unlocking his bike so early.

ME: Miguel, where are you going?
MIGUEL: I'm sorry, but I can't do this anymore; I give up. I'm going home.
ME: Home? Where are the girls? Your group, where are they?

MIGUEL: I guess they're still in the room doing whatever. They don't listen; they don't follow directions. I don't need this. I'm leaving.

Convincing Miguel that his desertion was problematic for several reasons consumed the next half hour. While he was not averse to hearing my comments, he seemed more confused and deflated. According to Miguel, the girls did not "take me seriously; they do nothing I tell them to, and I'm trying to help them."

Equipping girls from underserved communities with not one but multiple tools to become empowered activists is perilous work. We seek to provide girls skills and resources so they can dismantle the troubled system and create a better one. Accomplishing this feat requires girls to find themselves. This is not a solitary process. It is through interacting with each other and building alliances that COMPUGIRLS participants can gain the technical skills and other ingredients to recreate a more equitable world. I believe that all COMPUGIRLS participants can find their empowered selves.

Rather than focus on who the girls are, we aim to provide space for them to focus on who they can and should be. Posing questions to encourage girls to think more critically is one step in this process. However, this is not enough. Allowing girls to take over the space is also insufficient, as it suggests the mentor teacher is the only one who has the power to give up the context. Instead, we encourage girls to identify their limits and power so they can ask themselves and each other the right questions, even when there are no specific answers. It is the mentor teacher's responsibility to model the interrogatory model and reveal himself or herself in the struggle as a trusted ally. This requires the mentor teacher to possess a high level of critical consciousness[9] that thwarts a neoliberal agenda fixated on controlling girls. We are not saving them from themselves or shaming them into consciousness.

Like Ruth Nicole Brown's work in the organization Saving Our Lives, Hear Our Truths (or SOLHOT), COMPUGIRLS too "makes introspective thoughts sound louder. . . . Then we become aware of what we do not know" by articulating what we do and can know. And the knowing is not inextricably fixed to future potential. Brown puts it well. Even though she focuses on Black girls, her explication applies to all COMPUGIRLS participants: "Too often, Black girls are seen as valuable for who they will become as presumable citizens in the making, not for who they are as people marginalized, without the protections and privileges of being defined as an adult. . . . It is the potential of the collective—the entering into relationship—to build and create something beyond a self-serving good time" (2013, 187–88).

Although Miguel had successfully completed a graduate course with me, he struggled to link theory to practice. How should he provide girls the space to define themselves, even without his direct intervention? This question seemed to trouble Miguel to the point of self-excommunication. And his case is not unique, or even exclusively American. Soozandehfar and Noroozisiam noted in their study of preservice teachers in Iran instructors' preference to "describe themselves as being in authority for different reasons as to prevent chaos. They didn't seem to appreciate the learners' autonomy in terms of choosing issues and matters to be discussed, activities to be done and making changes to the materials" (2011, 1243).

It is far easier to theorize and write about critical pedagogy than to actually implement its tenets with real youngsters. Indeed, Miguel had done a fine job writing impressive reflective papers that more than adequately demonstrated a strong conceptual understanding of culturally responsive practices. Yet, Miguel was deeply offended and judged himself a failure because the girls refused to follow his directions or nod in assent to his leadership position. As long as culturally responsive practices were concepts, they were abstract and without substance that invaded the classroom. When they gained a body and the COMPUGIRLS participants personified elements of connectedness and reflection, Miguel could no longer dismiss his loss of power. His adulthood and professionalism were under attack, and he gave up. Miguel interpreted the girls' silence as disengagement and therefore rejection ("they don't want my help"). Rather than alter his practices or relinquish some of his perceived power, he gave up. Miguel tried to be his version of a critical pedagogue and "help" the girls. However, he perceived the youngsters as the only individuals who needed to make changes to their selves. It is difficult for adults to unshackle themselves from ideas that belittle the childhood experiences of girls who have been marginalized and who escape behind a wall of silence.

Critical feminist pedagogy in our space concerns how teaching and learning impacts both the adult and the youth. It is not enough for teachers, after-school professionals, and program developers to think that the only individuals who require saving are the youth. Adults need to be "saved" as well from their own self-aggrandized perceptions of power. Without interrogating our place in the learning process and how we perceive our own self, biases, and expectations as manifestations of the larger world order, we cannot engage in true critical pedagogy. To be a critical pedagogue, adults must value the girls' interpretations of the learning as it unfolds and be willing to co-constitute the knowledge enterprise.

Chhuon and Wallace (2014) provide important insight on how youth of color interpret instructional interactions. Although their exploration is not specific to girls, focusing on African American, Latino, and Asian American youth navigating urban high schools, they remind us of Nakkula and Toshalis's (2008) assertion that students prefer "developmental alliances"—teachers joining their students to contribute to students' growth as well as their own. "It is not enough for teachers to move students, as this movement is unilateral or unidirectional. Transformational learning occurs when students sense that they too have moved their teachers—through their efforts or accomplishments and through their deep engagement in the learning process" (19). Unfortunately, these authors also note that teachers often misread youth of color and their disengagement. The COMPUGIRLS group in this case, however, developed innovative strategies to confront Miguel's misunderstanding.

The girls were quite clear on what they wanted: guidance, not answers; time to find their voices and discover their skills; him to believe they could accomplish these activities and communicate these ideas without reproach. They saw themselves as an interdependent unit working toward a common end, the closing ceremony. Even Miguel's resistance did not cause them to disengage. When negotiations broke down, they remained unified.

For the second time that day, I called this group into my office. Thankfully, they did not realize Miguel had tried to permanently remove himself. I did not inform them of his true intent. Rather, we talked about how things were going since our last conversation earlier that morning.

ME: So, uh, things are better?
ALICIA: Oh, yes! Much, like, really, better.
RACHEL: Yeah, it's better, but—
DIANA: We're getting things done.
JULIE: But—
RACHEL: No, we're getting it done.

Since Rachel made a point to emphasize "we're," suggesting that progress was a result of the girls' work, I pursued.

ME: So, Miguel is helping you?

Unlike the rapid responses that became typical of our exchanges, an interesting pause hung in the air. Soundless, the girls averted my gaze. Instead, they looked at the floor and my desk, seemingly searching for words or hoping to escape this conversation. Almost ten seconds later, Alicia, a tall Latina whose height came close to my own five foot ten inches, boldly continued.

ALICIA: Miguel, is um, not, really, um, not—

DIANA: He gets so mad at us and, he, like, doesn't help us or anything, and—

RACHEL: He thinks he is helping, I think, maybe, but, I don't know, he—

DIANA: I don't think he understands what we are saying, and when we ask him a question I don't think he gets it or something and—

ALICIA: He gets mad at us and then, like, doesn't help at all. He just asks questions and, like, when we don't know the answer because he hasn't explained how we are to get the answer he, like, gets mad.

ME: Wait, you said you don't think he understands you?

DIANA: And we don't understand him most of the time because of his English.

While Miguel does have a heavy Spanish accent, I never experienced any problems understanding him. Additionally, none of his fellow mentor teachers demonstrated concern or difficulty comprehending his words. Nevertheless, three of the four girls are bilingual Spanish-English speakers, so I asked if they had tried to communicate in Spanish with Miguel.

DIANA: Yeah, we tried, yeah, but he won't speak to us in Spanish, even though we know Spanish too.

ALICIA: I thought it was maybe because Rachel doesn't speak Spanish, so—

JULIE: We translated everything for Rachel—

RACHEL: Plus I know enough, to, you know, like understand.

DIANA: But he won't respond in Spanish, only English, and we don't get it.

JULIE: I understand better when Diana explains things to me.

RACHEL: I go to Julie for help on Photoshop, not him.

ALICIA: Yeah, Miss, we can do it ourselves.

For the next twenty minutes, the girls and I brainstormed ways to work with Miguel. Since the summer session was quickly drawing to a close and the groups were focused on preparing their projects for the upcoming closing ceremony, we identified ways to better listen to their mentor teacher and not resist his support. They reluctantly agreed that he was indeed trying to assist them, although they did not appreciate his approach. Perceiving his demeanor as impatient and not providing them the support they expected caused the group to cease listening to him. His self-removal strategies may have provided him some emotional rest but also allowed the girls the necessary space to develop their consciousness on a different level. His departure did not lead to a breakdown in the learning. On the contrary, the girls used his absences to learn from each other.

Final Words

The girls assigned to Miguel did for one another what Charlotte did for everyone—that is, they attempted to build their activist agenda inclusive of self-sufficiency and accountability to individuals other than just themselves. Although performed differently, other girls recognized and valued these actions. The tension arose in how these different forms of activism and resistance were understood by surrounding adults. Miguel believed, like many educators, that in the cooperative learning space, there would be loud voices. Volume, in his mind, represented engagement. When the girls redefined the space and did not create a loud context, he coded their silence as a lack of interest and disengagement. Despite multiple attempts to get them to counter the very script many schools seek to delete—namely, the talkative, outgoing habits of mind and body—the girls wrote and owned a different set of behaviors defining activism and resistance in terms of inaudible fortitude. In doing so, they resisted not only Miguel's expectations but also the expectations of those who believe activism necessitates loud verbalizations. Charlotte subscribed to this same belief, although she worked in isolation to build the coalition of engaged girls.

While Miguel's struggles with the girls' actions could be attributed to his gender, I have noted over the years multiple examples of male mentor teachers being incredibly effective, encouraging girls to name their selves, space, and potential. Cofounder of the Oakland Men's project Paul Kivel describes how men work with young people to challenge violence from men against women and girls. These men acknowledge that fighting for girls to gain power inevitably means fighting for their power. Kivel accurately notes in analyzing his work a point some critical pedagogues wrestle with—namely, applying: "One of the most powerful ways to be an ally to young people is to take the time to listen to what they are saying and to help them articulate their questions" (2013, 223). He continues, describing a point that challenges the "savior" script that adults need to avoid: "We can be better allies if we shift our emphasis from raising teen's self-esteem to increasing their power. That in turn will allow the exuberance, insight and creativity of young people to contribute to better all our lives" (224).[10] To engage in this process requires adults and youth to (re)consider new roles for themselves and each other. Assuming these positions will require growth for both communities. As Miguel's story illustrates, this may be messy, uncomfortable, and not easily unpacked.

Girls' use of digital media, as reflections of how they live their lives away from technology, does not fit cleanly or clearly on a continuum in which girls are either victims or aggressors. Ringrose describes the commonplace neoliberal educational discourse of girls in which they are cast in an all-too-simplistic binary, as "either empowered consumers/winners or vulnerable victims of sexualised society" (2013, 4). Images of girls using digital media to harass other girls or to communicate trivial information concerning their day are artless attempts to justify adult power over female students.

For girls of color, adults use digital media as the proverbial carrot to protect the girls from themselves, each other, and their communities. In the COMPUGIRLS critical setting, digital media serves as the means by which girls can build a coalition of tech-savvy females who are in solidarity and producing socially just products. The technology becomes the means by which many girls connect to others, concurrently increasing their technological acuity. It is the vehicle by which the girls can remain in the shadows but ignite a collective change affecting current and future COMPUGIRLS participants to share in a nuanced technological experience. With minimal adult intervention, digital media becomes the glue that binds Black and Brown girls' interests to increase their technological knowledge in unprecedented ways. Their interpersonal relationships and collective action position digital media as a platform on which to build their associations and behaviors. As a result, activism is not a by-product of technology or an impediment.

Systematically, the Black and Brown girls discussed above constructed and operationalized habits that engendered activist selves. These images may recall biased notions of the almost-silent Black girl. The tropes of the self-sufficient girl resisting adult intervention may come into play. Such interpretations, however, miss the nuanced nature of how these images emerge and the role of digital media in maintaining a peer culture celebrating particular expectations. If we do not understand that Black girls can be impactful in their quietness, that some girls of color simply need a nudge rather than a direct push toward critical consciousness, and that resistance may include challenging the very efforts critical pedagogues construct, then we will never understand the level of noise that silence can carry for current and future generations of activists.

CHAPTER FIVE

I Have Something to Say

WHILE I HAVE SERVED as the executive director of COMPUGIRLS, many observers automatically assumed that because I am an African American woman, the program is targeted to African American girls. In reality, the percentage of African American girls participating in the program has never been influenced by my Black femaleness. Context played a more significant role than whether I or a non-Black COMPUGIRLS adult conducted the recruitment sessions. When the program appears in a state where the percentage of African Americans is low, it is not surprising that the majority of our participants represent racial or ethnic categories other than Black. It was in such a setting, one in which the K–12 population was 5 percent African American and 8 percent American Indian/Alaskan Native, that girls like Zaire, Sonia, Rihana, and Jade emerged.

In this chapter, I share stories of COMPUGIRLS participants navigating the program in two different contexts—one that was hosted at the university and the other on nearby tribal land, affectionately called the "rez." How the two sets of girls focused their attentions on "injustice" distinguished the settings in unique ways. In the end, all girls demonstrated a commitment to informing their communities about topics they believed remain invisible. However, making the invisible visible necessitated different partners to be engaged in the process. Who these partners were and how they contributed to the coalition and to what end differed across the two sites and challenged prescriptive notions of girls becoming change agents. There is no single definition of who is a change agent; this identity is fluid and contextual, correlating to the dynamic relationships built and developed in an acculturated setting.[1]

What is revealed below is how the girls engaged in this process with varying degrees of success, satisfaction, and support from each other.

Zaire

Navigating an economically stressed school system where the vast majority of students were of Mexican descent, Zaire, with her tall, thin frame, stood out as an African American girl. Her large oval eyes alternated between a look of drowsiness and one of alarm. At fifteen, her deep voice mimicked the cadence of an adult's. Words flowed with ease, reflecting a depth of ideas. Dressed in jeans or slacks and loose-fitting shirts, she rarely wore skirts. She had a flawless complexion that never appeared to need makeup on her medium brown skin, and Zaire's straightened hair always began in neat pigtails, only to have several wisps escape as the hours ebbed. Sometimes the satin cap covering her dark brown hair did a better containment job, and wearing it also allowed her gold earrings to shine more brightly. In all of the years I have known Zaire and her family, I can count on one hand how many times I heard her laugh.

This does not suggest that she was unhappy or possessed an unpleasant demeanor. Quick to approach any adult with an extended hand, her slim shoulders could often be found shaking from the frequent chuckle bubbling up from deep inside her. Zaire would be considered a serious teen who typically shared her opinion upon request. In preparing to present at the largest educational conference in our nation, Zaire had a lot to say.

Zaire applied to COMPUGIRLS the summer before her freshman year in high school, in 2007. Her handwritten essay was mildly critical and attuned to ethnic concerns many adult African American women express—that our experiences are not regularly heard by "others." Our program attracted her because it provided a space to tell her story. Identifying herself as a "girl of color," she did not talk specifically about her Black femaleness, although she was quite aware that "others" lacked knowledge about her life. While she never identified the "others" as she navigated all six courses throughout the two years spent in COMPUGIRLS, Zaire maintained a heightened sensitivity toward the "unjust situations" facing girls of color. Throughout her COMPUGIRLS experience, Zaire divided her time between listening very carefully to the other peers in her cohort, learning from them, and drawing attention to what she recommended others do with lessons learned. Technology became the platform on which Zaire sought to make her story (and others' stories) perceptible as a tactical move to inspire adults.

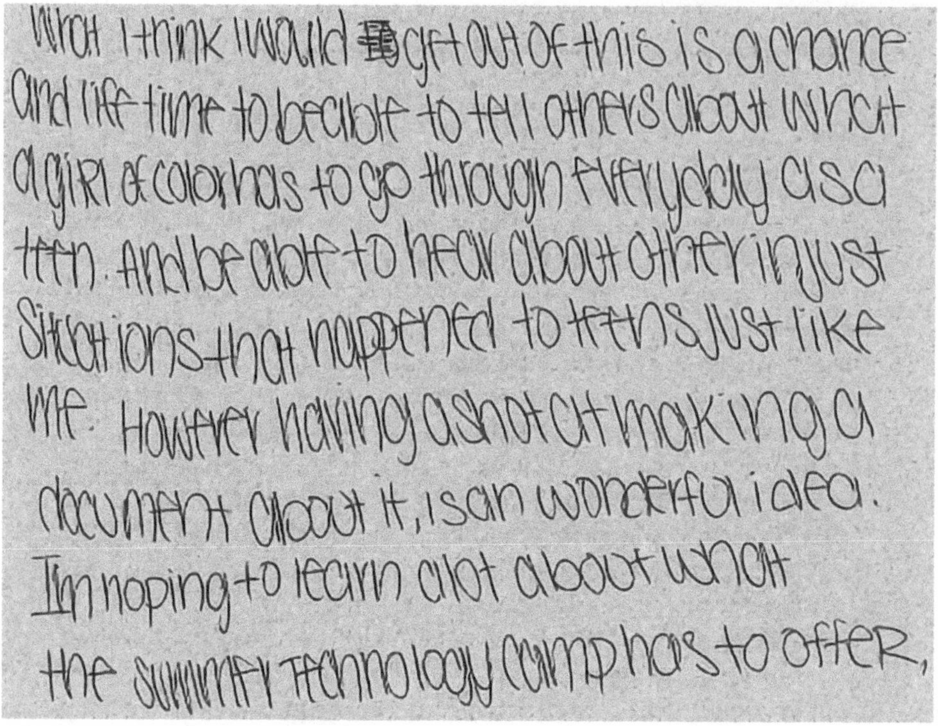

What I think I would be get out of this is a chance and life-time to be able to tell others about what a girl of color has to go through everyday as a teen. And be able to hear about other injust situations that happened to teens just like me. However having a shot at making a document about it, is an wonderful idea. I'm hoping to learn a lot about what the summer technology camp has to offer,

Figure 7. Zaire's application essay

Not All Skinny

Identifying how the Latina and African American girls in COMPUGIRLS shared similar experiences of subjugation inspired Zaire to not focus on our deficiencies. Rather, she became more interested in using technology to provide counter-narratives and solutions. By the time she enrolled in the Virtual Worlds course,[2] Zaire decided, "Well, I, uh, know that a lot of Black girls are large, like not really overweight, but big, like, and I, uh, don't see too many clothing stores in Teen Second Life[3] for us, like, the bigger girls. I don't even, you know, really see bigger avatars in Teen Second Life, but whatever. So, I want to have a clothing store, a virtual, you know, one in Teen Second Life for us." Zaire's proposal challenged the belief that online spaces promote what Nakamura (2002) calls "cybertypes."

Without much direction, Zaire understood how virtual spaces such as Teen Second Life (TSL) provide limited choices for representation and often mirror established stereotypes idealizing aesthetic beliefs of beauty. Tall and skinny female avatars may indicate the "distinctive ways that the Internet propagates, disseminates, and commodifies images of race and racism" (2002, 3),[4] but Zaire was not accepting those narrow images. When I asked Zaire about the catalyst for her idea, she had trouble articulating a reason. "I, uh, I don't know. But not everybody is skinny, and that is not fair." Zaire was being raised by a single mother who would be considered petite by any standard, and her younger siblings all had small frames. I did not initially observe Zaire talking with other COMPUGIRLS participants about her topic. However, when she presented the idea to the small group, all listeners marked her concept as ingenious.

For the girls navigating this cohort, they progressed to furthering their Virtual World creations in a continuing course. It was about this time that their self-sufficiency shone. The mentor teacher remarked how she could sit beside the group and serve as an observer since the girls were adept at carrying the conversation without much adult interference. Upon entering the college classroom, Yvette, Gennifer, Azure, Malia, and Zaire would quickly move their chairs into a tight circle. At times, the laptops balanced precariously on their laps, while at other moments the girls simply sat with a piece of paper and pen to take notes. It was during one of these sessions that Zaire presented her idea.

Charging the girls to build a culminating project, we encouraged them to incorporate all the digital production they had learned up until that point and try to remain within the same topics from the previous COMPUGIRLS experiences. We envisioned that their builds would contain revised versions of the video documentary and the game from Scratch, screenshots from The Sims, and demonstrations of their research. We required each girl to draft a written proposal, present it to their group, and gain feedback before curating their virtual space. Zaire's suggestion to create a "store" exceeded our expectations.

ZAIRE: Well, I, uh, want to build, like, wait, let me start again. I want to build a store and sell clothing for avatars that are not all skinny and stuff.

GENNIFER: But all the avatars are skinny, so who would buy them? I mean, I know I'm not small or anything, but, like, my avatar doesn't look like me.

YVETTE: Yeah, I agree with Gennifer, so why would you even do it?

Far from discouraged, Zaire convincingly argued how "none of us should have to wear stupid stuff, and in [Teen] Second Life we should be able to do what we want. I mean, like, if I can fly, then if I'm big I should be able to wear clothes I like. And I want to get into fashion design anyway, and I can design really cute outfits." For a moment she paused, and then words cascaded: "A lot of the clothes for, you know, bigger girls is unfashionable. Ugly. That is like punishing them because some people cannot help it. That's, no, not right."

To this, Gennifer and Yvette, who considered themselves "plump" and typically wore jeans and oversized T-shirts, wholeheartedly agreed. "That's why I wear jeans and stuff. You can wear whatever, cute things and all. I mean I don't really care, but still," Gennifer explained. Zaire did not demonstrate disturbance by being the "you" in their response, the "you" who seemingly was not bound by limits on the availability of "cute" clothing. Their remarks inspired her to move forward and contact a clothing designer in first life,[5] study fashion trends, and build a virtual store. Comments on how to market her store ensued. "How you goin' to advertise but not let people feel they are, you know, bad about themselves?" Malia wondered out loud.

"I don't feel bad because I need to get larger sizes!" Gennifer responded, to which Zaire said, "I will make the coolest clothes and fashions that the skinny ones will want too. Maybe this will make people create avatars that are more realistic, you know, not all skinny." Heads nodded in approval as Zaire scribbled on her paper, gaining sufficient support for her to begin typing her proposal.

Doing what she felt was "right" by creating a plus-size virtual store was not necessarily what we had in mind for the virtual build. Nevertheless, Zaire had identified an "injustice," conferred with her COMPUGIRLS sisters to garner support, and set out to change the virtual world. This form of activism, engaging in work that benefits others via digital spaces, was a relatively new phenomenon at this point in time. Tarana Burke's 2006 Me Too movement was one of the first to use the then-popular social media platform My Space to speak against sexual harassment. Unlike Burke, who is a survivor of sexual harassment, Zaire took on this topic because of its general significance, not as a personal fight. By choosing to protest against something that didn't necessarily apply to her, Zaire was demonstrating "the crucial interrelationship between body politics experienced in a local context and feminist actions whose efficacy relies on their translocal and transnational articulation." Thus, she was applying her "local stories of individual women to larger narratives of inequality" (Baer 2016, 17–18).

Although she did not enlist active or continued support from the other COMPUGIRLS participants, she did rely on them for input. They were her touchstones, individuals with whom she could share her frustrations, triumphs, and aspirations. The mentor teacher was not the "go-to" person for advice or direction. In fact, Zaire made clear her preference—to discuss issues, it was best to listen to her peers. Circling the chairs to create a ring of girls with heads drawn close to discuss, argue, and confront each other became the norm in this setting. The girls knew that they owned the space and would meet little to no resistance from the attending adult. In this setting, they could express themselves and their desire to explore a topic, even if it did not personally affect them. As long as a community was treated differentially, this was a cause for concern. Rather than simply criticize the discriminatory practice, girls like Zaire used it as an opportunity to change the tide. Notably, this was a learned response, since Yvette did eventually move away from her original topic on Indigenous culture to explore a subject that was more personal (see chapter 3). Zaire, on the other hand, remained dedicated to creating plus-size digital clothing until another opportunity presented itself. Unfortunately, this occasion also taught Zaire a disturbing truth about encouraging change.

Turn to Your Neighbor

Like we had done before, which resulted in the MIT trip Yvette and Gennifer took, we asked the girls to again elect two peers to present at the largest educational conference in the United States. At first, they wanted Yvette to attend, but she was quick to say, "No, we should pick someone else to have a turn. I and Gennifer want someone else to go, you know?" After much deliberation and a secret vote, Zaire and Elena were chosen. By that time, Zaire was seventeen years old. After two years in the program, she was more willing to share her opinion no matter the perceived status of the listener. I was not exempt from her critiques.

As COMPUGIRLS began to grow, I found myself spending less and less time in the classroom. Writing grants, meeting with potential funders, conferring with other scholars about our findings, and presenting our research both in writing and at conferences consumed time and removed me from the girls. Zaire was acutely aware of my absences. She made her displeasure clear. "You should really be in the classroom more. . . . We like your stories." Other girls in her cohort made similar comments: "We like our mentor teacher, but you know, we like it when you come in and talk." Even though I continued to have "rap sessions," a time when I requested mentor teachers to take a break so that girls could share with me what was or was not working well, the infrequency of my impromptu visits troubled me as well but not for the same reasons the girls shared. My concerns culminated from the following event.

Talking about COMPUGIRLS rather than creating opportunities for girls to talk for themselves seemed to conflict with the original intent of the program. Preparing girls to become techno-social change agents necessitates preparing them to interact with individuals beyond their community. Integral to this process is priming them to articulate their ideas to a host of individuals to invigorate change. We had already seen Yvette and Gennifer exercise their voices at MIT, expressing their views to the attending program developers. Zaire and Elena prepared for weeks to enter this space. Zaire particularly wanted "not just to talk, but can I try to get, you, know, folk to do something? Like I don't want to just talk and stuff."

She practiced her talk in front of her trusted peers to gain feedback, a requirement for any girl representing the collective. The critiques she received focused on whether her presentation served as the best example of the program. "We want people to see that we are not what they think," became a refrain shaping the suggestions for the elected representatives. The girls wanted Zaire and Elena to include more statistics and references to peer-reviewed articles and to highlight how well their topics demonstrated "cool" ways to show off girls' technical skills. Since the format required that they both present separately as part of a panel after I provided background information about COMPUGIRLS, they assumed different approaches but to the same ends. Once at the international conference, the adults' responses to each girl's presentation differed, reflecting a troubling discourse about budding scholar activists.

Elena would present immediately after me. Soft-spoken but very articulate, her peers and I encouraged her to speak up so all could hear her important words. With Spanish as her first and primary language, she often worried that she would forget words or, "you know, mix them up so no one knows what I'm saying." With a perpetual smile on her face, Elena's nerves were only mildly calmed when we agreed she could hold a "cheat sheet" during her seven-minute talk. Some girls balked at this concession: "But you know what you goin' to say already so you should do it without it and don't be lookin' down so much!" proclaimed Malia.

The admonishment did not change Elena's mind, so at the conference, she stood at the podium in front of nearly one hundred attendees, holding her three-by-five index cards. During her talk she glanced at them only once, preferring to use the live feed of her Teen Second Life project to describe its origins, purpose, and aspirations.

Elena's topic was child abuse. For hours outside of our semi-formal program sessions, she researched and identified some of the primary variables causing adults to abuse their children. As her research progressed, however, she shifted her focus to the psychosocial effects of child abuse on the victims. Upon learning that children can suffer from extreme depression that can lead to suicide, Elena became concerned with how to deal with the potential downward spiral for children suffering abuse. "I want people to know how dark it can be for some kids, how bad."

Concurrently, she was impressed by stories of kids' resiliency given effective support systems and treatment. Far more interested in proactive than reactive efforts, Elena identified the significance of a peer network that provided sustained opportunities for youngsters to talk with someone. Not that the same-age peers were ideal listening candidates, but Elena believed, "We should all know the phone numbers to give to people to call if they need help." Equally important, she researched and provided specific behavioral cues so that "if you see these, you know something is wrong and should do something, like ask or like listen or, you know, like give them the number to call."

For Elena, knowledge meant hope and a potential decrease in the incredible number of annual deaths of abused children. Either by the hands of an adult or by their own devices, Elena made sure her visual representation in TSL accurately depicted the disturbing number of victims alongside what could and should be the norm—that is, a childhood with no concerns other than cupcakes and candy. Granted, her vision of children's lives followed an idealistic script, filled with happiness and devoid of troubles and tribulations; yet, this representation was uplifting.

She explained her data collection methods, which included interviewing adult survivors, transcribing their words, conducting line-by-line coding, identifying categories, and recognizing themes that shaped her presentation, and made her closing statements: "In conclusion, I think we should, I mean, I liked using technology and Teen Second Life to tell this research and show what is the life of children who are abused and what it could be and that is why I created the cupcakes and other candy. And here are hotlines and ways to report child abuse or to help the children." While her recommendations were based on empirical research and followed an impressive set of methods, they did not disturb the audience's sensibilities in the way Zaire did, upon following Elena.

I had previously introduced Zaire in my opening remarks. Without hesitation, she stood up without a paper or card, having typed up her talking points ahead of time and left them on the podium. Like Elena, she adeptly manipulated the laptop to show screenshots of her Sims project (preferring not to showcase her TSL images). At the podium, Zaire stretched her hands on either side as if preparing to give a great speech.

As we had practiced, she began by thanking Elena for her presentation. With a careful cadence, she stated that her research questions led her to explore "the way men treated women in the workplace, men's attitudes about

Sexual Child Abuse Effects & Prevention

My research question is: What is the emotional impact on a parent whose child has been sexually abused and what can be done to prevent this type of abuse?

 I chose this topic to explore a different aspect of sexual child abuse because there are more stakeholders than just the direct victim. It is important to take the appropriate precautions to prevent lifelong effects on the whole family.

After the disclosure of a child's sexual abuse, the parent experiences a variety of emotions including grief, betrayal, and guilt.

My project focuses on ways to prevent sexual abuse, from either a family member or complete stranger.

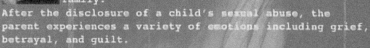

>>Teen
Second
Life<<

This is my avatar.
My name is
CaritaDeAngel
Lysette...

Project Proposal

In Teen Second Life, I am planning to create a building in the sky that looks like a cupcake, to give the sense of a child's world. Once you walk in, there will be a welcoming poster that describes the purpose of the building. There will be easels about, with statistics/data. There will also be little bubbles floating around that contain books in them and that reveal a story of either a parent or child when popped. Along the walls there will be a gallery of photos of children. In the corner, there will be a movie theater with dim lighting and numerous chairs, with a clip of a child who has been sexually abused telling their parents what happened and what the parent (and herself) could have done to prevent it. In another room, I would like to create a daycare-like room, which will be colorful and contain lots of toys. When some of the objects are touched, they will reveal a fact about childhood and how that childhood is destroyed after sexual abuse. There will be spiraling stairs that lead up to a divided room. One space will be the effects of those who don't get any help, and the other of those who do.

 Elena

Figure 8. Elena's research poster

women in the workforce, and popular ideas on how to get promoted in the workplace." Although she did not focus on one particular group of women, ignoring past recommendations from her peers to answer, "Which women? Do you mean Latina?," Zaire admitted that her interest in the topic stemmed from peer group conversations about "the way minorities get treated when it comes to getting a job or a house. I wondered about women and how they get treated differently—especially in how much they would make in the workplace if they were trying to make money to pay for an apartment." She drew on personal observations to test her own perceptions.

"I've watched a lot of TV shows and heard a lot of stories about how women are treated lower than men in the workplace. Women make less money in the same position as a man, are not respected for their ideas and minds as often, and sometimes get treated as sexual objects." Like Elena, Zaire described her methods using both primary and secondary data sources. "I used library databases and Google searches to find information on the topic. . . . I also conducted interviews and group discussions with adults and young people. I asked questions about people's personal experiences in the workplace and whether they believed gender discrimination exists."

Taking an approach quite similar to Charlotte's, Zaire programmed her Sims characters "to see how my characters could make more money in the workplace by getting promoted. I set it up so that both characters were working at the same place." Drawing on research from both popular press and peer-reviewed articles, Zaire created a quasi-experimental digital design:

> After I learned how to play the game, I created two separate Sims: a boy and girl character. I spent hours fixing the characters up and giving them aspirations so that their personalities would be similar. For the guy, I wanted him to have motivation to want a promotion, so I made his motivation about money. I made him a bachelor, and his strengths were based on his astrological sign, which made him strong, not lazy, and creative. For the woman, I also wanted her to have motivation to want a promotion, so I made her a single mother with two children. The reason she had a family is because I wanted her to be a hard worker, and the reason he didn't have a family is because I wanted them to have different types of motivation to work hard. She had the same strengths, but her aspirations were more family-oriented.

At this juncture, audience members began to squirm in their seats, while a few nodded their heads seemingly in agreement or surprise. Zaire did not appear to notice and began to digress a bit from her written words. "I learned that women are more family-oriented than men, and women having a family makes women more motivated, when it doesn't do much for men."

Zaire's interest in this topic caused her to read from a variety of sources, such as business magazines and marketing blogs. These resources allowed her to discover a surprising truth that she then applied to her Sims characters. "Then I looked up strategies to see how they could advance in the company faster. A strategy is a shortcut to get something faster than you would if you just played the game following all the rules. I found out there was a strategy that included sabotaging women so they would lose their job and the man could get a promoted. I used one of these strategies on my male character to see if it would work. It did."

The remainder of Zaire's presentation detailed her findings displaying hypermasculinized sexual undertones: "The guy was steady wooing girls. . . . In fact, he was creating more single moms because his strategy was designed to have him woo girls, make them come over, fall in love with him, and become obsessed with him to the point where they weren't going in to work anymore." Images of submissive women who "showed how females can become pets for men; women were literally on their knees while men dominated" appeared on the large screen.

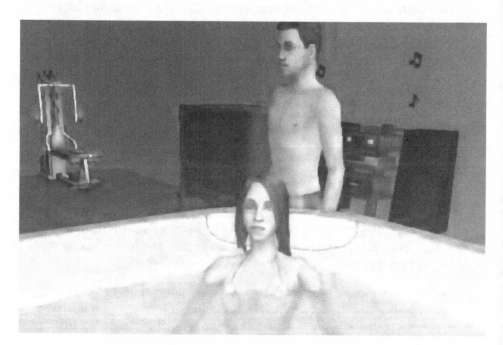

Figure 9. Zaire's Sims screenshot

Nearing the conclusion of her presentation, Zaire's notes indicated that she intended to say the following:

The Sims experience helped me understand women's treatment in the workplace better because I finally knew that what I was seeing on TV and in my research was true. I understood how situations come up that make it hard for women to get promotions or be treated fairly. . . . This project taught me that you can practically do anything with technology. It also taught me something about myself. It taught me that even though this world may seem like it's a man's world, we, as women, don't ever need to let that stop us from reaching our highest goals.

Extemporaneously, she supplemented her comments with words that caused the already riveted academic listeners to become disturbingly quiet. "I look around this room and see a lot of people, important people, who together could do something, really anything if we worked together. I want you to look at your neighbor, talk with your neighbor, and think about, talk about one or two things you think together you could do to address this problem of gender discrimination in the workplace."

Zaire's directions stood in the face of confused-looking audience members. "What are we supposed to do? Wait, I don't get it." And other comments demonstrating discomfort with her suggestion rocketed around the room. It was no surprise that when Zaire asked for people to share their ideas, she was met with questions about her presentation rather than with proposed solutions. Although she answered each inquiry gracefully, it was during our post-presentation conversation that her deflated spirit emerged.

"Why didn't they do anything? I mean, I wasn't clear or something? It's not like I expected a big movement or anything, but they could have at least talked to each other? Was I OK?" Zaire posed these and other questions to no one in particular at the debriefing session. And no one could truly answer her questions, except to say that she challenged people in a context that typically encouraged listening and not dialogue. Although Zaire demonstrated impressive skills with a clear path and vision, her challenge for the audience extended the contextualized bounds of customary presentation.

Although she did not racialize her research, preferring to simply focus on a single-unit analysis of gender, she demonstrated an important theme from Dillard's (2000, 2006, 2012) endarkened feminist epistemology—namely, the emphasis on community engagement. Zaire wanted her research to engage folks and did not rely on technology to tell the entire story. For her, The Sims was simply a vehicle to inspire thought, to assume a different stance. Realizing her own agency, that she "can do anything," may still represent the "can-do" attitude Anita Harris cautions in developing programs for girls. At the same time, Zaire realized and took notice of the tension between the interpersonal and its influence on the professional. In her analysis, women will remain the losers in this dynamic, as they are easily "wooed" by men. Without questioning this perceived reality, Zaire fed into the individuation myth—that women need to recognize their subjugation and can liberate themselves from male bravado. Greater effort needs to be spent challenging girls' notions of this image and their stress on the individual. However, in encouraging the audience to participate and dialogue, Zaire moved away from this trope, that she alone (and other individuals alone) can make change. She openly and courageously enlisted collective action. Unfortunately, her request fell on deaf ears, with audience members constrained by their own perceptions to consider the charge she laid before them. What becomes of girls like Zaire whose attempts to encourage a change fail in the moment?

Zaire epitomized the COMPUGIRLS participants' potential as change agents. She progressed from a quiet African American girl to one who articulately and consistently challenged scholars at international conferences. Her account presents the aspects of COMPUGIRLS that drew on her untapped resources, ultimately leading her to express complicated problems about the "other." For Zaire, becoming a change agent meant invigorating the scholarly community. I share this same belief.

While it pained me to decrease my time in the COMPUGIRLS space, I observed the need to explain what we were doing to the many communities to which I belonged. It can take years before academic, peer-reviewed articles appear in print, and even then, the readership is a small select group. Presenting at academic conferences, like the one described above, includes speaking with many of the same individuals who read the peer-reviewed articles—that is, a select group of scholars. Undoubtedly, these communities are important, and sharing our COMPUGIRLS work with them may influence research and education programs. However, granting agencies, parents, industries, tribal leaders, and policy makers, to name a few, are other social actors affecting COMPUGIRLS participants. I wanted to model to the girls my own change agency and ability to work with a multitude of individuals.

Crossing borders is challenging and required me to forge new partnerships, be vulnerable, learn new ways of communication, and, at times, accept defeat. Yet, how could I expect the girls to do anything more than what I was willing to do? For girls in the Indigenous community, many were also committed to change and engaging adult support to operationalize movement. The lines were drawn much more clearly on who could and should be included in community advancement efforts on the "rez."

In the COMPUGIRLS university setting, girls found commonality across racial and ethnic divides with Black and Latina girls coming together, bound by social justice. For some in this particular group, they believed their commitment to such issues of disparity was shared by all program participants and that if they all came together, COMPUGIRLS could enact a worldwide movement. Montserrat, introduced in chapter 1, stated, "I want there to be a COMPUGIRLS all over the world, like McDonald's, so that when people see the C and the G they will know it stands for COMPUGIRLS. Then we can see us taking over the world." This hope was significant, yet different contexts presented different realities and experiences. Some girls were far less interested in the global impact than in the work they could do in their own communities. The name of the program did not bind the girls together. Rather, it signaled that some girls in a particular context were interested in a social justice technology program.

Differences between the Native American COMPUGIRLS group and the cohorts at the university site populated mainly by girls of Mexican descent illustrate the need to disaggregate not only our data analysis but our approaches. As discussed below, girls in the local Indigenous community did not perceive any similarities with those at the university site, failing to see the commonalities in their difference. Yet, they too understood their Otherness. Making the invisible visible does not always involve non-community members.

The Rez

During the 2006–7 academic year, the same time I began working with girls on the reservation, only nine Native American/Alaskan Natives across the United States earned their PhD in computer science.[6] The data at that time did not indicate how many of these individuals were women. Not that earning any degree automatically opens doors through which girls of color can easily enter, but the jobs outlook for the few Native American women earning higher-level degrees does not bode well. In fact, a recent *New York Times* article points out that there are many reasons Black and Latino students who do actually major in and graduate with a computer science degree do not acquire jobs at technology firms.[7] One of the primary issues concerns perceptions. And although the *New York Times* does not consider the cultural lives of Native American youth, a notion persists that Native communities prefer nature and other nontechnical activities. Sometimes this supposed predilection is conveniently used to explain why so few Native American students enter technology. The data to corroborate this belief, however, remains conspicuously absent. Integrate gender with Native identity, and the taken-for-granted assumption is that Native American girls prefer cultural activities that exclude technology. While working as a guest on the rez, I found this notion to be erroneous.

An important component of culturally responsive practice centers on students' culture as a dynamic aspect of their overall identity. Identities are framed and reframed by individuals engaging in multiple activities and crossing numerous borders such as school, community, and home. Students' cultures and their identities are not extraneous or irrelevant to the learning experience but situated prominently as a source of knowledge. Often researchers describe these navigations as difficult for Indigenous individuals due to cultural differences. The "difficulty" comes not from cultural mismatches. Brayboy and Maughan's well-known *Harvard Educational Review* (2009) article makes it clear that how Indigenous communities acquire and enact knowledge is narrowly understood. Consequently, our culturally responsive efforts must take into account the unique, contextualized elements and knowledge systems of Indigenous peoples and tribal nations.

By their own admission and behaviors, Native American participants in this chapter wanted to learn about technology as long as it was purposeful. Many of the girls became inspired by discovering, to a great extent on their own, how a digital story, for example, could highlight assets in their community or illustrate a solution. Being labeled a change agent, activist, technologist, or any other term was far less important than revealing the "truths" about their community. The discovery process was significant to the girls because it directly or indirectly affirmed dimensions of their own culture that had been distorted, ignored, twisted, or forgotten.

My observations and interactions with the girls, their families, and tribal leaders documented a need for greater attention to be paid to how digital inclusion programs engage a marginalized community. As the following sections will illustrate, Native American girls in COMPUGIRLS possessed as much motivation and interest in technology as Black or Latina girls. How they operationalized their developing understanding of technology, girlhood, and community activism was a complex interplay. A unique set of stories concerning girls' abilities to navigate and take co-ownership of COMPUGIRLS set a stage for Native American girls to tell their own story and project a future that was compatible with goals attuned to the community's interest.

Their stories are not presented as "sentimental political stories" (Wanzo 2009) meant to pull on the readers' heartstrings. Rather, these accounts are filtered through my own subjectivities as one of the few African American females with whom the girls and the adults had contact, as a mother of a young girl, and as founder and director of this program. The following case stories are presented here to document what happens when lofty aims meet colliding cultural expectations. There were surprising turns as the girls claimed their space in COMPUGIRLS.

Crossing the Sites

Unlike the other cohorts, all ten girls attending COMPUGIRLS on the reservation belonged to the same community. They had grown up together, knew one another's families, and had attended the same schools, for the most part, since kindergarten. Their cultural-gendered identities were significantly influenced and formed by sustained interactions among parents, friends, and community. To be a member of this community meant each family identified as part of the tribe. We collaborated with the Boys and Girls Club site, mentioned in chapter 2, that had been located for several years in the rez's capital. A flat building surrounded by desert, it was the norm to see tumbleweeds and prairie dogs moving across the arid ground.

There were several pragmatic reasons we elected not to meet on the university campus like the other cohorts. First, transportation was a major issue. There was no public transportation system to transfer the girls from the community to the university. The Boys and Girls Club bus was always occupied and could not convey the girls thirty miles to the downtown campus. Second, the girls expressed trepidation about attending the university site. Alani, the primary mentor teacher at the rez, served as the spokesperson voicing their hesitation: "They don't want to go. I think it could be good, but they haven't been and don't know what to expect."

After the first year academic year (2007) and during the second summer (2009), we again broached the topic of having the girls make weekly visits to the university. During the time between the first request and the second, we had included several opportunities for the two cohorts to interact in hopes that both sets of girls would see their commonalities and differences. We hoped that providing girls this type of experience would assist them in both short-term and long-term success.

Yvette had already served as a peer mentor to the Indigenous cohort, driving the nearly forty minutes to the rez. Periodically, Malia or Kelly accompanied Yvette and co-led specific lessons. As one of the few African American girls with whom the girls came into contact, Malia had never visited the reservation. All three were excited about serving as near-peer mentors and spent time with Alani to discuss their roles. Kelly, one of the few White females in our program, elected to become a peer mentor because, "I mean, I've never even been down there and we are all in the same program. I know I've learned almost as much from other COMPUGIRLS as I have from the mentor teachers, and I like to tutor, so why wouldn't I go?" Malia reminded everyone "that we should be helping each other out and I want to go. They [the girls] can teach me; I don't know everything."

They sat with the girls from the community in small groups and provided feedback on their projects. During such exchanges, it was difficult to hear the conversations. There were marked differences among the girls from the rez. Sonia was outgoing and relatively talkative. Jessie was retiring and quiet. However, Yvette sparked the group, expressing real joy and satisfaction in driving round-trip to the reservation at least twice a week: "I think it is really cool, really great to be there. I mean, there is no reason we shouldn't all be together, you know, working together."

Bridging the distance between the university and rez sites was intentional but not universally successful. Finding a base to identify commonalities, given the wide disparity in perspectives, was not easy. Even though girls from both communities felt disenfranchised, they found it difficult to collaborate. The ground to build a common future failed to emerge, and the differences overshadowed similarities. The worlds of the underrepresented are by no means uniform, and their dissimilarities loom large, making it dangerous to generalize about individuals or their communities. Nevertheless, we trusted that digital products would be the vehicle to building the bridge. Most importantly, we were not interested in setting up structures in which the COMPUGIRLS university participants "helped" the rez girls because of the latter's lack of knowledge.

There were costs attached to the merger. Transporting university-sited girls to the rez was time consuming, required planning, and uprooted them from their customary environment. The girls from the rez took longer to complete the curriculum, not because of lack of interest or problems understanding and doing what was required but because cultural events and activities were added. COMPUGIRLS at the rez had a wider aperture than at the university. Tribal elders, especially women, hosted closed sessions with girls, and these often consumed an hour or more. The elders were assured that their input was valued and that the aims of our program did not supersede theirs. Tribal elders appreciated being able to piggyback on what they called a "training" program with access to young girls. The elders said, "We didn't think they [the girls] cared. It's good they are all together and we can teach them. This makes our job easier."

In addition to individual girls from the university site visiting their sister setting, we arranged specific opportunities for all participants to meet. Periodic field trips to local industry facilities broadened girls' understanding of the workforce. However, our closing ceremony allowed for unanticipated cross-pollination of ideas and cultural exchanges.

We alternated where we held the closing ceremony. At the conclusion of one course, we would charter buses to have all girls and their families travel to the tribal community, where the girls on the reservation organized the closing. For the next closing we reversed the process, inviting the girls and their family members from the rez to travel to the university. When the rez girls organized the closing, traditional foods were served, prayers in the Indigenous language opened the event, and music and musicians from the community played while girls presented their digital products and showcased their achievements. These cultural demonstrations highlighted contours of the rez that were probably foreign to participants from the university site. Most importantly, there was an elevation of the rez's culture, and girls from the rez enjoyed hearing the cultural overlaps. For instance, Rihana delighted in explaining to me how she included hominy in the traditional stew she prepared for the closing. And once I explained how my family, like many other Black folks with Southern roots, consumed hominy grits with cheese, butter, or chicken livers wallowing in a gravy slathered with onions, Rihana seemed intrigued: "Really? What does your hominy look like? Why would you eat it with liver?" This was one of the first of many subsequent times that Rihana's round face blushed with excitement when she realized other cultural groups celebrated important milestones.

Like other marginalized communities, Indigenous people have long been placed in positions to teach others (such as members of the dominant culture) about their culture.[8] An unfortunate result of this positioning is not understanding one's own background fully or deeply enough to question the need to cross borders. For girls on the reservation, COMPUGIRLS unexpectedly and simultaneously opened doors to understanding their own tribal culture as well as provided critical tools to evaluate how they could create a better community. COMPUGIRLS meetings were forums for the girls to tell their perspectives, their stories. Our program gained stature and acceptance because as the girls were learning how to be active in creating a better tribal political and social economy, they were not forsaking or downplaying their long and vaunted tribal heritage.

The interactions between Rihana and me, however, were not typical. When we were able to secure transportation for the rez participants to attend once-a-week meetings at the university, there was little contact between the groups. The Native American girls would sit in a corner working feverishly on their projects, while the other girls sat on the other side of the classroom in their small groups. During whole group instruction, the mentor teachers would address all, making sure to look at everyone, but the Native girls never offered to give their opinions, raise their hands, or share knowledge. Malia, Kelly, and Yvette would sit with the girls, but they too felt excluded: "They don't want to talk with me. I mean, I like, know them and everything, but they act like they don't. I guess I'll be leaving them if they don't want to talk," explained Malia, who seemed genuinely hurt by the lack of communication.

After a month of these failed attempts to have the girls see that they all belonged to one program, Alani advocated for the girls from her community. "They don't want to come. They don't feel right. They don't like, I don't know. They feel left out." When pressed to explain how we could salvage the situation in hopes of continuing the visits, she admitted, "It's OK for the girls [Yvette, Malia, and Kelly] to continue visiting us, but it just isn't working the other way. They look at all the stuff the [university] girls have, and they feel like they are being cheated. They feel sorta like forgotten, like the program isn't for them, like they are in a completely different program than the university girls—like they are getting more." Much to our surprise, the reservation girls coded the university site much like their schools, settings that Lomawaima (1994) aptly documents as having historically stripped away Native American identities and cultures.[9]

Alani's words came more and more rapidly as she continued explaining the situation, which, in her mind, was irreparable. The only solution was to cease transporting the girls to the university. To continue the visits would only make the girls feel more "forgotten." Herein lies an important tension that appears in many programs working with marginalized communities. Exposing participants to a site or a set of experiences different from those found in their culture or, exposing them to other individuals who do not share their cultural backgrounds, can deepen cultural schisms and prevent transformative measures from occurring. Without carefully considering the sociohistorical background and how these elements may be perceived from a cultural perspective, placing girls in situations or with individuals who may be well-intentioned can further disenfranchisement, reminding the girls of what they lack rather than what they can build. Careful attention needs to be placed on the role of physical spaces in encouraging or impeding these results.[10]

There was no high school on the rez. Instead, students attended one of the local educational institutions in the nearby city. For many, this was the first time they had left the community for any substantial period. Although each of the local high schools employed a Native American advisor responsible for shepherding the growing number of youngsters bused in from their homes, there was still much anxiety and misgivings attending these settings. Both parents and their children expressed similar concerns. As one tribal leader explained when describing his high school experience more than twenty years ago, "The Black kids were really bad to us. Made fun of us. Asked us where our tomahawks were. We didn't get along. We didn't fit in. We didn't even come together like we should have. We should have supported each other, even kids from other reservations. We're all Indians, and there shouldn't have been the divisions like that, you know?"

School was not the most pleasurable of experiences for the girls. While the majority of this small cohort had just begun high school, a few were still navigating the local middle school, fearing the inevitable removal from their community. The concern tended to focus on prolonged visits outside of their community. But weekend visits to the mall, if a parent or older sibling had access to a car, became a regular activity for them. These were short trips, lasting no more than an afternoon after the thirty-minute one-way car ride. Supplemented with visits to a grocery store larger than the only one present in the Nation's capital also caused girls to cross the cultural border between their land and that of the non-Native Other. Upon my visiting the local store and noting the overabundance of shelves stocked with various candy treats in colorful wrappers and minimal fresh fruit offerings, I was not surprised when the girls asked me to bring fruit to our meetings.

During one of these first meetings, I had the privilege of meeting Sonia.

Light-Skinned Outsider

According to Sonia and her mother, Sarah, they had "recently" moved to the rez from a midwestern community. In this case, "recent" meant nine years ago. Sonia had light-colored skin, light hazel eyes, and long, wavy, light-brown hair, and she and Sarah were both mindful of their outsider status both in this community and in their previous one. At various times Sonia and her mother identified themselves as Native American, Hispanic, and White. I learned from Sarah that the family always lived on a reservation but generally worked in nearby urban settings. Over the years, Sarah and I met at both preplanned and informal encounters. During a luncheon event for all rez parents, at the annual fair, and when dropping Sonia off at our weekly meetings, Sarah shared with me details about their outsider status: "We [my daughter and I] wouldn't always, be, you know, considered Indian. Because we're light and all and don't look dark like others, people would say we're not Indian. And then off the reservation, people didn't know what we were, we were Hispanic, or White, no not really White, but something. Our own family would wonder, you know, because we wanted to be educated. You know, go to school and get a job. I tell Sonia, 'You need to make something of yourself, but you are Indian. Don't matter what others say.'"

In contrast to Alani's comment about the reservation girls' unwillingness to communicate, Sonia, at fourteen years old, expressed in a nearly three-page, double-spaced typed response the anticipated effects of our lessons on her consciousness. Copied below in full, her words contain important themes about community engagement as well as limitations. Beginning with a well-articulated statement as to why she wanted to participate ("I'd like to participate in the COMPUGIRLS program because I'd like to explore further about computers and technology and possibly begin by establishing a career"), her words demonstrate important facets of herself that were not always as pronounced during peer interactions.

Our family enjoys watching movies and learning how they are made. It is also a priority to access the "special features" section and learn additional information about the different types or special ways of making a film. Our family visits our local Computer Technology Center where I'm always on a computer (when I have access) on the internet and this is where I assist members of this Community. I often assist my mother by preparing documents for her work and for us at home: memorandum, business correspondence, project materials, reports, etc. I've prepared slide shows, birthday cards, invitations, public notices, etc., all on software that is available here at the computer laboratory. I've been learning about computer capabilities since eight years of age at the CTC laboratory (Center for Technology Creation) in Sacaton. This Center is operated by Ms. Karla Peter who constantly inspires us to enjoy learning and continuing to learn even aside from school. My aunt also is employed with this department and she also teaches me so many useful things. Should they be busy, that's where I offer to assist or lend a hand. Chris Reed works at the lab also and we learn from all three of these dedicated staff. Every evening after school we drive to the CTC lab and begin homework, research, writing projects, and admittedly sometimes we might play some "games" if we have the time but mostly we must work. We enjoy being able to drive to this lab, but most students and children do not have the opportunity or resources to be able to come to the learning center each day as we do.

The difficult part is that of course this office has limited resources and we are only able to be here when the hours of operation are accessible and the lab is open. Later in the evenings or on weekend time we are not able to have any computer access due to not having available computers at our homes. Some of us might have a computer but are not able to afford having the internet to research or study. Also our homework assignments require printing (paper and supplies) and this is another difficulty. This makes studying difficult because this must be completed during the hours of operation and when the lab is not open we will not have access. Also most children here on the reservation do not even have a computer lab near their homes. We would like to have computer labs in each district on the reservation but this requires funding for the systems and operating funds.

Sonia reveals a responsibility to her community in helping out when she can while also stating her family plays an important role in nurturing her interest in "film making." Quick to affirm her strengths, Sonia comments on the limitations of her community. She acknowledges that access to technology is part of the larger issue, which also appears in terms of access to what others would consider basic supplies. Sonia notes that the lack of these materials is a systemic issue and without a systemic approach little will change.

At this time I am also enrolled in a Spanish course. This is a requirement at our high school because our high school curriculum is a college "bound" curriculum. This ideally requires constant computer and internet access. It would be so nice to have computer and internet access and headphones and access to contact my instructor and I must speak into a headset with a microphone recorder. Also we are required to download a program from the internet for me to be able to get the assignment completed and receive credit and uploaded "into or for" the online teacher. My grades would even improve if we were able to have access to a computer system or a laptop and become more familiar with the speaking, reading and writing this new language. We are trying but without internet access it is sometimes difficult. Especially when the only reason we do not have available computer access is due to various financial constraints and some students do not even have to worry about this.

I am also interested in learning how to repair computers, set up systems and programming. I've learned how to use computers pretty well and do not know everything but a lot of it. There were opportunities to use digital cameras before but do not know how to fully use them, having only had little experience with them. At this time I have been learning how to edit and make movies in the course offered at school. Most of the time I am the "crew"—I usually carry the camera and set up the scenes. It was good to have the opportunity to edit pictures at the computer lab in Sacaton, using the one picture scanner they have available. I am not fully experienced with the scanner but have used it to help others and my mother. When other people use it I help them and most have never used one before. I do not have any previous experience about iweb, nor have used Garageband but I have used itunes. I have an itunes account and an ipod. I know how to use itunes and how to download the songs onto the ipod but not everything the systems require. At the computer lab there was someone who had a family member pass away (deceased) and they needed to make a public notice "a sign" to let the community know about the unfortunate death. So they needed help immediately in making a flyer and of course the employees helped a lot. However at one point they got really busy (with other requirements) and I helped assist that particular person. Also another time a friend of our family was making an invitation for her sons' birthday party and she did not know how to use Microsoft publisher at all, so I helped her set it up and taught her how to use it for this purpose. They are so very thankful when I assist. I have also helped make banners for events.

Lately a family that we assist (disabled son with medical conditions) and care for had a computer that "crashed". It became full of viruses and worms. They did not know enough about computers to prevent this and they had precious data on this computer. Because I had some knowledge there was an opportunity for me to assist this family by showing them what type of data storage system we could use to hopefully store this data before the system was "cleared" because they could certainly lose this data if it was not stored on any devices. We found a data storage device, they were able to purchase this and I helped this family save their important, irreplaceable data. The computer will be repaired soon and they are so appreciative because of little cost and something that was meaningful to this family—their data.

It is examples such as this that make me consider the study of computers as a career. This will be a positive career also. Because this is something I definitely enjoy doing. Also I do not use computers to constantly play games. I've never done this constantly like some children and teenagers do. I will do this once in a while but really do not have the time. We do not own any of the game systems, etc. In this day and age, this is an important consideration because many children our age do this constantly. I see this in my friends and in other families that we are close to. We make comments but some children do enjoy game systems. I just wanted this review committee to understand this because some of us utilize computer systems and technology for reasons other than playing the various games available.

Sonia presented her computer interest as concerning more than production of film or troubleshooting programs. She expressed a keen interest in hardware. The final words in her essay reflected Sonia's perceived difference from her peers. Unlike other kids, she made note that she did not simply play games on the computer. Although game playing has been noted as a means to potentially introduce more kids to consider computer science as a career, Sonia did not see its relevance. She provided a more negative view, that game playing is mindless and unimportant.[11]

Throughout her year with COMPUGIRLS, her attention to her community was notable and impressive, but her rhetoric did not translate into observable actions. Sonia maintained an outsider status, separate from the girls. When required to pair with another and create a project, she chose to work in isolation. While she would occasionally provide assistance to other participants, these were rare instances. Girls did not seek her input or guidance. Although Sonia's projects were exemplary, reflecting much of the careful thought first apparent in her essay, she was not a sought-after member of the cohort. When she presented her final project, girls expressed their appreciation but were not overly excited or impressed.

Taking into account the remoteness of the reservation, Sonia became interested in how its geographic location contributed to certain health disparities, in terms of identification and treatment services. Although a relatively large amount of research has been conducted on Native American populations, diabetes, and obesity,[12] Sonia did not want to contribute to those topics; rather, "I'm interested in multiple myeloma, here, in our community." Standing in front of her fellow participants, she explained, "I know in my family, some of our own families, we, uh, know people who have multiple myeloma." Before Sonia could continue, she looked at the girls, some of whom glanced at her while most looked at the floor, slumped low in their seats. Sensing that no one understood the term describing this form of cancer, Sonia explained, "It is a form of cancer that attacks the bones. You know, old people get it, a lot.

But I've seen younger people, like people like my mother's age, get it." At this, several girls moved their bodies. Although they continued to slouch, a few arms uncrossed, and some sat up and took notice. Eyes began to gradually focus on Sonia.

"So, I'm looking at how this cancer affects our community. Is it different for us and how? I want to see what doctors have to say and see what needs to be done."

Sonia continued to stand in front of the half-circle while Alani asked the girls, "So, what do you think about this topic? I mean, this sounds important, and I've never heard of this before." Always giggling to express the conclusion of her thought, Alani looked from each girl to the other, patiently waiting for a response. There was a long period of silence.[13]

"I mean, that is interesting, I guess. I mean, I know this woman who is like my mother's age who has something wrong with her bones. It hurts real bad. I guess it could be that multiple thing." Other girls quietly chuckled at Bettina's replacement of the word "myeloma" with a more easily pronounce-able word such as "thing."

Sonia herself seemed amused but did not correct Bettina. Instead, she affirmed her comments. "Yeah, that's what I mean. It hurts real bad, and why anyone in their forties or fifties gets it doesn't make sense. Maybe we are exposed to something that we shouldn't be."

At this, Rihana whispered something under her breath, causing a few others to giggle nervously. "What's that, Rihana?" Alani asked.

Without hesitation: "I said, maybe something is in the air that we are breathing in or in the water or in something, I don't know." And this marked the first time I heard Rihana's voice.

Sonia's multiple myeloma project became an exemplar piece. She spent an incredible amount of time collecting and analyzing information about this topic. Although she began this topic alone, Jessie joined her in constructing the final product.

Jessie entered COMPUGIRLS about two weeks after the other girls began. We did not acquire an essay from Jessie; only the basic contact information was provided for her. At that point, most girls had completed data collection for their project and were dialoguing on how to present the information in an interesting way. The girls knew Jessie, but no one expressed an overwhelming desire to have her join the group. When Alani announced that Jessie would work with Sonia, Sonia's response of "OK" seemed enough for Jessie to sit down and listen to Sonia explain what she had accomplished thus far. With hair much shorter than Sonia's but having a pleasant rounded face and simple glasses set under her bangs, Jessie always seemed relaxed. She consistently allowed Sonia to present their work, although she stood next to her in front of the other girls. When working by themselves, Jessie would sit back in her chair watching Sonia's computer screen. She was content to listen to Sonia. Never did I see Jessie open the desktop in front of her. The notebook we provided each of the girls often remained in the same location at the end of the day as it appeared in the beginning, unopened and devoid of any writing. In the end, however, the concluding video documentary contained Jessie's crisp voice as well as Sonia's.

As a flute played traditional music from this community, we heard both Sonia and Jessie's voices describing how they collected information and what it meant to the community as a whole. Having interviewed a community member who also served as a health care provider, Sonia balanced their narratives with the adult's description of the issue.

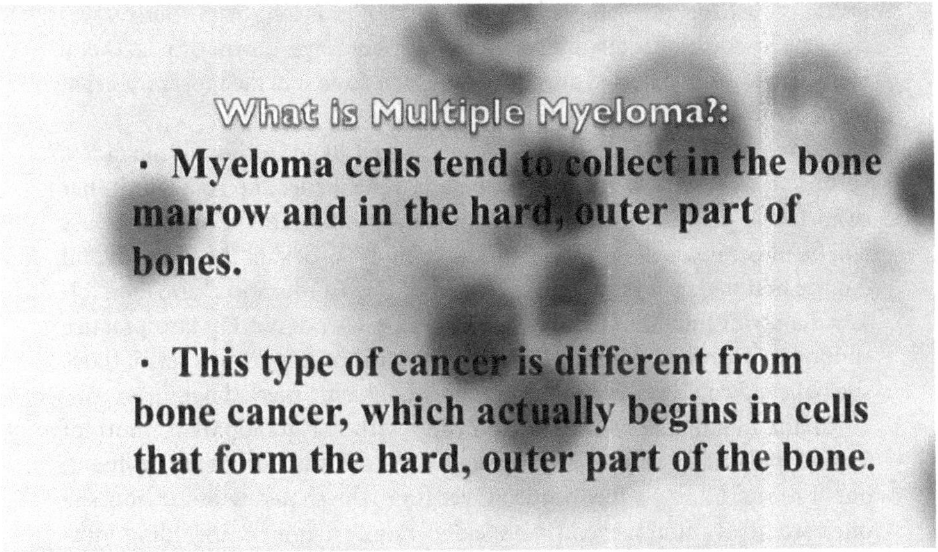

What is Multiple Myeloma?:
· **Myeloma cells tend to collect in the bone marrow and in the hard, outer part of bones.**

· **This type of cancer is different from bone cancer, which actually begins in cells that form the hard, outer part of the bone.**

Figure 10. Multiple myeloma slide by Sonia and Jessie

X-rays of bones broken from the cancer were supplemented with images Sonia took using Geographic Information System (or GIS) software to determine the nearest locations for community members to receive proper treatment once diagnosed. Realizing that the nearest facility was at least a ninety-minute ambulance ride away, Sonia and Jessie displayed all of this information in their video documentary.

Rihana

"Rihana" was an abbreviated version of her full name, the one she referenced only on her application and on the title slide of her video project. Beyond this information, specifics about why Rihana joined the program or what she hoped to accomplish were details she chose not to reveal at any point. With long brown hair framing her round face, her cheeks would burst into a smile quite often, causing her dark brown eyes to almost disappear. Of smaller-than-average height, Rihana was incredibly quiet and avoided eye contact.

For the first few weeks of the COMPUGIRLS program on the reservation, Rihana regularly attended. Although her eyes remained bloodshot and her mannerisms would suggest she was under some kind of influence, she did not miss a day of the program. Sitting no lower in her chair than the other girls, Rihana did not speak until the second week. Until then, she moved her head slowly to acknowledge whoever was talking, as long as the person was a peer. For adults, Rihana preferred to look sideways, down, or past them. Her sentences often trailed off, although she ensured that the most important parts of any conversation were heard.

Among her peers, Rihana seemed to be well-liked. Although much less verbose than Yvette, Rihana assumed a unique leadership role within her cohort, one that emphasized the significance of cultural maintenance. As will be illustrated below, Rihana did not simply "proclaim the ideals of and culture maintenance as an integral aspect of Native education" and then follow the script that Manuelito (2003) describes as not putting into practice support to include the ideals. With regular and constant contact with those she believed could teach her cultural norms, she manifested her views.

Rihana maintained a close relationship with her grandparents, both of whom spoke the Indigenous language. She admitted to not being fluent, but "I mean, I know a few words." Over time, she shared with me how she often attended cultural events with "elder" family members, including community district meetings. "I go to them with my grandmother. . . . We talk about a lot of things like, I don't know exactly, but a lot of what is going on. They are long." More than many of the other girls, Rihana was tuned in to the surrounding politics. Although her mother and father did not attend the closing ceremony, she became aware of a local fathers' group.

This group comprised men from the community who met regularly to discuss specific issues and develop ways to address them, and it was Rihana along with Alani who approached the men to work with COMPUGIRLS on the rez. "I thought it would be a good thing for them to come in and talk about our culture. I didn't know they were there," even though their meetings took place in the same Boys and Girls Club facilities every two weeks. Again, I was not privy to the information shared during their visit; however, Rihana expressed genuine excitement that one of the fathers agreed to play one of the traditional instruments at the girls' next closing ceremony. "He isn't charging or anything but will come and play the whole time if we want!" Her interactions with these men encouraged her to study over the course of two years language and culture loss in her community. Rihana intentionally approached this topic as a way to oppose what she and the girls believed to be one of many troubling stereotypes of them and their culture.

Rihana was less concerned with how outsiders perceived them but was far more interested in how community members saw each other. In general, Rihana and her peers were more introspective and focused their attentions on how tribal elders viewed the Indigenous youngsters. This may partially explain the reasons behind the limited interactions once the girls came to the university space. Nevertheless, after about the third week of the digital storytelling course (Course I), following the visits from the fathers' group and a female tribal leader, there was a noticeable change in Rihana. With much clearer eyes, she began to sit up a bit more in her chair.

Although she did not take notes, she opened her laptop more quickly than before. When asked about her action, she replied, "I'm looking for images about our culture."[14] Over the course of the digital storytelling experience, Rihana crafted an incredible project that informed her Scratch game and virtual world products. She wanted to illustrate to the community elders that youngsters are very interested in learning their culture and language, though many adults did not believe this was the case. With Alani's guidance, Rihana created a survey instrument used with over fifty respondents in the community. The intent of the survey was to assess how elementary- and middle-school-aged children (ages six to thirteen) thought of their culture and language. Rihana was acutely interested in whether they wanted to learn their language and how much they actually knew. Although we demonstrated to Rihana the ease of SurveyMonkey as a free software program that can organize and provide descriptive statistics of closed-ended survey questions, she understood that the vast majority of her respondents would not have access to a computer to answer the questions. Instead, Rihana printed several copies of her survey, and rather than seek approval from the principals of the elementary and middle schools, neither of whom were Native Americans, she preferred to approach youngsters during less formal events.

While walking into the Boys and Girls Club, attending community meetings, or on her way to school, Rihana carried the surveys with her, which contained five questions. Once she reached what she believed was the appropriate sample size, she began inputting the data into an Excel file. Her plan was to display the results in interesting and colorful pie graphs and charts "to show what I got. It was interesting so, you know, we should see it." This was Rihana's first step in revealing that the youngsters in her community *did* want to speak the language but not learn it through conventional means. Specifically, kids admitted that learning the language in school was the least interesting way they could think of.

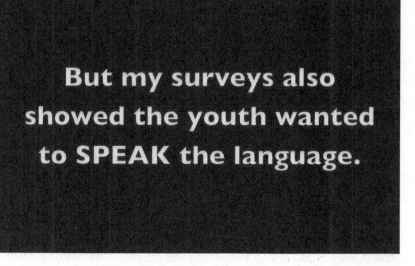

Figure 11. Language slide by Rihana

Rihana dedicated the Scratch course to addressing her survey respondents' desire to learn the language. She believed a logical next step was to teach users how to count in her Indigenous language. To accomplish this she worked independently from the other girls and called on the knowledge of the elders. Correct pronunciation and intonation were achieved after countless consultation sessions with her grandmother. In the end, she recorded her grandmother's voice rather than use her own. By all accounts, her game was a success.

The closing ceremony revealed the product, and in a gallery-type setting, the nearly one hundred attendees at the community-based event played her game on the borrowed laptop. Rihana stood next to her creation and explained to all onlookers the genesis for creating this product: "I learned that the kids want to learn the language, but schools are not teaching it to them. We cannot let it die, and it will if we don't teach the young."

Once she revealed her results, one ceremony attendee exclaimed, "I didn't know they, you know, the kids care to learn our ways. Now I know, now I know. We have a senior group who can help teach them. They are always looking for things to do, and they are some of the last ones who can speak it [the Indigenous language]."

Rihana was disinterested by what non-Indigenous individuals thought about her topic or her community as a whole. She was mindful of the cultural expectations set by her own community. On the first screen of her Scratch project, she coded, "In our culture, we are told it is not acceptable to share our language." Rihana expressed disagreement with this notion for the sake of preservation:

Figure 12. "Who We Are" by Rihana

Without using the academic term, Rihana's actions illustrated Kovach's elaboration that Indigenous epistemology "is about giving back to the community" (2010, 11). One way researchers can contribute to this is through sharing their work in order to be used by others. Chilisa adds that the colonized should be the center for the production and storage of information and knowledge produced about them (2012, 56).

Indeed, Rihana did not rely on other participants, for the most part, in actualizing her project. She did, however, spend an enormous amount of time with Alani and her grandmother, fleshing out the pieces of this project. In this context, COMPUGIRLS participants engaged in parallel work. They occupied the same space as each other and listened to the whole group instruction or engaged in near-peer mentoring, but they did not use the setting or the program as a tool by which to bond.

Since the girls saw each other in school and in the community, they did not see a need to know each other in a different space. Although less articulated in Rihana's cohort, future COMPUGIRLS participants on the rez came together, coalesced by their marginalization as Native Americans. Repeatedly, girls expressed concern that "they [non-Natives] think we are druggies and drink [alcohol]." Some girls admitted their belief that "Native Americans that do that [drink alcohol] are not respecting the land." Jade, for instance, eloquently voiced this and other views about perception and the power of being visible in non-Native spaces.

Better to Be a Feminist Than a Prostitute

As the youngest participant in her cohort, Jade's twelve-year-old voice was quite powerful. She frequently moved her body as she spoke, demonstrating comfort and self-confidence with her average height. Her wavy hair displayed red tips that reflected the ombre trend popular at the time. Everyone seemed to know Jade as she entered the clubhouse; most girls and boys greeted her warmly. Quick to engage in conversation, her speech was purposeful, rarely failing to transmit her opinion, whether asked for or not.

Jade came to understand that in her school space, even with concerted efforts to place value on Native cultures, such strategies did not always produce the anticipated results.[15] She explained that her school had an "American Indian" school counselor, but since that advisor's departure, Jade felt as though the school had fewer American Indian students. She continued to explain that with the decreasing numbers of American Indians at her school, the climate had become more chilly toward them: "We're not as welcome as we used to be. . . . More people are looking down on us." This recognition did not dampen Jade's hope but also did not inspire her to seek or develop a coalition with other COMPUGIRLS participants.

Like Sonia and Rihana, Jade preferred to focus her energies on calling attention to the invisible, rarely talked about discourse that rested on assumptions of young Native individuals. She used her voice to identify what lay below the surface, wanting to express what had been bottled up and reveal its power and applicability. The COMPUGIRLS program on the reservation did not provide the community girls a space to come together and build the type of coalition that emerged in the university setting, a coalition that was driven by the desire of each participant to move the globe in unique and impactful ways. Girls like Jade focused on revealing what was missing from their developing consciousnesses through a critical lens and by working alongside one another to take down the veils of disbelief. Their efforts were not about igniting a community to act, even though this was sometimes a result (as was the case of Rihana's work), but about opening new or forgotten areas of knowledge that enhanced appreciation and utilization of tribal culture.

Although not specific to Native women, Jade often critiqued how others saw marginalized females. When discussing women in music videos, she stated that "they're not presentable; they're not fully dressed or acting respectable. . . . It's disrespectful, and then men think that we're all like that . . . not just disrespecting yourself but other women out there in the world. . . . They're making it look like we're stupid and don't know how to act." Her mentor teacher asked, "What about equality? In comparison with the other gender," to which Jade responded, "That's probably why they look down on us, especially in high positions, because in the music videos they see women acting like that." When her mentor teacher asked her, "What can you do it about?," she retorted with, "If we're going to do something about it, you can't do anything bigger than our community; we could, probably, but who would listen to us? We're just random people trying to do something about it." Another girl added, "And we would be labeled as feminists," to which Jade replied, "Better to be labeled feminists than prostitutes."

Jade did not particularly like the label "feminist." She was conflicted by maintaining cultural traditions. From where she stood, nothing could be worse than irreverence for the "old" ways. Those who grasped for modernity not only rejected the former mores but settled for an inferior, degrading lifestyle. Not everything about the "other" culture was good, and women were especially vulnerable to losing their dignity. When Jade castigated some women who looked like prostitutes, she was casting a wide net and intended to caution young girls of impending danger. But she wasn't too happy at the thought of her sisters becoming feminists, which was a little better but still not compatible with images of a mature, responsible tribal woman.

Coming Together

Zaire and Elena believed that their immediate peer-centered/girl-centered community was strong, solidified, and far less dependent on engaging support from adults in their immediate context than on other girls. COMPUGIRLS participants at the university were committed to building each other up, with or without the assistance of adults hired to provide resources and opportunities to engage in critical activist work (see Miguel's story in chapter 4). But they yearned to make a global impact.

In neither the university nor the reservation site did we find dysfunctional, disaffected teens. They didn't need assistance to discover their worth, and they had large loyalties and concerns that transcended carnal pleasure or moping. They had a variety of stances relating to adults. They rejected the approach that adults were commissioned to "save" the girls from themselves and each other. For Zaire and other attendees at the university site, they did not seek adult acceptance, per se, but support in actualizing the vision they had discovered as a result of their research. Zaire's peers encouraged her and Elena to cross borders and to make visible their concerns in the hopes of enlisting adults. To step outside of their protective COMPUGIRLS culture (for example, going to an international conference) was acceptable because they knew they could return to the safe space of our program. We recognized this idea of COMPUGIRLS being a safe space after the first cohort.

One recent participant remarked, "I would describe it [COMPUGIRLS] as being, like, lots of fun and new stuff and very much like an environment that allows you to thrive. . . . It's very supportive." For many participants, there was safety in being able to speak their minds without recrimination, after comprehending that accountability and criticism are not synonymous. Girls understood they would need to present their ideas to each other and be able to articulate how their proposals affected their communities. Being visible and heard in the program's protected space was not necessarily enough but was a good beginning for initiating the type of change they wanted to see. It was paramount that the participants be visible to their peers.

But visibility did not always become expressed recognition. Respect of voice, knowledge, and adhesion to a community took precedence. How girls made use of these terms, however, was not consistent between the two sites. What was constant was that girls didn't gravitate toward acceptance of community goals as superior to all others without question. To be sure, encouraging and preparing the girls to engage in critical thinking didn't shelter the entire program from the same scrutiny and evaluation that other elements of the experience received. In the spaces occupied by the programs, there were safe havens but also arenas where virtually everything was contested. Adults didn't know and certainly could not determine the direction or flow of the program. The dynamic was not in the hands of or subject to the control of adults. At times this created confusion and dismay for mentor teachers.

Whether to scholars at an international conference or to tribal elders, COMPUGIRLS was invested in making topics apparent to demonstrate the "truth" about one's culture. This was a strategy COMPUGIRLS on the reservation developed. In any event, both sets of girls persevered to articulate their perceived lives, even if it meant working at odds with and in seeming isolation from each other. Neither curriculum nor occupying the same space was a strong enough force to shape critical thinking. Outcomes couldn't be predicted, and even within the same peer group individual choices played no small role. Tuning COMPUGIRLS to fluid considerations was absolutely necessary. This not only prescribed adult supervision and input but also reflected seriousness in conferring to the girls maximum control of the teaching-learning process. Outsiders to the reservation, including Sonia and the near-peer mentors, experienced difficulty with this concept, as did the reservation cohort when forced to visit the university setting. There was a tangled interplay in COMPUGIRLS operations that was always changing and in some cases did not fit neatly with theoretical considerations.

CHAPTER SIX

Where Are They Now

IT WOULD BE ARROGANT to assume COMPUGIRLS was the sole reason the girls in the preceding chapters were able to produce such impressive research projects through mutually constitutive process, create innovative digital products, and develop heightened critical inquiries and praxes to confront social injustices. Along those same lines, the girl-selected topics, ways we collected findings, and types of implementation methods varied across regions and time. Sadly, we did not have the capacity or the financial resources to conduct systematic longitudinal tracking. Since 2017, and thanks to a thoughtful postdoctoral fellow working with me, we do have some summative data (see appendix). Even with the absence of continued data, COMPUGIRLS' expansiveness continues as we partner with organizations and institutions around the world. Within all of our work, we recognize that COMPUGIRLS was and is an instrument and alone does not empower the girls. The stories in this narrative should reveal that the girls' emergent identities were not solely the result of the program.

While the characteristics of the site certainly did have an influence, the peer cultures and the cultural knowledge of the individuals also played critical roles in developing girls' consciousness as change agents and technologists. One of the many consequences of their participation in this program was an expansion of girlhoods of color. Strikingly apparent to both mentor teachers and closing ceremony attendees, girls' interest in immediate and global cultures and how they could transform these spaces took center stage. When constructing new identities, girls battled each other, outsiders, and well-meaning adults. It was important that the girls not demonize those of their culture who blocked social change or limited their participation by labeling them as disinterested in their own communities. Some of our future work will explore which specific programmatic elements influence participants' domain-specific self-concepts.

I would also be a Pollyanna to think that this is not a provocative tale of subversion. For some, the COMPUGIRLS phenomenon is one to be feared. A critical mass of girls of color becoming technologically savvy and equipped to critique and change the status quo with insightful thoughts and the ability to build a coalition can seem troubling. Even for professional educators, the COMPUGIRLS' approach may be problematic. As has been pointed out, regardless of philosophical foundations, handing supervision and control to girls may be too daunting for some.

The stories featured here provide different images of success. Our program touched a relatively small number of girls from high-needs areas. To some extent, I regret our relatively limited reach. Two years after its launch, Black Girls Code reached 3,000 girls. By 2019, seven years after its founding, Girls Who Code provided programming to 300,000 girls, with half of the participants from "underrepresented groups." Techbridge's after-school and summer programs included 7,000 girls. In contrast, during more recent years, COMPUGIRLS' programming tends to host 150–300 girls per year. The reasons behind our relatively shallow breadth reflect my situated positionality as a scholar-activist.

The time it takes to build and maintain long-term partnerships with communities, schools, and girls is not inconsequential. Developing trust with disenfranchised communities requires all of one's self. And even though I, too, am multiply marginalized, my Black femaleness did not grant me automatic acceptance with all the communities I wished to serve. Establishing rapport with participants, their schools, and their communities took time both before and after I fulfilled other professional obligations (such as teaching, mentoring students, and committee work).

And since COMPUGIRLS relies exclusively on external grants, writing and talking about the program are critical activities. For better or worse, funders tend to support well-known initiatives. Consequently, I felt compelled to present to and dialogue with various audiences to ensure COMPUGIRLS remains in the forefront of minds. Upon receiving a 2014 White House STEM Access Champion Change award for COMPUGIRLS, we could argue that the efforts paid off. Still, lessons learned from this more-than-a-decade-long initiative have evolved over time.

Results of the program's impact may not apply to all or most high-needs areas, because there are significant variations among these school districts. Certainly, our program doesn't open the door fully to girls from these communities in terms of being prepared for technological careers. Some girls, without prodding and after demonstrating competence with computer skills, turned away and sought other non-STEM occupations. The primary aim of COMPUGIRLS is to provide girls the basic building blocks for entering and succeeding in any field they choose. Although I am concerned that so few girls of color are entering technology-related fields, COMPUGIRLS has a much wider lens. Measuring our accomplishments according to numbers of girls entering STEM fields cannot be the only barometer of success.

Success is difficult to map in an educational enterprise, largely because change happens over time and not all change is of the same quality. Qualitative data was instrumental to this project and should not be discounted. Much can be learned from listening to girls of color and observing them as potent forces rather than as broken vessels. Of course, assuming an asset lens necessitates a definition of change not universally understood or accepted. One of the yardsticks we used was to determine the value of social change to the community. What if social change is equated with the identification and treatment of disease that is affecting some lives in a tribal community? Is the pinpointing of the disease sufficiently broad enough in scope to warrant the label of social change? What we learned from this encounter was that judgments brought to COMPUGIRLS, no matter how carefully they have been aligned with theory, may not fit the situation. Perceptions of students are more important to outcomes than the best-laid plans of curriculum developers or adult mentor teachers.

Like Denner and Guzman state in the introductory chapter to their edited book on Latina girls, I, too, am "not naïve enough to suppose that the girls in this book are 'problem free.' Many come from households and communities where limited resources, fear of crime, and physically demanding work create daily stress and health problems. However, the girls in these chapters are more prepared than many to confront life's challenges because they are actively engaged in transforming systems of oppression and creating their own language of well-being" (2006, 5).

We are not concerned with merely with digital inclusion but with disruption. More girls of color may enter technology and at the same time maintain their cultural identities if provided sustained opportunities to capitalize on the cultural richness of their selves, build on their insider knowledge as members of multiple communities, learn to appreciate the varying shades of their identities, and concurrently learn technology to advance the common interest of their contexts. The type of trouble we seek involves what Cox describes as "locating the radical potential in all efforts—intentional, accidental, and otherwise" so that girls can develop "outside of normatively scripted modes of self-improvement and social mobility" (2015, 31).

The program not only provides space for such counter-normative efforts but also upsets distance between constructs, communities, and supposed truisms. By requiring girls to critique images produced by digital media, I maintain the same condition Ruth Brown articulates as beneficial when working with Black girlhood in her Saving Our Lives, Hear Our Truths project: "to also make visible the responsibility of the viewer to hold a productive uncertainty about what is being seen and to prompt discussions about challenging institutional norms and interpersonal actions that do not recognize the humanity of Black girls" (2013, 100). Brown continues demonstrating the importance of engaging Black girls in interrogating and contesting normalized raced-gendered images of themselves, as misrecognition can occur even among the marginalized. She reminds us that our race-gender does not inoculate anyone from the stereotypical images meant to confirm and exacerbate our oppression. Without space and resources for, in our case, girls of color to acquire the skill and language to recognize, contest, and ultimately undermine these images with innovative manifestations of their cultural knowledge, unjust copies of girlhood prevail.

In part, the digital products become important vestiges of their narratives. Whether the girls' digital stories, animations, or games, and whether through Scratch or Virtual Worlds or The Sims, these presentations are reconceived as social justice ends. At the same time, these creations, no matter how impressive, are simply part of the complex puzzle of how the girls see themselves and their capabilities in the constellation of possibilities.

Nevertheless, both this book and the COMPUGIRLS program take seriously McPherson's clarion call: "We need to create structures and supports—from hands-on tools to open peer-to-peer systems to curricula—that mobilize the gains in imagination, creativity, and hope that our interactions with mutable, variable technologies animate. We need to study and foster the excitement and engagement we palpably note when children engage digital media, but we need to do more than that. We also need to 'cultivate' and 'grow' this excitement in very particular directions with a mind to ethical and socially just outcomes lest it only be harvested for corporate profit" (2008, 13).

One of the delimiting factors of COMPUGIRLS is its applicability to a Western context. I have received calls of interest to expand COMPUGIRLS to other countries. Indeed, in 2015, I founded a research unit, the Center for Gender Equity in Science and Technology (CGEST), to coordinate and broaden COMPUGIRLS and related work. CGEST institutionalizes the program through research, advocacy, and new capacity building initiatives. As of 2020, we have developed or are in the process of establishing new COMPUGIRLS courses: a human-centered robotics curriculum; a place-based computational thinking experience for Native Hawaiian and Pacific Islander girls; an in-school co-educational course for high school students in rural districts; culturally responsive computational professional development for Ireland's teachers; cybersecurity courses for Native American girls. And with this increase in programming, we look to the knowledge gained from the original cohorts as a bedrock of our actions. Yet, the findings presented herein cannot automatically extend to other girls of color nationally or abroad.

How would this culturally responsive computing curriculum operate in Kenya? What kind of identities would emerge if COMPUGIRLS appeared in Costa Rica, where social justice issues are inextricably woven within the very fabric of everyday life? If girls sought social change in a country that grants women and girls few rights, a setting in which demands for disruption could lead to severe punishment or death, should COMPUGIRLS strive to stir action?

Ten Years Later

A decade is not a long period to interpret results of an educational program. Nevertheless, I include what two participants thought about this work in its manuscript stage and how they gauged the impact of the program on their lives and careers ten years after participating. Although these two accounts were not from any of the African American COMPUGIRLS participants, I include comments from some of their e-mails in response to bell hooks's suggestion from her "Revolutionary Black Women" essay in order to inspire the subjectivity of other women of color.

Kelly

I just graduated with a Bachelor's of Science in Anthropology and a Bachelor's of Science in Psychology. I am preparing for an archaeology field school this summer in Belize. I will be applying for a straight Ph.D. program in archaeology this fall in preparation to start in the fall of 2017.

I think COMPUGIRLS has helped me immensely throughout my high school and college career. I was in COMPUGIRLS throughout high school, had an internship through COMPUGIRLS the summer before my senior year, and worked for COMPUGIRLS as an REU [undergraduate research assistant][1] for the first part of college. I have had the chance to do everything from learn and participate with mentor-teachers, help teach a class myself, do research, and even co-write a chapter of a book with a fellow COMPUGIRL. All of these experiences were because of my connection through the program.

I feel like I learned a lot as a student in COMPUGIRLS, and I truly think it gave me a leg-up when I started college. We learned digital storytelling and research skills before our colleagues did that proved useful throughout college. As an employee through COMPUGIRLS, I was given the opportunity to conduct research on the program, help new students, and publish my experiences as a low-income female in the education system. Overall, I really do think COMPUGIRLS helped reshape my life for the better and gave me many opportunities that I would not have had otherwise. Overall, it made me better prepared for college, graduate school, and life.

I am still Facebook friends with many of the girls that were in my cohort and many of the girls that were in the program while I worked for it earlier in my college career. We still connect and support each other through our mutual high school and college experiences. One of the great things about COMPUGIRLS is that it created a big family for many of us to connect and support each other. Once a COMPUGIRL, always a COMPUGIRL!

Montserrat

Yes, I feel like you represented the stories well. The part where you were describing Yvette during the orientation was very well written. I felt like it was my experience being described, I thought it was very cool that you were able to convey that.

Also, I'm sure you have enough cited material, but when you talked about her refusal to attend school it reminded me of Herbert Kohl's "I Won't Learn From You" . . . [in which] he talks about students CHOOSING to not learn. "Not learning produces thoroughly different effects. It tends to strengthen the will, clarify one's definition of self, reinforce self-discipline, and provide inner satisfaction . . . Not-learning tends to take place when someone has to deal with unavoidable challenges to her or his personal and family loyalties, integrity, and identity." He also talks . . . how he had to un-learn racist and sexist language because a student of his had chosen to not-learn that type of language.

Charlotte's story is another great choice for this piece. I liked how you were able to show Yvette's "I do belong here" attitude and juxtapose it with Charlotte's quieter and more withdrawn personality.

I also enjoyed reading the Miguel story. It is bold of you to share these difficult moments and wonderful because it can help others think about the difficulties they come across.

Overall, I highly enjoyed reading about the different girls' stories and experience in COMPUGIRLS. It is coming along quite nicely! . . .

The most helpful [lesson I learned in COMPUGIRLS] would be the confidence in technology and leadership because it allowed me to continue to be a technological leader in my classes. Additionally, my experience as a REU. By working as an undergraduate research assistant, I was able to have practice in writing peer-reviewed research papers, learn how to conduct studies, observe and help graduate researchers which inspired me, with the push of Dr. Scott,[2] to work towards my Ph.D. It no longer seems as daunting or impossible. Moreover, this entire experience is what encouraged me to apply for the Fulbright scholarship, something that I would definitely have not applied for on my own. . . .

I love all of the stories that you told about the M-Ts [mentor teachers] and emphasized how instrumental they were to our successes. I think this was true throughout all cohorts of COMPUGIRLS and was very vital to what made COMPUGIRLS such a family. This ties into another point that I am glad that you highlighted—the importance of COMPUGIRLS becoming a space that belongs to the students. This definitely became true because when the adults relinquished some of their "authority" over us, we felt that our ideas were valued and our thoughts were important. I am glad you discuss these at length through Yvette's story!

I loved the story about Charlotte using a male voice to display what she found with her Sims. It was sad, but very powerful in highlighting some of the problems that girls face when trying to be assertive and present in front of a crowd. She felt much more comfortable hiding behind a male voice, as these tasks are often associated with a male and not a female. I also could really appreciate the story involving Miguel's group (especially because I remember him since I was in that cohort)! I think it was a powerful story showing how not only the girls needed to create their own space, but it highlighted many of the problems that many mentor-teachers might have coming from a standard educational background. It really showed how the role of mentor-teacher is NOT the same as a standard educator, and I think highlights one of the many things that makes COMPUGIRLS unique.

I like how you use Zaire's story to show how the girls grow and become change agents throughout the course. I know as a student, we thought of this as one of the most important things that we learned in the program, and I think Zaire's story highlights change and growth very nicely. I also really enjoyed the section about the Rez. I remember it how you describe it, no matter what we did collectively as a larger group, we often secluded Rez girls from the downtown girls—albeit not intentionally. I think this speaks to a larger cultural difference and presses how the Rez girls were facing many similar, but also many different cultural and technological challenges.

I remember interning at "the Rez" and seeing how little technology they had access to in general. It is a very different environment and can be difficult to connect those bridges back to the cohort from downtown. As far as I know, Rihana's story was accurate. I worked with her a bit on her project and she on mine—we both MC'ed the same Closing Ceremony. Her project was very interesting and highlights an important difference that the girls on the Rez faced (something very few girls downtown could relate to).

Looks good!

Responsively and Onward

Not all of the program graduates felt the same level of success as Kelly and Montserrat. As young women in their twenties, some former participants felt that because they did not complete an undergraduate degree they had failed. Others expressed a recognizable resentment, the kind too many young people express when they realize that one program, no matter how long, cannot fully prepare them for life's bumps and bruises that women of color experience in our peculiar way. Others felt a calling to engage in social justice work and majored in poverty studies and political science, readying themselves to earn a law degree. One young woman did not feel obliged or in any way sorry that she did not continue her education past high school. Instead, building websites for early childhood programs while developing databases for such institutions became her passion and life's work. In general, none of the girls followed predictable scripts often assigned to females from under-resourced areas, but there was a common chord running through most of their narratives—the need to act beyond participating in the program.

For COMPUGIRLS participants, activism involved learning how to resist majoritarian scripts of potential. Traditional measures of success meant little to most of them. Getting good grades, regularly attending school, entering postsecondary school, and even majoring in computer science were far less interesting pursuits than engaging in activities that revealed new truths about their culture, self, or others. In this sense, participants defined activism in terms of how their researched actions affected a community. Community was not necessarily or consistently bound by geographic, tribal, racial, or ethnic borders. What a much more complex image of girlhood than typically presented for girls of color.

Harris (2004b) reminds us that girlhood is typically defined by consumption, victimization, and maintenance of a flawed social system. It is through images of passive consumption that the notion of girls as disempowered and defeated persists. These images are typically assigned to White girls. Absent the most recent body of reports[3] that tend not to appear in peer-reviewed social science outlets such as journals with high impact factors, the media maintains their successes at perpetuating the images of the hypersexual, defiant, loud-talking Black girls; hypersexual, heavily accented Latina girls; and drug- or alcohol-dependent, quiet Native American girls who dare not leave the rez. For those girls who "get out" and succeed, their fight-the-odds appearances come as a result of individual, solitary endeavors. Resistance for girls of color in this digital age rarely includes collective action, movement, or the significance of their peer system.

Escapism—moving far away from one's cultural backgrounds, families, and communities—and solitude become distinguishable markers designed to shape the contours of success for our girls. Narratives of how the lone girl overcame her fatherless home or survived her overworked mother's emotional distance and poor school resources leave the researcher and well-meaning after-school program director with a comforting but overly simplified roadmap devoid of girls' insights. Statements such as "If I can identify the most salient variables from her life that make a positive impact—variables that are rarely extant in her community—then change can occur" or "If I can integrate that same variable into an after-school or summer program, an experience that looks much different from what the girls are accustomed to, then we may see some gains" not only assume the all-too-present deficit approach but make it exceedingly difficult to genuinely understand the completeness of experiences, the importance of voice, and the potential of "these" girls' activism. For the most part, the COMPUGIRLS participants resisted becoming or embodying who the surrounding world believed they were or could be and at times opposed what their mentor teachers held as their "true" identities.

Often, the girls' resistance involved quietly opposing the curriculum we set before them. At other moments, resistance meant exploring more deeply cultural beliefs and expectations. All in all, COMPUGIRLS participants crafted their own scripts that did not necessarily take into account race, gender, and social class all at one time. Social class and tribal membership might have intersected and influenced the interpretation of affordances and lack of resources to highlight; gender and social class converged at other moments and within some analyses of earning potential. Forming one's identity as a youth activist assumed greater clarity than developing a professed consciousness or identity as a girl-of-color activist. Race and ethnicity were more elusive for many COMPUGIRLS participants. Unless specifically teased out, identity remained a fluid concept, contested for what it meant in terms of possibilities, yet unexamined regarding how it contributed to other sociocultural factors influencing their experiences. Its perceived absence, however, did not dampen girls' desire to act out their intentions as individuals who made the invisible visible using means often coded as symbols of passive defeat. Resistance was not necessarily a "loud" demonstration that involved protests or name-calling. For these girls, resistance and, as a result, their girlhoods were shaped by tensions between the positioning of the technical skills and the power skills.

To the best of my knowledge, none of the COMPUGIRLS graduates from the first two cohorts majored in computer science. This does not suggest that they lacked the computational thinking skills or aptitude to lead, supervise, or innovate with digital media. Instead, the girls graduated from the program with a much stronger sense of themselves as change agents. For them, change required gaining access to communicative tools that could deconstruct what was in order to reconstruct new images of what could be. Digital stories, games, and builds within virtual worlds served as a means to display their understanding, interpretations, and calls to action. Technology was not the solution but a way to demonstrate the multitude of pathways toward more equitable worlds. Consequently, their stories illustrated that while recognizing their own marginality might have been part of the process, it was not the catalyst.

Girls come to understand, in varying degrees, that gender, social class, and/or tribal membership may position them outside the dominant mainstream but does not disempower them from furthering their communities or changing their selves. In this sense, they are all innovators proposing new systems of thinking, images, and results. For some, this involves reinventing themselves completely, while for others it is simply acquiring the language to express the discovery of their contextualized identities. This harkens back to Unger's (2000) point of "positive marginality," neatly demonstrating that there is much positive activity in those marginalized spaces. Hence, these girls are not merely dispossessed beings requiring a prescient hero. They may lack access to resources and opportunities to unpack their and others' experiences, but this can be resolved with strategic planning that is culturally responsive.

Providing girls space to create their own systems, flexible enough to include their developing consciousnesses even when their identities do not follow conventional notions of intersecting variables, should be at the heart of social inclusion projects. Concurrently, as program developers, we need to question our own intentions and pause when including strategies aiming to "expose" girls of color to anything or anyone. Without understanding how these moments can be perceived, the unexamined features that the well-meaning field trip may implicitly convey—the unspoken statement that said "you don't belong"—may do more harm than good in terms of empowering girls of color. Program development needs to be culturally responsive, just as the pedagogical efforts that make up the program are.

At Last

When we fail to recognize both big and small critical acts of resistance, Collins's *Another Kind of Public Education* reminds us of the consequences: "If denied the opportunity to hear and read the ideas of figures such as [Martin Luther] King, or to see pictures of the sole student staring down tanks in Tiananmen Square, or to engage in conversations via social networks in mediated communities, we can easily remain without a vision and be denied the skills to realize a vision even if we could develop one" (2009, 180–81).

These wise words apply to COMPUGIRLS as a program and as a book.

As we refine our offerings, expand to other national and international sites, and witness more and more girls enter college and the workforce, we reaffirm our values:

- Populating the "pipeline" with more Black and Brown female bodies fails to fix the race-gender parity problems in technology. There needs to be a seismic transformation for an inclusive system to exist.
- Change requires a redefinition of success. Achievement must include how well we challenge images of what is and our ability to reconstruct those images to depict what could and must be.
- All programs, including those for girls from high-needs districts, must be intentionally driven by culturally responsive methods. And those methods need to apply intersectionality as a frame to understand power, relationality, critical inquiry, and critical praxis in the way they nurture girlhoods of color.

Michelle Obama's words in her significant book, *Becoming*, aptly summarize my present and future work: "If there's one thing I've learned in life, it's the power of using your voice. I tried my best to speak the truth and shed light on the stories of people who are often brushed aside" (2018, n.p.). For those of us invested in dissolving oppressive systems, we must hear our girls and understand their girlhoods of color in this digital age. This is an act of love. This is COMPUGIRLS.

Epilogue

RECENTLY, I PRESENTED EARLIER versions of this manuscript at a well-known university. To a crowd of approximately sixty world-renowned top-notch scientists, engineers, astronomers, and physicists, I concluded in my typical manner, requesting questions. One male listener stated, "I get it that you want these girls to go out and do great things and create their own STEM businesses or STEM industries, but we need them here [at the university]. And to be honest, our environment is not going to change any time soon. It is going to be hostile. So, what do you say to them? We need them here now. Plus they won't be able to start their own thing unless they come here first." I made the following response that contextualized the work we have done as well as that yet to be accomplished.

> We do not believe becoming a techno-social change agent requires girls to first become interlopers. Silently navigating a space that does not expect them to dismantle its structural constraints is of no interest to COMPUGIRLS participants and graduates. Rather than minimize our program's existence and our impact, we encourage girls to use digital tools that embrace and enhance the necessary disruption to transform any hostile environment. To this end, they must engage in this process through asset-building approaches, coalitions, and reflection on who they are, who they can be, and who they will become in the next digital age. Although digital media is not the silver bullet that society believed it would be at COMPUGIRLS' origination, it does provide much needed space for authorship.

The writing of this book took much longer than I anticipated—nearly eight years. Along the path of revisions, there has been a swell of diversity and inclusion activities with and for girls of color. Black Girls Code launched in 2011. CODeLLA, with a focus on Latina girls ages eight to thirteen, began in 2014. And as recently as 2018, the American Indian Science and Engineering Society, in collaboration with the Women of Color in Computing Research Collaborative,[1] initiated a project to create curriculum for Native high school girls attending Native-serving schools. At the same time, there has been more interest in and understanding of how intersectionality as a framework can and should influence social action.

Of note is Patricia Hill Collins's 2019 book, *Intersectionality as Critical Social Theory*, in which constructs of relationality, power, and resistance are unpacked to invigorate transformational change. Additionally, the National Science Foundation's ADVANCE program[2] expects proposals to apply an intersectional approach when suggesting ideas for systemic change in institutions of higher education. As the NSF is one of the largest federal funders of STEM programs, its inclusion of this requirement speaks volumes about intersectionality's stronghold. Sadly, these gains have not led to an appreciable improvement in the technology workforce for women of color.

Annually, some of the biggest organizations release reports indicating the number of women (read: White women) as well as women and men of color in their workforce. A Women of Color in Computing Research Collaborative data brief synthesized these reports along with other statistics and research to illustrate the gross race-gender disparities from entry level to leadership positions in Silicon Valley (McAlear et al. 2018). Although progress has been almost nonexistent, we have seen a recent boom in new girl-centered programs. Some assume a culturally responsive approach and, to varying degrees, gain success. The impact of these collective efforts over time is not abundantly clear. However, my COMPUGIRLS experience has caused me to note another troubling current running through many of these attempts at diversity.

Elsewhere, a colleague and I discuss how a disproportionate number of digital inclusion programs result in a "sharecropper model."[3] Drawing on W. E. B. Du Bois's description of sharecropping, we argue how many of these efforts may seem as if they encourage emancipatory action when a closer examination reveals they result in strengthening a system in which the target audience will never own the technology industry. Ensuring that scholars, program developers, and even conferences for and with women of color in computing remain siloed is one way the system continues to ensure underrepresentation prevails. Without coordination among these efforts, a coding camp, an affinity group, a residential program, or some other attempt to diversify technology may seem desirable, when in actuality such efforts reinforce the system in which race- or gender-marginalized groups lack competencies to transform the infrastructure.

Even after more than two decades' worth of work, I still reflect about our program's impact. COMPUGIRLS has established sites in several states and worked with various nonprofit organizations, school districts, and tribal leaders. We continue to expand nationally and internationally. New research methods to assess our impact have emerged; more nuanced questions about intersectionality shape our efforts. We are working to include more up-to-date hardware and software than presented in this book and spread our culturally responsive curriculum in ways that address a given context's needs. We are also incredibly mindful of building our own coalitions and are engaged in programming with parents and how to prepare industries to work with girls and their communities.

In my estimation, there are too many well-meaning industry folk who want to be mentors to students or teachers in underrepresented communities but have limited knowledge as to how effective interactions should be. However, and relevant to the male interrogator's question above, we are also working to cultivate more male allies. All of these efforts are in tandem with building a unified front, steeped in research and targeting policy makers to translate theory to critical praxis.

A thousand or so girls have completed at least one course with COMPUGIRLS, and I maintain contact with several from the original cohort. Many of the graduates' present-day lives have caused me to take pause and question the long-term effects of the program presented in this book. Specifically, a number of the girls were unable to apply their COMPUGIRLS skills in real-world employment. Some expressed their feelings of failure because they did not pursue a STEM career. Presently, we[4] are questioning how our initial efforts failed to consider long-term objectives.

Our work continues, as do the questions of how girls make sense of their experiences in programs such as COMPUGIRLS. As an admirer of critical race theory, I appreciate Derrick Bell's "racial pessimism" and recognize that programs like COMPUGIRLS will not eradicate racism, sexism, or any other ism in our society. However, I maintain my mantra, to comfort the disturbed and disturb the comfortable, and hope that our continued pursuit for equity will move the needle further for COMPUGIRLS, participants' children, and the next generation of scholars claiming equality for all.

Appendix

Types of COMPUGIRLS Activities

Dates— Active Years	Region	Type of COMPUGIRLS Program	Methods of Data Collection	Grant Awarded For
2007–8	Southwest	Pilot program to develop curriculum for out-of-school models	Informal and formal interviews; observations; external evaluation of program objectives being met	Program development
2008–14	Southwest	Out-of-school program	Pre- and post-surveys assessing girls' self-regulatory, academic possible selves; future time perspectives; informal and formal mentor teacher interviews; external evaluation of program objectives being met	Program development and research

Dates— Active Years	Region	Type of COMPUGIRLS Program	Methods of Data Collection	Grant Awarded For
2012–18	Southwest, Northeast, Far West	Out-of-school scale-up programs	Ethnographic observations of girls; pre- and post-surveys assessing girls' self-regulatory, academic possible selves; future time perspectives; informal and formal mentor teacher interviews; external evaluation of program objectives being met	Program development and research
2015– present	Southwest, Midwest, Pacific Islands	In-school co-educational pilots; out-of-school programs with new curriculum (e.g., robotics, cybersecurity, astrophysics); research grants to develop culturally responsive quantitative methods, curriculum for industry mentors, and curriculum for parents	Pre- and post-surveys; focus groups; interviews with mentor teachers and students; psychometric analyses; validity and reliability testing of new instruments	Program development and research

Notes

Preface

1. Irvine uses the plantation image in her 2003 book, *Educating Teachers for Diversity*. This metaphor refers to scholars viewing and treating research participants, particularly those from under-resourced contexts, as objects. Like slaveowners on America's plantations during slavery, researchers use participants' minds and bodies to benefit their academic careers. Subtle acts such as publishing data without sharing results with participants, speaking for the participants rather than inviting them to narrate their own stories, and not inviting anyone from the community to speak up and back to the researcher's interpretations serve as examples of this dynamic.

Introduction

1. Although Corsaro and Molinari's 2005 book, *I Compagni*, was not the first to present Reggio Emilia, it was one of the most celebrated accounts to describe how the preschool experience informed peer cultures well beyond the preschool years.

2. At the time, we and the girls themselves used "Latina." The remainder of this book employs "Latina" to honor the tenor of the times.

3. The well-known report that resulted from this meeting, titled *The Double Bind: The Price of Being a Minority Woman in Science*, was authored by Shirley Malcolm. Sadly, the descriptions of how women of color fared in the sciences are the same more than forty years after its publication. Indeed, in an updated 2011 article coauthored by Shirley Malcolm and Lindsey Malcolm, they again reveal the multitude of issues that women of color continue to face even after earning their science degrees.

4. Ong and her colleagues found that between 1970 and 2008, there were only a little more than 100 research articles published about women of color in STEM (Ong et al. 2011).

5. LinkedIn founder Reid Hoffman attributes his success, in part, to a master's degree in philosophy; the founders of Flickr and Hunch—Caterina Fake and her partner Stewart Butterfield, who went on to develop Slack—have both a BA and an MA in philosophy; angel investor Chris Dixon also has a BA and an MA in philosophy.

6. Created in 2015, the Girl Effect (https://www.girleffect.org/) is an international initiative focused on empowering some of the most vulnerable girls in developing countries. Digital media centers its efforts as it provides girls access to technology in order to change their communities in unprecedented ways.

7. NSF ITEST (#0833773) was the first of eight grants the National Science Foundation awarded for COMPUGIRLS' specific programming and research. It should be noted, however, that the first granting agency to support COMPUGIRLS was the Arizona Community Foundation. Thanks to its award, we were able to pilot a 2007 cohort.

8. Lee's report "Bridging Digital Divides between Schools and Communities" (2020) gives a history of how federal efforts spent considerable amounts of money to furnish schools with technology. Gathering data from two under-resourced urban and rural school communities, Lee illustrates how providing schools with computer equipment and professional development fell short of giving students from these communities all that was needed for their success. Her report demonstrates how thirty years' worth of funding has done little for students like those we aimed to recruit for COMPUGIRLS.

9. In Collins's *On Intellectual Activism*, she describes how the different domains of power operate as unexamined forces. Her analysis provides the necessary language to reveal and ultimately dismantle the oppression caused by this web. Power is organized as "(1) a structural domain, where social institutions of a society, such as banks, hospitals, schools, corporations, retail establishments, government agencies, and health care, routinely discriminate in favour of whites and against everyone else; (2) a disciplinary domain, where modern bureaucracies regulate race relations through their rules and practices, primarily surveillance; (3) a cultural domain, where ideologies, such as white supremacy, patriarchy, and heterosexism, are constructed and shared; and (4) an interpersonal domain that shapes social relations between individuals in everyday life" (2013, 72).

10. Bobb and Brown's chapter in the 2017 book *Moving Students of Color from Consumers to Producers of Technology* reveals that 40 percent of African American and "Hispanic" students earn computer science degrees from for-profit schools of higher education. Completion at these institutions provides these graduates with skills for technical maintenance and as service providers. In contrast, the number of Black and Hispanic students who attend the top ten computer science programs is abysmally small (3 percent), yet they acquire skills to be innovators, producers, and technological leaders hired by the most prestigious of companies. Bobb and Brown argue that providing students of color entry into tech is important but should not serve as the end goal. "The tech sector will have created a *technology ghetto* if Black and Hispanic workers are only trained to work in quadrant III," made up of the lowest-paid, least influential tech jobs (252).

11. The 2015 report, *Double Jeopardy? Gender Bias against Women of Color in Science,* provided convincing data on how women of color who had successfully completed degrees and worked in a science field consistently confronted race-gender-ethnicity biases. Although the results are not specific to computer science, all women of color in the sample were forced to deal with the resulting discriminatory practices based on their perceived incompetence, hypermasculinity, lack of emotional regulation, or maternal inclinations.

12. The "can-do" girl (contrasted with the "at-risk" girl described by Harris) succeeds in life by virtue of her internalized and individualistic optimism, self-assuredness, and proactive reinventing of herself as a successful girl who is not constrained by conventional gender norms or by social structures (Harris 2004b, 13).

13. I concur with Sue's definition of microaggressions, particularly its relation with power: "brief, everyday exchanges that send denigrating messages to certain individuals because of their group membership." The "power of microaggressions lies in the invisibility to the perpetrator, who is unaware that he or she has engaged in behavior that threatens and demeans the recipient of such a communication" (2013, 15–16).

14. Standpoint theory is integral to critical feminist theory, particularly Black feminist thought. Since the standpoints of women of color are typically obscured, preventing a complete understanding of how the matrix of power works to further oppress peoples, accessing the vision of women of color is not only an act of love but necessary for our self-preservation and emancipation.

15. It would be impossible to list all of the microaggressions and acts of racism, sexism, and homophobia in which women of color are the perpetual targets. However, in 2018 a Kapor-funded report, *Tech Leavers Study,* surveyed 2,000 individuals who voluntarily left their tech jobs. The work revealed that "underrepresented men and women of color experienced stereotyping at twice the rate of White and Asian men and women; 30% of underrepresented women of color were passed over for promotion. Experiencing and observing unfairness was a significant predictor of leaving due to unfairness, and the more bullying experienced, the shorter the length of time that employees remained at their previous company" (Scott, Klein, and Onovakpuri 2017, 3).

16. Culturally responsive computing is a particular pedagogical approach that COMPUGIRLS assumed. Our employment of culturally responsive computing includes what Nkrumah (2021) describes as the ARC approach. In short, all COMPUGIRLS activities excite asset building, reflection, and connectedness.

17. Not all COMPUGIRLS sites follow this particular sequence of courses.

Chapter One. COMPUGIRLS' Development

1. In an attempt to make the program and its participants stand out, originally we intentionally used all uppercase letters for "COMPUGIRLS." As the years progressed, this stylistic choice changed to distinguish earlier iterations from later program titles, represented as "CompuGirls."

2. Not only was my dress coded incorrectly, but my entire appearance came into question. Administrators' concerns did not become clear to me until years after this initial contact. It seems that suspicions about my age led some to question my ability to understand issues about race and urban education. Interestingly, not until I revealed my upbringing in an African American church did the skepticism diminish (for more on this phenomenon, see Scott [2012]).

3. Epstein, Blake, and González explain, "Across all age ranges, participants viewed Black girls collectively as more adult than white girls. Responses revealed, in particular, that participants perceived Black girls as needing less protection and nurturing than white girls, and that Black girls were perceived to know more about adult topics and are more knowledgeable about sex than their white peers" (2017, 8). They go on to say that between the ages of ten and fourteen, these adult-perceptions peak. The implications of these beliefs influence the interconnectedness of power and relationships Black girls have with adults: "Simply put, if authorities in public systems view Black girls as less innocent, less needing of protection, and generally more like adults, it appears likely that they would also view Black girls as more culpable for their actions and, on that basis, punish them more harshly despite their status as children" (8).

4. Years later, my colleagues and I published an article in which we describe the "Charlie Brown Syndrome" (Scott, Sheridan, and Clark 2014). This phenomenon appears when digital inclusion program developers fail to include parents in their activities. Ignoring "nondominant" parents' import, devaluing their knowledge, and relegating their culture as inconsequential have been most apparent in urban schools disproportionately populated with Black and Latinx students (see, for a recent example, Barajas-López and Ishimaru [2020]).

5. In the 2015 informative report *Black Girls Matter: Pushed Out, Overpoliced and Underprotected*, authors Crenshaw, Ocen, and Nanda draw on national statistics and regional data to make this point. U.S. Department of Education statistics show that Black girls are suspended six times as often as White girls; in comparison, Black boys are three times more likely than White boys to be excluded from school (Crenshaw, Ocen, and Nanda 2015, 18). Additionally, studies in Boston and New York public school districts estimate that Black girls were expelled at ten and fifty-three times the rate of White girls, respectively.

6. Elsewhere, I document how these girls believed surrounding districts, mainly White, did not want them. The girls were quite clear that they feared rejection at multiple levels—physical, social, and cultural—if they were forced to attend another school (see Scott [2003]).

7. Of the ways Anzaldúa describes to think about coalition building, three are relevant for COMPUGIRLS: "bridge," "drawbridge," and "island." These refer to the ways sociohistorically oppressed individuals are used as a mediator with the majority (White) culture, whether we are engaged (down like a "bridge"); withdrawn like a "drawbridge," so that we can get a "breather from being a perpetual bridge without having to withdraw completely"; or functioning as an "island" by sometimes not being

visible (1990, 224). For our purposes, interacting with the dominant White culture was of little concern, particularly since the only White individuals were teachers in the girls' schools. Associations with each other in this all-Black context still provided occasions for girls to serve as bridges, providing information, support, and advocacy at different points in time.

8. Haraway's definition of situated knowledge fits well: "the partial understanding of the world that each person develops based on their embodied experiences." She continues with a warning while maintaining the significance of recognizing situated knowledge: "I am arguing for politics and epistemologies of location, positioning, and situating, where partiality and not universality is the condition of being heard to make rational knowledge claims. These are claims on people's lives. I am arguing for the view from a body, always a complex, contradictory, structuring, and structured body, versus the view from above, from nowhere, from simplicity. Only the god trick [of claimed omniscience and objectivity] is forbidden" (1988, 589).

9. Critiquing norms of false objectivity, Collins argues that "such criteria ask African-American women to objectify ourselves, devalue our emotional life, displace our motivations for furthering knowledge about Black women, and confront in an adversarial relationship those with more social, economic, and professional power" (2008, 256). However, Collins comments on how Black women represent nimble and resourceful "access to another epistemology that encompasses standards for assessing truth that are widely accepted among African-American women" (256). What is most important in this context is the girls learn that their insider knowledge and their epistemologies are important to the achievements of each other.

10. As described in Taft's *Rebel Girls*, "The changes they [girls] imagine are about creating a world that is better for many people, not just improving their own abilities to deal with and overcome the problems they see in the world" (2010, 26). For many graduates like Montserrat, change is not conducted on an individual level but must include others and benefit a community.

11. Both the sample lesson and more details about it appear in our article; see Scott and Garcia (2016).

Chapter Two. COMPUGIRLS' Emergence

1. The girls and their parents did not refer to themselves as Native American. Instead, they called themselves by their tribal affiliations. To maintain confidentiality, however, I will use the term "Native American," understanding the phrase is not representative of their self-perception.

2. I use the term "power skills" rather than "soft skills" to "acknowledge the importance of unlocking the hidden curriculum for students naturally gifted but structurally handicapped" (David Johns, personal communication, May 28, 2016).

3. In this instance, the "we" refers to the White male external evaluator who joined the research team years after the initial cohort. Interestingly, he found that few girls hesitated in describing to him their perspectives. Even though there were no White

male students in COMPUGIRLS, during one-on-one conversations with the evaluator, participants were forthright sharing their opinions with him. I interpret their lack of reluctance as a sign of ownership. In the girls' eyes, the evaluator remained external to the cultural happenings of COMPUGIRLS.

4. By 2010, the Black population hovered around 4 percent. Arizona was one of only eighteen states "in which the number of prime-age black men living in households actually outnumber black women," according to a *New York Times* article (https://www.nytimes.com/2015/04/22/upshot/areas-with-large-black-populations-have-the-smallest-shares-of-black-men.html).

5. It was in 2016 that the Oregon circuit court ruled Jaime Shupe could legally identify as nonbinary.

6. Grillo (2013) defines this more thoroughly: "Essentialism is the notion that there is a single woman's, or Black person's, or any other group's, experience that can be described independently from other aspects of the person—that there is an 'essence' to that experience. An essentialist outlook assumes that the experience of being a member of the group under discussion is a stable one, one with a clear meaning, a meaning constant through time, space, and different historical, social, political, and personal contexts" (1995, 19).

7. In a 2017 *New York Times* article, Ashkenas, Park, and Pearce argue that Black and Hispanic students are more underrepresented at top universities today when considered as a proportion of the total eligible population: "Even after decades of affirmative action, black and Hispanic students are more underrepresented at the nation's top colleges and universities than they were thirty-five years ago, according to a *New York Times* analysis. The share of black freshmen at elite schools is virtually unchanged since 1980. Black students are just six percent of freshmen but fifteen percent of college-age Americans. . . . More Hispanics are attending elite schools, but the increase has not kept up with the huge growth of young Hispanics in the United States, so the gap between students and the college-age population has widened."

8. Collins and Bilge identify two important points about power relations: they are mutually constructed and reinforcing, and they need to be examined both at intersections and across domains. "First, intersectional frameworks understand power relations through a lens of mutual construction. In other words, people's lives and identities are generally shaped by many factors in diverse and mutually influencing ways. Moreover, race, class, gender, sexuality, age, disability, ethnicity, nation, and religion, among others, constitute interlocking, mutually constructing or intersecting systems of power. Within intersectional frameworks, there is no pure racism or power. Rather, power relations of racism and sexism gain meaning in relation to one another" (2016, 26–27). And "second, power relations are to be analyzed both *via their intersections*, for example, of racism and sexism, as well as *across domains of power*, namely structural, disciplinary, cultural, and interpersonal. The framework of domains of power provides a heuristic device or thinking tool for examining power relations" (27, emphasis in original).

9. Hunter defines colorism as "the process of discrimination that privileges light-

skinned people of color over their dark-skinned counterparts. Colorism is concerned with actual skin tone, as opposed to racial or ethnic identity" (2007, 237). Colorism can be practiced by all people, regardless of ethnic or racial background.

10. Scratch is a block-based coding language developed at MIT to give children early access to computer programming. "Scratch is a programming language and an online community where children can program and share interactive media such as stories, games, and animation with people from all over the world. As children create with Scratch, they learn to think creatively, work collaboratively, and reason systematically. Scratch is designed and maintained by the Lifelong Kindergarten group at the MIT Media Lab." See the description on the Scratch website (https://scratch.mit.edu/parents/).

11. The Sims, launched in 2000, is a sandbox game; there is no one particular objective, save for creating an environment and personalities for virtual characters. Sihvonen's 2012 book provides an accurate description that is applicable to our purposes: "The Sims is a life simulation game, almost like a computerized dollhouse. Players create characters, give them personalities, build them domiciles, find them jobs, entertain them, feed them, and even make them sleep and bathe. Characters interact and sometimes even fall in love, get married and have children" (9).

12. Gorski, among other scholars, describes the digital divide in its traditional sense as "inequalities in access to computers and the Internet between groups of people based on one or more social or cultural identifiers" (2005, 5). More recent studies illustrate that the divide has less to do with access to hardware than availability of a curriculum that encourages innovation and critical thinking.

13. These are described as "preparatory privilege" by Margolis (2008b, 79–84)—critical factors like early access and experiences with computers, as well as support by adults.

14. Margolis, Goode, and Flapan (2017) distinguish between "identifying-talent" and "building-talent" approaches for broadening participation in computer science. "Identifying-talent" approaches can be useful for diversifying participation but are vulnerable to an overly narrow "pipeline focus" that conflates "high potential" with "preparatory privilege" whereby some students have earlier access to and support for using computers. Meanwhile, the "building-talent" approach rejects "fixed mindset" thinking that feeds deficit models and instead "addresses the individual assumptions we make on a personal level, as well as efforts to confront structural inequities that deny equal access to educational opportunities, especially for students of color in underserved schools" (4–5). In other words, "building-talent" pursuits, like COMPUGIRLS, presume that every girl, when given not just access to technology but also culturally responsive mentoring, is capable of growing and excelling as a technological agent.

15. In February 2018, the New School's provost and chief academic officer, Tim Marshall, discussed how a liberal arts education is imperative given the changing technological landscape. Firstly, in noting some of the major technology leaders in the world, all of whom graduated with liberal arts degrees, he argues that having the

ability to create technology may transform society, but understanding the implications of that transformation is gained through a liberal arts education. The first type of skills will provide short-term success, but the long-term benefits come from a liberal arts education as this type of learning teaches students "to think, communicate, collaborate, design, and make their—and our—futures" (Marshall 2018). His points represent an age-old debate concerning the utilitarian nature of a vocational versus liberal arts education.

16. In a coedited book, *Indigenous and Decolonizing Studies in Education*, Smith, Tuck, and Yang connect Indigenous research methods to relational validity: "Creating and maintaining respectful and mutually beneficial relationships between researchers and Indigenous communities (even when the researcher comes from the community) is of utmost importance" (2019, xi).

17. Everett uses the term "black technophobia" to give name to the pervasive myth that a reason for low representation and participation of Black people in technology is that they just aren't interested in or don't like technology (2002, 132). A similar questionable label has also been applied to describe Indigenous people. Specifically, Di Chiro (2007) contextualizes "science-phobia" as the wariness of Indigenous communities toward science activities given the history of "biocolonialism," such as the privatization of genetic and natural resources under private property law or the exploitation of Indigenous culture and heritage in the name of scientific research.

18. Parkhurst et al. show that rural American Indian/Alaskan Native communities have the lowest use of broadband internet at home and rely largely on mobile forms of access, like smartphones. For example, "although 52 percent [of AI/AN households] indicated computer usage, only 31 percent had broadband Internet adoption. Rural AI/AN households trailed well behind the rural U.S. household's averages for both computer use (70 percent) and broadband adoption (57 percent)" (2015, 219).

19. Drawing from hooks's "Radical Black Female Subjectivity" (RBFS), which "is indicative of not only coming into an empowered understanding of one's self, but through that process also coming to be engaged in and committed to collective struggles against oppression" (1990, 15), "RBF*IS* [Radical Black Female Inter-Subjectivity] emphasizes the role of inter-textuality in connecting Black women intellectuals across place and time and beyond the reproduction of text. This push beyond creates pedagogical 'homeplaces'—spaces where the next generation of Black women intellectuals are created/developed/commissioned to the struggle against injustice" (Edwards and Baszile 2016, 88).

20. Culturally responsive computing practices are pedagogical strategies that center students' knowledge and experiences on rigorous computational thinking goals. These practices include reflective activities to understand power dynamics in the digital age as well as opportunities to connect with others whose identities are complex and multifaceted. The strategies in a culturally responsive computing context aim to nurture participants' abilities to innovatively use technology for social justice purposes (Scott, Sheridan, and Clark 2014). See also Eglash et al. (2013).

Chapter Three. This Isn't Like School

1. Blazer explains: "Some parents feel intimidated and unwelcome at school. Many parents had negative school experiences themselves or are so unfamiliar with the American culture that they do not want to get involved or feel unsure about the value of their contributions. Barriers are also created by parents who have feelings of inadequacy or are suspicious of or angry at the school" (2005, 3).

2. In a study of Philadelphia magnet schools intended to increase diversity, Saporito found that "despite this goal, the few white students who remain in the public school system still avoid integrated neighborhood schools by using the magnet school choice program" (2003, 198). This was largely a result of school choice that allowed for "out-group avoidance," White families leaving schools with high Black student populations and attending other schools instead. Frankenberg, Siegel-Hawley, and Wang explain that "while segregation for blacks among all public schools has been increasing for nearly two decades, black students in charter schools are far more likely than their traditional public school counterparts to be educated in intensely segregated settings. At the national level, seventy percent of black charter school students attend intensely segregated minority charter schools (which enroll 90–100% of students from under-represented minority backgrounds), or *twice* as many as the share of intensely segregated black students in traditional public schools. Some charter schools enrolled populations where 99% of the students were from under-represented minority backgrounds" (2010, 4).

3. Lerner, Dowling, and Anderson contextualize personhood as part of the civic growth of a young person: "within a developmental systems model of the person—context regulatory processes involved in healthy youth development, and in positive and productive adult personhood, young people and their communities are involved in a bidirectional relationship wherein community assets are both products and producers of the actions of engaged young people" (2003, 178).

4. Martin demonstrates how among preschool-age children, girls learn that modulating their voices, engaging in more formal activities rather than in relaxed, informal tasks, and assuming less physical space gain more positive peer and teacher responses than not doing these things. Boys, on the other hand, are expected to use their bodies in more physically demanding ways and occupy more physical space with more assertive and aggressive movements (1998, 508). Winkle-Wagner (2009, 116) and Mahalik et al. (2005, 418) expand on these types of "feminine norms" to include passivity and silence.

5. Ringrose explains that when girls do succeed, or exceed performance of boys, due to leveling of educational institutions through supportive programs, changing of pedagogy to be less masculine, and other measures, what then arises is fear of "feminization" of schooling or "failing boys panic," revealing that equal performance by girls is seen as an aberration that must come at the cost of boys' educations (2013, 21).

6. Smith and Marx's work provides one of the earliest critiques of technological determinism, challenging the notion that technology is or should serve as the "key governing force in society" (1994, 2).

7. The widely cited Pew-commissioned study by Lenhart and Madden (2007) illustrated that girls tend to use digital media to interact with their peers more frequently and regularly than their male counterparts. However, this information does not take into account racial or social class differences. How Latina girls—for instance, from areas like the one Yvette navigates—use digital media is narrowly understood.

8. Cultural capital is defined by Bourdieu thusly: "Cultural capital can exist in three forms: in the embodied state, i.e. in the form of long-lasting dispositions of the mind and body; in the objectified state, in the form of cultural goods (pictures, books, dictionaries, instruments, machines, etc.), which are the trace or realization of theories or critiques of these theories, problematics, etc.; and in the institutionalized state, a form of objectification which must be set apart because, as will be seen in the case of educational qualifications, it confers entirely original properties on the cultural capital which it is presumed to guarantee" (1986, 243). Bourdieu also describes how cultural capital is necessary to use machines (technology) effectively: "To possess the machines, he only needs economic capital; to appropriate them and use them in accordance with their specific purpose he must have access to embodied cultural capital; either in person or in proxy" (247). Selwyn interprets the interaction of Bourdieu's "cultural capital" with technology use: "Yet we can also see that there are specific technological forms of cultural capital useful to the 'information age' such as technological skills, competencies and 'know-how' as well as socialisation into the 'technoculture' via family and the household. Such forms of cultural capital can be seen, for example, as the difference between having access or ownership of a technology and engaging with and making meaningful use of that technology" (2002, 13).

9. Roberts's pivotal 1997 book, *Killing the Black Body*, was one of the first to chart the history of policing and surveillance that Black female bodies have undergone for quite some time. Blake and his colleagues' 2011 analysis demonstrated that Black girls are disproportionately disciplined for not conforming to conventional (White, middle-class) ideals of femininity. More recently, Cammarota (2004) detailed through ethnographic methods similarly troubling unfair treatment and neglect of young Latinas.

10. Kennelly (2009) theorizes how feminist theory and Bourdieu's concepts of capital contribute to youth agency, arguing that political agency rests on relationships and a habitus that comes from family influence or networks formed outside of the home. Integral to the former are "cultural guides" who assist new members to understand the valued capital and alternative norms.

11. For example, Mary Carpenter and Annette Akroyd Beveridge were described as "cultural missionaries" by Ramusack (1990) for attempting in the late 1800s to mold the lives of Indian widows to fit the Victorian British values in which they were steeped, yet they saw themselves as merely applying universal values to people in need.

12. Graham Greene was a prominent English novelist of the twentieth century whose fiction often included deep themes related to Catholicism; his stories were grouped into serious literature and thrillers, known as "entertainments."

13. James Michener was a Pulitzer Prize–winning author whose book *Tales of the South Pacific* was adapted by Rogers and Hammerstein into the musical *South Pacific*.

14. Looking at the trend toward imposing standards on schools and the subsequent impact on multicultural education efforts in the late 1990s, Bohn and Sleeter argue that "pluralizing the teaching force, giving teachers real opportunities to explore multicultural issues, and treating members of the teaching corps as professionals who can make informed decisions about teaching and curriculum are approaches that have far more potential to improve schools than searching for a 'magic bullet' in the form of top-down standards" (2000, 159). Cochran-Smith (2003) discusses how both professionalization (top-down) of multicultural teacher training and deregulation (bottom-up) of the same offer benefits and disadvantages. Professionalization could standardize the quality of teachers to be better able to engage multiculturally but also could exclude many potential teachers (especially teachers from diverse ethnic backgrounds themselves). Meanwhile, deregulation could increase access for these same potential teachers but risks underpreparing them based on local resources and governance. The Bilingual Education Act is an example of a top-down attempt to promote bilingual education, but because it provided only funding but not a specific directive, instruction under its auspices often fell short of this goal, instead emphasizing transitions to English speaking and writing (Ovando 2001).

15. In the Italian school context of Reggio Emilia, Corsaro and Molinari describe how art, literature, and self-expression merged to manifest each preschool student's personal story. Individualized books contained three years' worth of photos, descriptions, and other artifacts from the children's school and family lives. Like the books, the COMPUGIRLS closing ceremony was an occasion where "the past is overwhelmed by the anticipation of the future and the children's movement to a new stage of their lives" (2008, 256). For the participants, the "new stage" involved opportunities to apply their growing understanding of self, community, and technology. This type of future excited the girls.

16. Collins and Bilge demonstrate the use of an intersectional lens by analyzing the 2014 FIFA World Cup held in Brazil using four domains of power—interpersonal, disciplinary, cultural, and structural: "Using intersectionality as an analytic lens highlights the multiple nature of individual identities and how varying combinations of class, gender, race, sexuality, and citizenship categories differentially position each individual. Regardless of the love of soccer, these axes of social division work together and influence one another to shape each individual biography" (2016, 8).

17. Research by Snibbe and Markus comparing self-control choices by high school and college graduates finds a difference in the manifestation of personal control, whereby "the model of agency that is most prevalent in BA contexts emphasizes expressing uniqueness and exerting environmental control, whereas the model of agency that is most prevalent in HS contexts emphasizes maintaining personal in-

tegrity (e.g., honesty, loyalty, reliability, cross-situational consistency) and exerting self-control" (2005, 703).

18. Compare this to the definition of privilege offered by Khan as "a sense of self and a mode of interaction that advantage [elite students]," rather than an entitlement to things that elites have, like wealth, "breeding," and social status (2011, 14).

19. Although "social justice" has generally referred to an interest in identifying and correcting injustices and unfairness in society, such as through addressing gender, racial, ethnic, and class disparities, the term has recently taken on new meaning through the colloquial term "social justice warrior." In August 2015, "social justice warrior" was added to Oxford Dictionaries with the definition "a person who expresses or promotes socially progressive views," but it is also classified as an "informal, derogatory noun." As reported by the *Washington Post* (Ohlheiser 2015), the term used to carry positive connotations but somehow flipped in definition through online movements like Gamergate (where a large collective of video game players claimed that feminism and other "social justice" interests negatively influenced game design and review practices) to mean something negative.

20. Corsaro and Johannesen describe an initiation ritual among Russ (Norwegian high-school-graduating youth) that both brings the participants into a tradition but also allows the students to contribute to it: "As the students put their mark on and add to the variation and richness within the tradition, they contribute to their own sense of belonging to their particular school as well as to a differentiation within the Russ community in terms of cohort, school, and also color (red, blue, or black). This differentiation does not alienate the *Russ* from each other but rather creates a strong sense of we-ness and ownership within the tradition. The collective nature of the ritual, and the public display of the name embraced by each *Russ* for this period in their lives, contributes to this shared sense of we-ness among all *Russ*" (2014, 338). This type of in-group and within-group identity formation does not address power relations in the way that Anzaldúa's "coalition building" describes, but it does recognize difference even while celebrating solidarity and belongingness within a system.

21. In Scratch, Sprites are images powered by the user's instructions. The Scratch cat is the most common, but as Scratch has evolved, so have the breadth of images.

22. In 2011, the International Society for Technology in Education and the Computer Science Teachers Association defined computational thinking as

a problem-solving process that includes (but is not limited to) the following characteristics:

- Formulating problems in a way that enables us to use a computer and other tools to help solve them
- Logically organizing and analyzing data
- Representing data through abstractions such as models and simulations
- Automating solutions through algorithmic thinking (a series of ordered steps)
- Identifying, analyzing, and implementing possible solutions with the goal of achieving the most efficient and effective combination of steps and resources

- Generalizing and transferring this problem solving process to a wide variety of problems.

See https://cdn.iste.org/www-root/ct-documents/computational-thinking-operational -definition-flyer.pdf?sfvrsn=2.

23. From an address presented at a graduation commencement at Wellesley in 2012.

24. In my 2016 coedited book, *Women Education Scholars and Their Children's Schools* (Scott and Henward), a legion of female education scholars from across the globe describe our own trials and tribulations navigating our children's schools. What is interesting from this collective are the common chords running through the chapters. Across geographic differences and cultural uniqueness, each author describes how her professional knowledge, race-ethnic, gender, ability, and other social identities all intersect, affecting her effectiveness to advocate for her children.

Chapter Four. Sounds of Silence

1. Bordo acknowledges the body as both a medium and a metaphor for and as a text of culture, but also "as a practical, direct locus of social control" (1989, 13).

2. A "case story" combines aspects of the case study method and storytelling, which brings tradition, artistry, and imagination (Ackerman and Maslin-Ostrowski 2002, 145). This allows for vicarious learning through others' living written and oral accounts of their experiences.

3. This SIMS' iteration allowed users to observe and record their characters' be- haviors.

4. Physical movement initiated and controlled by children in education spaces has been found to improve cognition. It is critical for children to define a "projected space." See Seitz (1992).

5. For examples, see Burke (2007); Hall and Damico (2007); Cavanagh (2007); Jackson et al. (2008); Kuhlemeier and Hemker (2007); and Frehill et al. (2007).

6. Rhode, Cooke, and Ojha (2012), in an article in *The Atlantic*, reveal that even in Mann's home state of Massachusetts, income inequality is a significant contributor to inequitable education across the population.

7. Another example is the National Center for Women and IT's 2012 *Girls in IT* report (Ashcraft, Eger, and Friend 2012).

8. Merriam and colleagues explain, "The notion of positionality rests on the as- sumption that a culture is more than a monolithic entity to which one belongs or not" (2001, 411). For example, Villenas (1996) reflects on her complex positionality as both colonized (Chicana graduate student in a White institution) and colonizer (educated researcher with institutional backing studying Latino communities).

9. "Critical consciousness" is used by Freire to describe people's ability to "intervene in reality in order to change it" (2005, 4) because it represents "things and facts as they

exist empirically," in contrast to "naïve consciousness," which "considers itself superior to facts, in control of facts, and thus free to understand them as it pleases" (39).

10. This aligns with Edwards's "ally for social justice" type (contrasted with "ally for self-interest" or "ally for altruism"), defined as "individuals acting as Allies for Social Justice [who] work with those from the oppressed group in collaboration and partnership to end the system of oppression" (2006, 51). As Patton and Bondi explain, "Allies for social justice recognize the interconnectedness of oppressive structures and work in partnership with marginalized persons toward building social justice coalitions. They aspire to move beyond individual acts and direct attention to oppressive processes and systems. Their pursuit is not merely to help oppressed persons but to create a socially just world which benefits all people" (2015, 490).

Chapter Five. I Have Something to Say

1. Lueck and Wilson define acculturation as "cultural changes resulting from primary contact between distinct ethnic groups, influenced by dominating social norms in society on the one hand and by an assertion of ethnic traits on the other. Acculturation has been further defined as the process by which individuals incorporate beliefs, behaviors and values from the new host culture into the context of beliefs, behaviors and values of the native culture. The acculturation process involves different levels of modification, survival, adaptation, domination, resistance, and stress" (2011, 187). See also Redfield, Linton, and Herskovits (1936); and Berry (2006).

2. Virtual Worlds is a multi-user online program like Second Life that is offered by the nonprofit AcaCon as a virtual environment for educational and nonprofit use. In it, users can choose and design an avatar, move around in a digital world, create objects called "perms," and utilize other features of digital reality programs.

3. Teen Second Life was first offered on February 14, 2005, as a "teen-only" version of Second Life, available to users aged thirteen through seventeen. It was later closed down in 2011, and accounts were transferred to the regular Second Life community (or held until the user reached sixteen years of age).

4. Willet found that even though girls exercise agency in claiming to reject media images of girls and women as skinny and sexy, they are still influenced by social norms and discourses: "The girls draw on discourses around individuality, self-confidence and proper parenting to argue that they make conscious decisions about what to wear and to demonstrate that they have healthy attitudes about their bodies. The girls' arguments demonstrate their agency, but neoliberal discourses frame their arguments and construct positions which demand autonomous, rational and unitary selves" (2008, 432). These stereotypical images also impact the people who use these avatars, as found by Fox, Bailenson, and Tricase (2013), who discovered that people owning more sexualized avatars engaged in more self-objectification through what is known as the "Proteus effect" (Yee and Bailenson 2007).

5. "First life" is a term used to refer to what is commonly called "real life" or "off-line" life prior to generating an online digital presence. Boellstorff's (2008) ethno-

graphic account within his *Coming of Age in Second Life: An Anthropologist Explores the Virtually Human* reveals how Second Life users feel a tension between first and second life. His analysis demonstrates how users of Second Life feel constrained in first life, thereby identifying their online personas and experiences as liberatory.

6. This data comes from the thirty-seventh annual CRA Taulbee Survey. Numbers represent the 186 responses of 234 PhD-granting departments surveyed in the United States and Canada. It was not until 2013 that Taulbee's data were disaggregated by race and gender (Jakita Thomas, personal communication, April 21, 2020).

7. Bui and Miller (2016) discuss a multitude of factors other than technical skills that affect Black and Latino students' entering technology companies. The majority of factors reference either perceptions of a technology company's climate or the actual climate and culture that is anti-inclusive.

8. White described this as "tokenism," where "many students-of-color feel that their words and ideas take on greater significance in the classroom context and beyond, especially when discussing matters of race, history, economic class, and culture. Minority students often find that they are expected to speak for the entirety of their cultures' experiences" (2011, 253). Jones, Castellanos, and Cole, in a study of minority student experiences at university, describe how "students felt the expectation of having to know 'all about their culture' and being viewed as 'experts in their culture.' They were called on in class to discuss 'What Latinos think . . . or to simply provide the *minority* perspective'" (2002, 31). Cook-Lyn (1997) explains how many early Native American scholars in the 1970s and 1980s were hired and placed in university departments to provide the "Indian Voice," to offer "minority input" to give the appearance of balancing out overwhelmingly White professionals, and to be "all things to all people." This publicly recognized tokenism had the additional effect of undermining the perceived value of their work. The admonition "It is not my job to educate you" has become a common rejection of this assumed responsibility to teach others not from one's culture or identity, largely present in social media discourses like Facebook, Twitter, and Tumblr. This is a rejection of previous generations' activism, which included a responsibility to address ignorance with education about lived experiences.

9. Lomawaima and McCarty detail the troubled history of American schools and their role in destroying Native American identities and cultures through "Americanization":

> The "civilized" nation assumed that its right to dispossess Native nations went hand in hand with a responsibility to "uplift" them, and mission and federal "Indian schools" were established as laboratories for a grand experiment in cultural cleansing, Christian conversion, and assimilation of laborers and domestic workers into the workforce. The so-called civilization of American Indians, at times simply termed "Americanization," mandated the transformation of nations and individuals: Replace heritage languages with English; replace "paganism" with Christianity; replace economic, political, social, legal, and aesthetic institutions. Given the American infatuation with the notion that

social change can best be effected through education, schools have logically been vested with the responsibility for Americanizing Indigenous peoples as well as immigrants. (2006, 4)

10. Uline and Tschannen-Moran, in a survey of Virginia middle schools, identified significant connections between the quality of facilities, and student achievement, and school climate:

The manner in which a school building is designed, managed, and maintained sends a message to its occupants and the community beyond, speaking volumes about the value placed on activities transpiring within its walls. . . . At the same time we seek to improve science laboratories and integrate state of the art technology systems, we should also pay particular attention to the ways in which various learning spaces encourage or impede daily interactions between and among students, teachers and parents. If carefully conceived, the separate spaces of a school reinforce each other physically and aesthetically, creating rich environments where interpersonal relationships can flourish. Within such spaces, occupants find themselves comfortable enough to take the individual and collective risks requisite to most meaningful interaction and learning. (2008, 67)

11. This perspective stands in stark contrast to research advocating the value of educational games (Rosas et al. 2003; Habgood and Ainsworth 2011) and even non-educational games (Gee 2003; Shaffer 2006; Prensky 2006) in promoting interest in learning with children.

12. For examples, see Li et al. (2009); Lillioja et al. (1993); and Nelson et al. (1996). Importantly, there is a host of strategies and programs targeting Native American populations, as they have been found to be "at higher risk for becoming obese and suffering from obesity-related illness compared with other populations." What is most notable is that "prevention methods have not been successful with this group, especially intervention attempts aimed at children, which have been few and ineffective" (Wann et al. 2015, 118). The unsuccessfulness of the efforts should not be seen as the fault of the victims but as a reflection of how well (or not) the strategies take into account cultural aspects of the population in need.

13. In *The Handbook of Intercultural Discourse and Communication*, Paulston, Kiesling, and Rangel (2012) detail how the Western Apache Native American Indian community uses silence during "socially ambiguous situations." Girls from the community featured in this project did not seem to apply silence in the same way but as a means to gather their thoughts. I noticed when interacting with adults from this community that long pauses were the norm.

14. I purposely have not shared these images, in order to maintain the confidentiality of this community. Although I received approval from the Tribal Council and had regular oral reports to give about our progress, I decided to not share the name of this community.

15. There are four levels of integration of ethnic content, according to Banks (1989,

192): contributions (focus is on heroes, holidays, discrete cultural elements), additive (content, concepts, themes, and perspectives are added to curriculum without structural changes), transformation (structure of curriculum is changed to shift perspectives to those of ethnic groups), and social action (students make decisions on important social issues and work to solve them). Most "inclusive" curricula do only the first two, which, while laudable, do not offer lasting change or sustainability for students of diverse cultures.

Chapter Six. Where Are They Now

1. Thanks to support from the National Science Foundation, three COMPUGIRLS graduates became undergraduate research assistants. While attending my university as undergraduate students, these women participated in and created their own research projects. Their work often led to coauthored papers and presentations at national and international conferences.

2. Montserrat referred to me in the third person.

3. Some recent reports have emerged from both federal and academic sources and have been released online. For example, in November 2015, the White House Council on Women and Girls published the "Advancing Equity for Women and Girls of Color" report. Additionally, the NAACP's Legal Defense and Education Fund collaborated with the National Women's Law Center to produce "Unlocking Opportunities for African American Girls."

Epilogue

1. Funded by Pivotal Foundation, the Women of Color and Computing Research Collaborative is a partnership between the research center I founded—the Center for Gender Equity in Science and Technology—and the Kapor Foundation. Support allowed us to fund a series of grantees and senior academic fellows to conduct research on women of color and computing.

2. NSF's ADVANCE program funds university-wide projects that "broaden the implementation of evidence-based systemic change strategies that promote equity for STEM faculty in academic workplaces and the academic profession. The NSF ADVANCE program provides grants to enhance the systemic factors that support equity and inclusion and to mitigate the systemic factors that create inequities in the academic profession and workplaces." See the NSF website at https://www.nsf.gov/funding/pgm_summ.jsp?pims_id=5383 (last accessed 4/26/2021).

3. Originally, I presented this idea in a keynote address at the University of Oregon's Fourth Gender and STEM Network Conference in Eugene. After revising the speech, we published the piece; see Scott and Elliott (2020).

4. In this case, "we" refers to the over thirty associate and affiliated faculty members, postdoctoral fellows, graduate students, undergraduate students, and staff that make up the Center for Gender Equity in Science and Technology.

References

Ackerman, R. H., and P. Maslin-Ostrowski. 2002. *The Wounded Leader: How Real Leadership Emerges in Times of Crisis*. San Francisco: Jossey-Bass.

Adair, V. C. 2002. "Branded with Infamy: Inscriptions of Poverty and Class in the United States." *Signs* 27, no. 2: 451–71.

Ainsworth-Darnell, J. W., and D. B. Downey. 1998. "Assessing the Oppositional Culture Explanation for Racial/Ethnic Differences in School Performance." *American Sociological Review* 63, no. 4: 536–53.

Aitchison, C., P. Hopkins, and M. Kwan, eds. 2007. *Geographies of Muslim Identities: Diaspora, Gender and Belonging*. Burlington, Vt.: Ashgate.

Ali, S., H. Mirza, A. Phoenix, and J. Ringrose. 2010. "Intersectionality, Black British Feminism and Resistance in Education: A Roundtable Discussion." *Gender and Education* 22, no. 6: 647–61.

Alsubaie, M. A. 2015. "Hidden Curriculum as One of Current Issue of Curriculum." *Journal of Education and Practice* 6, no. 33: 125–28.

Anzaldúa, G. 1990. "Bridge, Drawbridge, Sandbar or Island: Lesbians-of-Color Hacienda Alianzas." In *Bridges of Power: Women's Multicultural Alliances*, edited by Lisa Albrecht and Rose M. Brewer, 216–33. Philadelphia: New Society Publishers.

Ashcraft, C., E. Eger, and M. Friend. 2012. *Girls in IT: The Facts*. Boulder: National Center for Women and IT.

Ashkenas, J., H. Park, and A. Pearce. 2017. "Even with Affirmative Action, Blacks and Hispanics Are More Underrepresented at Top Colleges Than 35 Years Ago." *New York Times*, August 24. https://www.nytimes.com/interactive/2017/08/24/us/affirmative-action.html.

Baer, H. 2016. "Redoing Feminism: Digital Activism, Body Politics, and Neoliberalism." *Feminist Media Studies* 16, no. 1: 17–34.

Balsamo, A. 2011. *Designing Culture: The Technological Imagination at Work*. Durham, N.C.: Duke University Press.

Banks, J. A. 1989. "Approaches to Multicultural Curriculum Reform." *Trotter Review* 3, no. 3, article 5. Available at http://scholarworks.umb.edu/trotter_review/vol3/iss3/5.

Banks, J. A., and C. A. M. Banks, eds. 2010. *Multicultural Education: Issues and Perspectives*. 7th ed. Hoboken, N.J.: Wiley.

Barajas-López, F., and A. M. Ishimaru. 2020. "'Darles El Lugar': A Place for Nondominant Family Knowing in Educational Equity." *Urban Education* 55, no. 1: 38–65.

Becker, J. D. 2007. "Digital Equity in Education: A Multilevel Examination of Differences in and Relationships between Computer Access, Computer Use and State-Level Technology Policies." *Education Policy Analysis Archives/Archivos Analíticos de Políticas Educativas* 15: 1–38.

Berry, J. W. 2006. "Acculturative Stress." In *Handbook of Multicultural Perspectives on Stress and Coping*, edited by Paul T. P. Wong and Lilian C. J. Wong, 283–94. New York: Springer.

Bettis, P., and N. G. Adams. 2005. *Geographies of Girlhood: Identities In-Between*. Mahwah, N.J.: Lawrence Erlbaum.

Black Girls Code. 2020. "What We Do." https://www.blackgirlscode.com/what-we-do.html.

Blake, J. J., B. R. Butler, C. W. Lewis, and A. Darensbourg. 2011. "Unmasking the Inequitable Discipline Experiences of Urban Black Girls: Implications for Urban Educational Stakeholders." *Urban Review* 43, no. 1: 90–106. https://doi.org/10.1007/s11256-009-0148-8.

Blazer, C. 2005. *Literature Review on Family Involvement: The Home-School Partnership*. Miami: Miami-Dade County Public Schools.

Bobb, K., and Q. Brown. 2017. "Access, Power, and the Framework of a CS Education Ecosystem." In *Moving Students of Color from Consumers to Producers of Technology*, edited by Y. Rankin and J. Thomas, 245–60. Hershey, Pa.: IGI Global.

Boellstorff, T. 2008. *Coming of Age in Second Life: An Anthropologist Explores the Virtually Human*. Princeton, N.J.: Princeton University Press.

Bohn, A. P., and C. E. Sleeter. 2000. "Multicultural Education and the Standards Movement: A Report from the Field." *Phi Delta Kappan* 82, no. 2: 156–59.

Bordo, S. 1989. "The Body and the Reproduction of Femininity: A Feminist Appropriation of Foucault." In *Gender/Body/Knowledge: Feminist Reconstructions of Being and Knowing*, edited by A. Jaggar and S. Bordo, 13–33. New Brunswick, N.J.: Rutgers University Press.

Bourdieu, P. 1983. "Okonomisches Kapital, Kulturelles Kapital, Soziales Kapital." In *Soziale Ungleichheiten*, edited by R. Kreckel, 183–98. Göttingen, Germany: Schwartz.

———. 1986. "The Forms of Capital." In *Handbook of Theory and Research for the Sociology of Education*, edited by J. Richardson, 241–58. New York: Greenwood.

Brayboy, B. M. J. 2005. "Toward a Tribal Critical Race Theory in Education." *Urban Review* 37, 5: 425–46. https://doi.org/10.1007/s11256-005-0018-y.

Brayboy, B. M. J., and E. Maughan. 2009. "Indigenous Knowledges and the Story of the Bean." *Harvard Educational Review* 79, no. 1: 1–21.

Brown, R. N. 2013. *Hear Our Truths: The Creative Potential of Black Girlhood*. Urbana: University of Illinois Press.

Buckingham, D., and R. Willett. 2013. *Digital Generations: Children, Young People, and the New Media*. Abingdon, U.K.: Routledge.

Bui, Q., and C. C. Miller. 2016. "Why Tech Degrees Are Not Putting More Blacks and Hispanics into Tech Jobs." *New York Times*, February 25.

Burke, R. J. 2007. "Women and Minorities in STEM: A Primer." In *Women and Minorities in Science, Technology, Engineering, and Mathematics: Upping the Numbers*, edited by R. J. Burke and M. C. Mattis, 3–27. Cheltenham, U.K.: Edward Elgar.

Burke, R. J., and M. C. Mattis, eds. 2007. *Women and Minorities in Science, Technology, Engineering and Mathematics: Upping the Numbers*. Cheltenham: Edward Elgar.

Burton, L. M., S. P. Kemp, M. Leung, S. A. Matthews, and D. Takeuchi, eds. 2011. *Communities, Neighborhoods, and Health: Expanding the Boundaries of Place*. Vol. 1. New York: Springer Science and Business Media.

Cacioli, J.-P., and A. J. Mussap. 2014. "Avatar Body Dimensions and Men's Body Image." *Body Image* 11, no. 2: 146–55. https://doi.org/10.1016/j.bodyim.2013.11.005.

Cammarota, J. 2004. "The Gendered and Racialized Pathways of Latina and Latino Youth: Different Struggles, Different Resistances in the Urban Context." *Anthropology and Education Quarterly* 35, no. 1: 53–74.

Carastathis, A. 2014. "The Concept of Intersectionality in Feminist Theory." *Philosophy Compass* 9, no. 5: 304–14.

Cavanagh, S. 2007. "Science Camp: Just for the Girls." *Education Week* 26, no. 45: 26–28.

Cheryan, S., A. Master, and A. N. Meltzoff. 2015. "Cultural Stereotypes as Gatekeepers: Increasing Girls' Interest in Computer Science and Engineering by Diversifying Stereotypes." *Frontiers in Psychology* 6:1–8.

Cheryan, S., V. C. Plaut, P. G. Davies, and C. M. Steele. 2009. "Ambient Belonging: How Stereotypical Cues Impact Gender Participation in Computer Science." *Journal of Personality and Social Psychology* 97, no. 6: 1045.

Chhuon, V., and T. L. Wallace. 2014. "Creating Connectedness through Being Known: Fulfilling the Need to Belong in U.S. High Schools." *Youth and Society* 46, no. 3: 379–401.

Chilisa, B. 2012. *Indigenous Research Methodologies*. Thousand Oaks, Calif.: Sage.

Cochran-Smith, M. 2003. "Standing at the Crossroads: Multicultural Teacher Education at the Beginning of the 21st Century." *Multicultural Perspectives* 5, no. 3: 3–11.

Cockburn, C. 1992. "The Circuit of Technology: Gender, Identity and Power." In *Consuming Technologies: Media and Information in Domestic Spaces*, edited by R. Silverstone and E. Hirsch, 33–42. London: Routledge.

Colby, S. L., and J. M. Ortman. 2015. *Projections of the Size and Composition of U.S. Population: 2014 to 2060*. U.S. Census Bureau, March 2015. http://www.census.gov/content/dam/Census/library/publications/2015/demo/p25-1143.pdf.

Cole, R. W. 2008. *Educating Everybody's Children: Diverse Teaching Strategies for Diverse Learners*. Alexandria, Va.: ASCD.

College Board. 2014. *The 10th Annual AP Report to the Nation: Computer Science*. http://media.collegeboard.com/digitalServices/pdf/ap/rtn/10th-annual/10th -annual-ap-report-subject-supplement-computer-science-a.pdf.

Collins, P. H. 1999. "Moving beyond Gender: Intersectionality and Scientific Knowledge." In *Revisioning Gender*, edited by M. M. Ferree, J. Lorber, and B. B. Hess, 261–84. Thousand Oaks, Calif.: Sage.

———. 2000. *Black Feminist Thought*. New York: Routledge Classics.

———. 2006. *Black Sexual Politics: African Americans, Gender, and the New Racism*. New York: Routledge.

———. 2008. *Black Feminist Thought: Knowledge, Consciousness, and the Politics of Empowerment*. New York: Routledge.

———. 2009. *Another Kind of Public Education: Race, Schools, the Media, and Democratic Possibilities*. Boston: Beacon Press.

———. 2013. *On Intellectual Activism*. Philadelphia: Temple University Press.

Collins, P. H., and S. Bilge. 2016. *Intersectionality*. Malden, Mass.: Polity Press.

Combahee River Collective. 1986. *The Combahee River Collective Statement: Black Feminist Organizing in the Seventies and Eighties*. New York: Kitchen Table: Women of Color Press.

Cook-Lyn, E. 1997. "Who Stole Native American Studies?" *Wicazo Sa Review* 12, no. 1: 9–28.

Cooper, D. 1998. *Governing out of Order: Space, Law, and the Politics of Belonging*. New York: Rivers Oram Press.

Corsaro, W. A., and B. O. Johannesen. 2014. "Collective Identity, Intergenerational Relations, and Civic Society: Transition Rituals among Norwegian Russ." *Journal of Contemporary Ethnography* 43, no. 3: 331–60. https://doi.org/10.1177/0891241613498419.

Corsaro, W. A., and L. Molinari. 2008. "Policy and Practice in Italian Children's Transition from Preschool to Elementary School." *Research in Comparative and International Education* 3, no. 3: 250–65. https://doi.org/10.2304/rcie.2008.3.3.250.

Cox, A. 2015. *Shapeshifters: Black Girls and the Choreography of Citizenship*. Durham, N.C.: Duke University Press.

Crabtree, R., D. A. Sapp, and A. C. Licona. 2009. *Feminist Pedagogy: Looking Back to Move Forward*. Baltimore: Johns Hopkins University Press.

Crenshaw, K. 1991. "Mapping the Margins: Intersectionality, Identity Politics, and Violence against Women of Color." *Stanford Law Review* 43, no. 6: 1241–99.

Crenshaw, K., P. Ocen, and J. Nanda. 2015. *Black Girls Matter: Pushed Out, Overpoliced and Underprotected*. New York: African American Policy Forum and Center for Intersectionality and Social Policy Studies, Columbia University. https://www .atlanticphilanthropies.org/wp-content/uploads/2015/09/BlackGirlsMatter_Report .pdf.

Cronberg, T. 2003. *Transforming Russia: From a Military to a Peace Economy*. New York: IB Tauris.

Currie, D., D. M. Kelly, and S. Pomerantz. 2009. *"Girl Power": Girls Reinventing Girlhood*. New York: Peter Lang.

Davis, A. Y. 1994. "Afro Images: Politics, Fashion, and Nostalgia." *Critical Inquiry* 21, no. 1: 37–45.

Denner, J., and B. Guzman, eds. 2006. *Latina Girls: Voices of Adolescent Strength in the U.S.* New York: NYU Press.

Di Chiro, G. 2007. "Indigenous Peoples and Biocolonialism: Defining the 'Science of Environmental Justice' in the Century of the Gene." In *Environmental Justice and Environmentalism: The Social Justice Challenge to the Environmental Movement*, edited by R. Sandler and P. C. Pezzullo, 251–83. Cambridge, Mass.: MIT Press.

Dillard, C. B. 2000. "The Substance of Things Hoped for, the Evidence of Things Not Seen: Examining an Endarkened Feminist Epistemology in Educational Research and Leadership." *International Journal of Qualitative Studies in Education* 13, no. 6: 661–81.

———. 2006. *On Spiritual Strivings Transforming an African American Woman's Academic Life.* Albany: State University of New York Press.

———. 2012. *Learning to (Re)member the Things We've Learned to Forget: Endarkened Feminisms, Spirituality, and the Sacred Nature of Research and Teaching.* New York: Peter Lang.

Duckworth, A. 2016. *Grit: The Power of Passion and Persistence.* New York: Scribner.

Edwards, K. E. 2006. "Aspiring Social Justice Ally Identity Development: A Conceptual Model." *NASPA Journal* 43, no. 3: 39–60.

Edwards, K. T., and D. T. Baszile. 2016. "Scholarly Rearing in Three Acts: Black Women's Testimonial Scholarship and the Cultivation of Radical Black Female Inter-Subjectivity." *Knowledge Cultures* 4, no. 1: 85–99.

Eglash, R., J. E. Gilbert, V. Taylor, and S. R. Geier. 2013. "Culturally Responsive Computing in Urban, After-School Contexts: Two Approaches." *Urban Education* 48, no. 5: 629–56. https://doi.org/10.1177/0042085913499211.

Elias, N., and J. L. Scotson. 1994. *The Established and the Outsiders: A Sociological Enquiry into Community Problems.* 2nd ed. London: Sage.

Epstein, R., J. J. Blake, and T. González. 2017. *Girlhood Interrupted: The Erasure of Black Girls' Childhood.* Washington, D.C.: Georgetown Law, Center on Poverty and Inequality.

Evans-Winters, V. E., and J. Esposito. 2010. "Other People's Daughters: Critical Race Feminism and Black Girls' Education." *Journal of Educational Foundations* 24, nos. 1/2: 11–24.

Eveleth, R. 2015. "Genetic Testing and Tribal Identity." *The Atlantic*, January. https://www.theatlantic.com/technology/archive/2015/01/the-cultural-limitations-of-genetic-testing/384740/.

Everett, A. 2002. "The Revolution Will Be Digitized: Afrocentricity and the Digital Public Sphere." *Social Text* 20, no. 2: 125–46.

Faulkner, W. 2001. "The Technology Question in Feminism: A View from Feminist Technology Studies." *Women's Studies International Forum* 24, no. 1: 79–95.

Federal Inventory of STEM Education Fast-Track Action Committee, the Committee on STEM Education, and the National Science and Technology Council. 2011.

The Federal Science. Technology, Engineering, and Mathematics (STEM) Education Portfolio. https://files.eric.ed.gov/fulltext/ED542910.pdf.

Fine, M., with E. Tuck and K. W. Yang. 2013. "An Intimate Memoir of Resistance Theory." In *Youth Resistance Research and Theories of Change*, edited by E. Tuck and K. Wayne Yang, 46–58. New York: Routledge.

Fordham, S. 1993. "'Those Loud Black Girls': (Black) Women, Silence, and Gender 'Passing' in the Academy." *Anthropology and Education Quarterly* 24, no. 1: 3–32.

———. 2014. "Are (Black) Female Academics Ignored?" Center for American Progress, August 6. https://www.americanprogress.org/issues/race/news/2014/08/06/95248/race-and-beyond-are-black-female-academics-ignored/.

Fordham, S., E. Tuck, and G. Dimitriadis. 2013. "What Does an Umbrella Do for the Rain? On the Efficacy and Limitations of Resistance." In *Youth Resistance Research and Theories of Change,* edited by E. Tuck and K. W. Yang, 97–106. New York: Routledge.

Fortier, A.-M. 1999. "Re-Membering Places and the Performance of Belonging(s)." *Theory, Culture and Society* 16, no. 2: 41–64.

Fox, J., J. N. Bailenson, and L. Tricase. 2013. "The Embodiment of Sexualized Virtual Selves: The Proteus Effect and Experiences of Self-Objectification via Avatars." *Computers in Human Behavior* 29, no. 3: 930–38. https://doi.org/10.1016/j.chb.2012.12.027.

Frankenberg, E., G. Siegel-Hawley, and J. Wang. 2010. *Choice without Equity: Charter School Segregation and the Need for Civil Rights Standards.* Los Angeles: Civil Rights Project/Proyecto Derechos Civiles at UCLA. https://www.civilrightsproject.ucla.edu.

Freeman, C. 2000. *High Tech and High Heels in the Global Economy: Women, Work, and Pink Collar Identities in the Caribbean.* Durham, N.C.: Duke University Press.

Frehill, L. M., N. Di Fabio, P. Layne, A. T. Johnson, and S. Hood. 2007. "Women in Engineering." *Society of Women Engineers* 53, no. 3: 1–24.

Freire, P. 2005. *Education for Critical Consciousness.* New York: Continuum.

Gay, G. 2010. *Culturally Responsive Teaching: Theory, Research, and Practice.* New York: Teachers College Press.

Gee, J. P. 2003. *What Video Games Have to Teach Us about Learning and Literacy.* New York: Palgrave Macmillan.

Gibson, K. S. 2017. "Student Teachers of Technology and Design: Can Short Periods of STEM-Related Industrial Placement Change Student Perceptions of Engineering and Technology?" *Design and Technology Education: An International Journal* 17, no. 1: 1360–1431.

Girls Who Code. n.d. "About Us." Accessed February 9, 2021. https://girlswhocode.com/about-us/.

Giroux, H. A. 2012. *Disposable Youth, Racialized Memories, and the Culture of Cruelty.* New York: Routledge.

Gonick, M. 2001. "What Is the 'Problem' with These Girls? Youth and Feminist Pedagogy." *Feminism and Psychology* 11, no. 2: 167–71.

———. 2006. "Between 'Girl Power' and 'Reviving Ophelia': Constituting the Neo-liberal Girl Subject." *NWSA Journal* 18, no. 2: 1–23.

———. 2012. *Between Femininities: Ambivalence, Identity, and the Education of Girls.* Albany: State University of New York Press.

Gonick, M., E. Renold, J. Ringrose, and L. Weems. 2009. "Rethinking Agency and Resistance: What Comes after Girl Power?" *Girlhood Studies* 2, no. 2: 1–9.

Gorski, P. 2005. "Education Equity and the Digital Divide." *Association for the Advancement of Computers in Education Journal* 13, no. 1: 3–45.

Green, G. P., and A. Haines. 2015. *Asset Building and Community Development.* Thousand Oaks, Calif.: Sage.

Grillo, T. 1995. "Anti-Essentialism and Intersectionality: Tools to Dismantle the Master's House." Berkeley Law Scholarship Repository. https://doi.org/10.15779/Z38MC6W.

Gunderson, E. A., G. Ramirez, S. C. Levine, and S. L. Beilock. 2012. "The Role of Parents and Teachers in the Development of Gender-Related Math Attitudes." *Sex Roles* 66, nos. 3–4: 153–66. https://doi.org/10.1007/s11199-011-9996-2.

Habgood, M. P. J., and S. E. Ainsworth. 2011. "Motivating Children to Learn Effectively: Exploring the Value of Intrinsic Integration in Educational Games." *Journal of the Learning Sciences* 20, no. 2: 169–206. https://doi.org/10.1080/10508406.2010.508029.

Hall, D. T., and J. Damico. 2007. "Black Youth Employ African American Vernacular English in Creating Digital Texts." *Journal of Negro Education* 76, no. 1: 80–88.

Hand, M., and B. Sandywell. 2002. "E-Topia as Cosmopolis or Citadel: On the Democratizing and De-Democratizing Logics of the Internet, or, Toward a Critique of the New Technological Fetishism." *Theory, Culture and Society* 19, nos. 1–2: 197–225.

Haraway, D. 1988. "Situated Knowledges: The Science Question in Feminism and the Privilege of Partial Perspective." *Feminist Studies* 14, no. 3: 575–99. https://doi.org/10.2307/3178066.

Harmon, A. 2010. "Indian Tribe Wins Fight to Limit Research of Its DNA." *New York Times*, April 21. http://www.nytimes.com/2010/04/22/us/22dna.html?pagewanted=all&_r=0.

Harris, A. 2004a. *All about the Girl: Culture, Power, and Identity.* London: Routledge.

———. 2004b. *Future Girl: Young Women in the Twenty-First Century.* New York: Routledge.

———. 2011. "Beyond the 'Transitions' Metaphor: Family Relations and Young People in Late Modernity." *Journal of Sociology* 19: 561–77.

Harris-Perry, M. V. 2011. *Sister Citizen: Shame, Stereotypes, and Black Women in America.* New Haven, Conn.: Yale University Press.

Henriksen, D., et al. 2015. "Rethinking Technology and Creativity in the 21st Century: Transform and Transcend: Synthesis as a Trans-disciplinary Approach to Thinking and Learning." *TechTrends* 59, no. 4: 5–9.

Herrera, S. G. 2010. *Biography-Driven Culturally Responsive Teaching.* New York: Teachers College Press.

hooks, b. 1984. *Feminist Theory from Margin to Center.* Boston: South End Press.

————. 1990. *Yearning: Race, Gender, and Cultural Politics.* Boston: South End Press.

————. 1994a. *Teaching to Transgress: Education as the Practice of Freedom.* New York: Routledge.

————. 1994b. *Outlaw Culture: Resisting Representations.* New York: Routledge.

————. 1997. *Cultural Criticism and Transformation.* Video file. https://www.youtube .com/watch?v=zQUuHFKP-9s.

Hunter, M. 2007. "The Persistent Problem of Colorism: Skin Tone, Status, and Inequality." *Sociology Compass* 1, no. 1: 237–54. https://doi.org/10.1111/j.1751–9020.2007 .00006.x.

Irvine, J. J. 2003. *Educating Teachers for Diversity: Seeing with a Cultural Eye.* Vol. 15. New York: Teachers College Press.

Jackson, C., C. Paechter, and E. Renold, eds. 2010. *Girls and Education 3–16: Continuing Concerns, New Agendas.* Berkshire, UK: Open University Press.

Jackson, L. A., Y. Zhao, A. Kolenic, H. E. Fitzgerald, R. Harold, and A. Von Eye. 2008. "Race, Gender, and Information Technology Use: The New Digital Divide." *Cyber-Psychology and Behavior* 11, no. 4: 437–42. https://doi.org/10.1089/cpb.2007.0157.

Jocson, K. 2013. *Cultural Transformations: Youth and Pedagogies of Possibility.* Cambridge, Mass.: Harvard Education Press.

Jones, L., J. Castellanos, and D. Cole. 2002. "Examining the Ethnic Minority Student Experience at Predominantly White Institutions: A Case Study." *Journal of Hispanic Higher Education* 1, no. 1: 19–39.

Kahne, J., E. Middaugh, and D. Allen. 2014. *Youth, New Media, and the Rise of Participatory Politics.* Oakland, Calif.: Youth and Participatory Politics Research Network.

Kennelly, J. J. 2009. "Youth Cultures, Activism and Agency: Revisiting Feminist Debates." *Gender and Education* 21, no. 3: 259–72.

Khan, S. 2011. *Privilege: The Making of an Adolescent Elite at St. Paul's School.* Princeton, N.J.: Princeton University Press.

Kivel, P. 2013. *Living in the Shadow of the Cross: Understanding and Resisting the Power and Privilege of Christian Hegemony.* British Columbia: New Society Publishers.

Klein, H. K., and D. L. Kleinman. 2002. "The Social Construction of Technology: Structural Considerations." *Science, Technology and Human Values* 27, no. 1: 28–52.

Kohl, H. R. 1994. *"I Won't Learn from You": And Other Thoughts on Creative Maladjustment.* New York: New Press.

Kovach, M. E. 2010. *Indigenous Methodologies: Characteristics, Conversations, and Contexts.* Toronto: University of Toronto Press.

Krishna, V. V. 1997. "Science, Technology and Counter Hegemony—Some Reflections on the Contemporary Science Movements in India." In *Science and Technology in a Developing World*, edited by T. Shinn, J. Spaapen, and V. Krishna, 375–411. Dordrecht: Springer Netherlands. https://doi.org/10.1007/978–94–017–2948–2_13.

Kuhlemeier, H., and B. Hemker. 2007. "The Impact of Computer Use at Home on Students' Internet Skills." *Computers and Education* 49, no. 2: 460–80. https://doi .org/10.1016/j.compedu.2005.10.004.

Kurtzleben, D. 2016. "People Keep Talking about 'The Establishment.' What Is It, Anyway?" National Public Radio, February 11. https://www.npr.org/2016/02/11/466049701/how-establishment-became-the-buzzword-of-the-2016-election.

Kwon, S. A. 2013. *Uncivil Youth: Race, Activism, and Affirmative Governmentality.* Durham, N.C.: Duke University Press.

Ladson-Billings, G. 2014. "Culturally Relevant Pedagogy 2.0: a.k.a. The Remix." *Harvard Educational Review* 84, no. 1: 74–84. https://doi.org/10.17763/haer.84.1.p2rj131485484751

Lenhart, A., and M. Madden. 2007. *Teens, Privacy and Online Social Networks.* Washington, D.C.: Pew Internet and American Life Project.

Lerner, R. M., E. M. Dowling, and P. M. Anderson. 2003. "Positive Youth Development: Thriving as the Basis of Personhood and Civil Society." *Applied Developmental Science* 7, no. 3: 172–80. https://doi.org/10.1207/S1532480XADS0703_8.

Li, S., H. J. Shin, E. L. Ding, and R. M. van Dam. 2009. "Adiponectin Levels and Risk of Type 2 Diabetes: A Systematic Review and Meta-analysis." *JAMA* 302, no. 2: 179.

Lillioja, S., D. M. Mott, M. Spraul, R. Ferraro, J. E. Foley, E. Ravussin, W. C. Knowler, P. H. Bennett, and C. Bogardus. 1993. "Insulin Resistance and Insulin Secretory Dysfunction as Precursors of Non-Insulin-Dependent Diabetes Mellitus: Prospective Studies of Pima Indians." *New England Journal of Medicine* 329, no. 27: 1988–92.

Lincoln, Y. S., and E. G. Guba. 1985. *Naturalistic Inquiry.* Beverly Hills, Calif.: Sage Publications.

Lloyd, S. 2013. "Sara Baartman and the 'Inclusive Exclusions' of Neoliberalism." *Meridians* 11, no. 2: 212–37.

Lohan, M., and W. Faulkner. 2004. "Masculinities and Technologies." *Men and Masculinities* 6, no. 4: 319–29.

Lomawaima, K. T. 1994. *They Called It Prairie Light: The Story of Chilocco Indian School.* Lincoln: University of Nebraska Press.

Lomawaima, K. T., and T. L. McCarty. 2006. *"To Remain an Indian": Lessons in Democracy from a Century of Native American Education.* New York: Teachers College Press. http://public.eblib.com/choice/publicfullrecord.aspx?p=4873352.

Lorde, A. 1984. "Age, Race, Class, and Sex: Women Redefining Difference." In *Sister Outsider*, 114–23. New York: Ten Speed Press.

———. 2007. *Sister Outsider: Essays and Speeches.* Berkeley, Calif.: Crossing Press.

Lueck, K., and M. Wilson. 2011. "Acculturative Stress in Latino Immigrants: The Impact of Social, Socio-Psychological and Migration-Related Factors." *International Journal of Intercultural Relations* 35, no. 2: 186–95. https://doi.org/10.1016/j.ijintrel.2010.11.016.

MacKenzie, D., and J. Wajcman. 1999. "Introductory Essay: The Social Shaping of Technology." In *The Social Shaping of Technology*, edited by D. MacKenzie and J. Wajcman, 3–27. Buckingham, Eng.: Open University Press.

Mahalik, J. R., E. B. Morray, A. Coonerty-Femiano, L. H. Ludlow, S. M. Slattery, and A. Smiler. 2005. "Development of the Conformity to Feminine Norms Inventory." *Sex Roles* 52, no. 7: 417–35. https://doi.org/10.1007/s11199-005-3709-7.

Malcom, L., and S. Malcom. 2011. "The Double Bind: The Next Generation." *Harvard Educational Review* 81, no. 2: 162–72.

Malhi, R. S., and A. C. Bader. 2015. "Engaging Native Americans in Genomics Research." *American Anthropologist* 117, no. 4: 743–44. https://doi.org/10.1111/aman.12369.

Mann, H. 1848. *Twelfth Annual Report to the Secretary of the Massachusetts State Board of Education.* Commonwealth of Massachusetts: State Board of Education.

Manuelito, K. D. 2003. "Building a Native Teaching Force: Important Considerations." *ERIC Digest.* ERIC Publications.

Margolis, J. 2008a. "Introduction: The Myth of Technology as the 'Great Equalizer.'" In *Stuck in the Shallow End: Education, Race, and Computing*, 1–16. Cambridge, Mass.: MIT Press.

———. 2008b. *Stuck in the Shallow End: Education, Race, and Computing.* Cambridge, Mass.: MIT Press. http://site.ebrary.com/id/10246370.

Margolis, J., J. Goode, and J. Flapan. 2017. "A Critical Crossroads for Computer Science for All: 'Identifying Talent' or "Building Talent,' and What Difference Does It Make?" In *Moving Students of Color from Consumers to Producers of Technology*, edited by Y. Rankin and J. Thomas, 1–23. Hershey, Pa.: IGI Global.

Marshall, T. 2018. "STEM May Be the Future—but Liberal Arts Are Timeless." *Quartz.* February 27. https://qz.com/1215910/stem-may-be-the-future-but-liberal-arts-are-timeless/.

Martin, K. A. 1998. "Becoming a Gendered Body: Practices of Preschools." *American Sociological Review* 63, no. 4: 494–511.

Maton, K. I., F. A. Hrabowski, and C. L. Schmidt. 2000. "African American College Students Excelling in the Sciences: College and Postcollege Outcomes in the Meyerhoff Scholars Program." *Journal of Research in Science Teaching* 37, no. 7: 629–54.

Matsuda, M. 1991. "Beside My Sister, Facing the Enemy: Legal Theory out of Coalition." *Stanford Law Review* 43, no. 6: 1183–92.

McAlear, F., A. Scott, K. Scott, and S. Weiss. 2018. *Data Brief: Women and Girls of Color in Computing.* https://www.wocincomputing.org/wp-content/uploads/2018/08/WOCinComputingDataBrief.pdf.

McPherson, T. 2008. "A Rule Set for the Future." In *Digital Youth, Innovation, and the Unexpected*, edited by Tara McPherson, 1–26. Cambridge, Mass.: MIT Press

Merriam, S. B., J. Johnson-Bailey, M.-Y. Lee, Y. Kee, G. Ntseane, and M. Muhamad. 2001. "Power and Positionality: Negotiating Insider/Outsider Status within and across Cultures." *International Journal of Lifelong Education* 20, no. 5: 405–16. https://doi.org/10.1080/02601370120490.

Mirza, H. S. 2013. "'A Second Skin': Embodied Intersectionality, Transnationalism and Narratives of Identity and Belonging among Muslim Women in Britain." *Women's Studies International Forum* 36: 5–15. https://doi.org/10.1016/j.wsif.2012.10.012.

Modi, K., J. Schoenberg, and K. Salmond. 2012. *Generation STEM: What Girls Say about Science, Technology, Engineering, and Math.* New York: Girl Scout Research Institute.

Mohanty, C. T. 2003. *Feminism without Borders: Decolonizing Theory, Practicing Solidarity.* Durham, N.C.: Duke University Press.

Monroe, B. J. 2004. *Crossing the Digital Divide: Race, Writing, and Technology in the Classroom.* New York: Teachers College Press.

Nakamura, L. 2002. *Cybertypes: Race, Ethnicity, and Identity on the Internet.* London: Routledge.

———. 2008. *Digitizing Race: Visual Cultures of the Internet.* Vol. 23. Minneapolis: University of Minnesota Press.

Nakkula, M. J., and E. Toshalis. 2008. *Understanding Youth: Adolescent Development for Educators.* 2nd ed. Cambridge, Mass.: Harvard Education Press.

National Academy of Science. 2010. *Expanding Underrepresented Minority Participation: America's Science and Technology Talent at the Crossroads.* Washington, D.C.: National Academies Press.

National Science Foundation. 2012. "Science and Engineering Indicators 2012." http://www.nsf.gov/statistics/seind12/.

National Science Foundation, National Center for Science and Engineering Statistics. 2015. *Women, Minorities, and Persons with Disabilities in Science and Engineering: 2015.* Special Report NSF 15–311. Arlington, Va.

Nelson, R. G., P. H. Bennett, G. J. Beck, M. Tan, W. C. Knowler, W. E. Mitch, . . . and B. D. Myers. 1996. "Development and Progression of Renal Disease in Pima Indians with Non-Insulin-Dependent Diabetes Mellitus." *New England Journal of Medicine* 335, no. 22: 1636–42.

Nkrumah, T. 2021. "Promoting Diversity, Equity, and Inclusion in STEM: A Culturally Responsive Computing Framework." Conference on Religion, Ethics, and Science (CORES) 2021, Arizona State University, February.

Noble, S. U. 2013. "Searching for Black Girls: Old Traditions in New Media." Ph.D. diss., University of Illinois. https://www.ideals.illinois.edu/handle/2142/42315.

Noguera, P., S. Ginwright, and J. Cammarota. 2006. *Beyond Resistance! Youth Activism and Community Change: New Democratic Possibilities for Practice and Policy for America's Youth.* New York: Routledge.

Obama, M. 2018. *Becoming.* New York: Crown.

Ohlheiser, A. 2015. "Why 'Social Justice Warrior,' a Gamergate Insult, Is Now a Dictionary Entry." *Washington Post,* October 7. https://www.washingtonpost.com/news/the-intersect/wp/2015/10/07/why-social-justice-warrior-a-gamergate-insult-is-now-a-dictionary-entry/?utm_term=.861dcea8c070.

Ong, M., C. Wright, L. Espinosa, and G. Orfield. 2011. "Inside the Double Bind: A Synthesis of Empirical Research on Undergraduate and Graduate Women of Color in Science, Technology, Engineering, and Mathematics." *Harvard Educational Review* 81, no. 2: 172–209.

Orfield, G., J. Kucsera, and G. Siegel-Hawley. 2012. *E Pluribus . . . Separation: Deepening Double Segregation for More Students.* Los Angeles: The Civil Rights Project.

Ovando, C. J. 2001. "Language Diversity and Education." In *Multicultural Education:*

Issues and Perspectives, edited by J. A. Banks and C. M. Banks, 268–91. 4th ed. New York: John Wiley and Sons.

Paris, D., and H. Alim. 2014. "What Are We Seeking to Sustain through Culturally Sustaining Pedagogy? A Loving Critique Forward." *Harvard Educational Review* 84, no. 1: 85–100. https://doi.org/10.17763/haer.84.1.982l873k2htl6m77.

Parkhurst, N. D., T. Morris, E. Tahy, and K. Mossberger. 2015. "The Digital Reality: e-Government and Access to Technology and Internet for American Indian and Alaska Native Populations." In *Proceedings of the 16th Annual International Conference on Digital Government Research*. May, 217–29. https://doi.org/10.1145/2757401.2757424.

Patton, L. D., and S. Bondi. 2015. "Nice White Men or Social Justice Allies? Using Critical Race Theory to Examine How White Male Faculty and Administrators Engage in Ally Work." *Race Ethnicity and Education* 18, no. 4: 488–514. https://doi.org/10.1080/13613324.2014.1000289.

Paulston, C. B., S. F. Kiesling, and E. S. Rangel. 2012. *The Handbook of Intercultural Discourse and Communication*. Malden, Mass.: Wiley-Blackwell.

Penley, C., and A. Ross, eds. 1991. *Technoculture*. Vol. 3. Minneapolis: University of Minnesota Press.

Perna, L., V. Lundy-Wagner, N. D. Drezner, M. Gasman, S. Yoon, E. Bose, and S. Gary. 2009. "The Contribution of HBCUs to the Preparation of African American Women for STEM Careers: A Case Study." *Research in Higher Education* 50, no. 1: 1–23.

Phippen, J. W. 2015. "How One Law Banning Ethnic Studies Led to Its Rise." *The Atlantic*, July 19. https://www.theatlantic.com/education/archive/2015/07/how-one-law-banning-ethnic-studies-led-to-rise/398885/.

Phoenix, A. 2010. *Ethnicities: The Sage Handbook of Identities*. London: Sage.

Prensky, M. 2006. *"Don't Bother Me Mom, I'm Learning!" How Computer and Video Games Are Preparing Your Kids for Twenty-First Century Success and How You Can Help!* St. Paul: Paragon House.

President's Council of Advisors on Science and Technology. 2012. "Engage to Excel: Producing One Million Additional College Graduates with Degrees in Science, Technology, Engineering, and Mathematics." https://obamawhitehouse.archives.gov/sites/default/files/microsites/ostp/fact_sheet_final.pdf.

Rails Girls. n.d. "Rails Girls—Get Started with Tech." Accessed February 9, 2021. http://railsgirls.com/.

Ramusack, B. N. 1990. "Cultural Missionaries, Maternal Imperialists, Feminist Allies: British Women Activists in India, 1865–1945." *Women's Studies International Forum* 13, no. 4: 309–21.

Rankin, Y., and J. Thomas, eds. 2017. *Moving Students of Color from Consumers to Producers of Technology*. Hershey, Pa.: IGI Global. https://doi.org/10.4018/978-1-5225-2005-4.

Redfield, R., R. Linton, and M. J. Herskovits. 1936. "Memorandum on the Study of Acculturation." *American Anthropologist* 38, no. 1: 149–52.

Reed, T. V. 2014. *Digitized Lives: Culture, Power, and Social Change in the Internet Era*. New York: Routledge.

Rhode, D., K. Cooke, and H. Ojha. 2012. "The Decline of the Great Equalizer." *The Atlantic*, December.

Ringrose, J. 2013. *Postfeminist Education? Girls and the Sexual Politics of Schooling*. New York: Routledge. http://public.eblib.com/choice/publicfullrecord.aspx?p=1016157.

Ringrose, J., and E. Renold. 2012. "Slut-Shaming, Girl Power and 'Sexualisation': Thinking through the Politics of the International SlutWalks with Teen Girls." *Gender and Education* 24, no. 3: 333–43.

Roberts, D. E. 1997. *Killing the Black Body: Race, Reproduction, and the Meaning of Liberty*. New York: Vintage Books.

Rosas, R., M. Nussbaum, P. Cumsille, V. Marianov, M. Correa, P. Flores, and M. Salinas. 2003. "Beyond Nintendo: Design and Assessment of Educational Video Games for First and Second Grade Students." *Computers and Education* 40: 71–94.

Rusk, N., M. Resnick, R. Berg, and M. Pezalla-Granlund. 2008. "New Pathways into Robotics: Strategies for Broadening Participation." *Journal of Science Education and Technology* 17, no. 1: 59–69. https://doi.org/10.1007/s10956-007-9082-2.

Saporito, S. 2003. "Private Choices, Public Consequences: Magnet School Choice and Segregation by Race and Poverty." *Social Problems* 50, no. 2: 181–203. https://doi.org/10.1525/sp.2003.50.2.181.

Scott, A., F. Klein, and U. Onovakpuri. 2017. *Tech Leavers Study*. Kapor Center for Social Impact. https://mk0kaporcenter5ld71a.kinstacdn.com/wp-content/uploads/2017/08/TechLeavers2017.pdf.

Scott, A., and A. Martin. n.d. *Gender and Racial Stereotype Endorsement and Implications for STEM Outcomes among High-Achieving Underrepresented Adolescent Females*. Kapor Center. Accessed February 12, 2021. https://www.kaporcenter.org/gender-and-racial-stereotype-endorsement-and-implications-for-stem-outcomes-among-high-achieving-underrepresented-adolescent-females/.

Scott, K. 1999. "First-Grade African-American Girls' Play Patterns." Ph.D. diss., Rutgers University.

———. 2003. "A Case Study: African-American Girls and Their Families." In *The State of Black America 2003*, by the National Urban League, 181–96. [Washington, DC]: National Urban League.

———. 2012. "Lessons Learned: Research within an Urban African American District." *International Journal of Qualitative Studies in Education* 25, no. 5: 625–43.

Scott, K. A., and S. Elliott. 2020. "STEM Diversity and Inclusion Efforts for Women of Color: A Critique of the New Labor System." *International Journal of Gender, Science and Technology* 11, no. 3: 374–82. genderandset.open.ac.uk/index.php/genderandset/article/view/646.

Scott, K. A., and P. Garcia. 2016. "Techno-Social Change Agents: Fostering Activist Dispositions among Girls of Color." *Meridians* 15, no. 1: 65–85.

Scott, K. A., and A. Henward, eds. 2016. *Women Education Scholars and Their Children's Schools*. New York: Routledge.

Scott, K. A., K. M. Sheridan, and K. Clark. 2014. "Culturally Responsive Computing: A Theory Revisited." *Learning, Media and Technology* 40, no. 4: 412–36.

Seitz, J. A. 1992. "The Development of Bodily-Kinesthetic Intelligence in Children: Implications for Education and Artistry." *Holistic Education Review* 5, no. 2: 35–39.

Selwyn, N. 2002. *Defining the "Digital Divide": Developing a Theoretical Understanding of Inequalities in the Information Age.* Cardiff, Wales: School of Social Sciences, Cardiff University.

Shaffer, D. W. 2006. *How Computer Games Help Children Learn.* New York: Palgrave Macmillan.

Sihvonen, T. 2012. *Players Unleashed! Modding The Sims and the Culture of Gaming.* Amsterdam: Amsterdam University Press.

Smith, L., E. Tuck, and K. Yang, eds. 2019. *Indigenous and Decolonizing Studies in Education: Mapping the Long View.* New York: Routledge.

Smith, M. R., and L. Marx. 1994. *Technological Determinism in American Culture: Does Technology Drive History? The Dilemma of Technological Determinism.* Cambridge, Mass.: MIT Press.

Snibbe, A. C., and H. R. Markus. 2005. "You Can't Always Get What You Want: Educational Attainment, Agency and Choice." *Journal of Personality and Social Psychology* 88, no. 4: 703–20.

Soozandehfar, S. M. A., and E. Noroozisiam. 2011. "Which One Speaks Better? The Field-Dependent or the Field-Independent?" *Language in India* 11, no. 2: n.p.

Sue, D. W. 2013. *Microaggressions in Everyday Life: Race, Gender, and Sexual Orientation.* Hoboken, N.J: Wiley. http://rbdigital.oneclickdigital.com.

Taft, Jessica K. 2004. "Girl Power Politics: Pop-Culture Barriers and Organizational Resistance." In *All about the Girl: Culture, Power, and Identity,* edited by Anita Harris, 69–78. New York: Routledge.

———. 2006. "'I'm Not a Politics Person': Teenage Girls, Oppositional Consciousness, and the Meaning of Politics." *Politics and Gender* 2, no. 3: 329–52.

———. 2010. *Rebel Girls: Youth Activism and Social Change across the Americas.* New York: NYU Press.

TallBear, K. 2013. *Native American DNA: Tribal Belonging and the False Promise of Genetic Science.* Minneapolis: University of Minnesota Press.

Tapscott, D. 1998. *Growing Up Digital.* New York: McGraw-Hill.

Taylor, C. 1994. *Multiculturalism.* Princeton, N.J.: Princeton University Press.

Tuck, E. 2009. "Suspending Damage: A Letter to Communities." *Harvard Educational Review* 79, no. 3: 409–27. https://doi.org/10.17763/haer.79.3.n0016675661t3n15.

———. 2012. *Urban Youth and School Pushout: Gateways, Get-Aways, and the GED.* New York: Routledge.

Tuck, E., and K. W. Yang. 2014. "R-Words: Refusing Research." In *Humanizing Research: Decolonizing Qualitative Inquiry with Youth and Communities,* edited by D. Paris and M. T. Winn, 223–48. Thousand Oaks, Calif.: Sage Publications.

Tuck, E., K. W. Yang, eds. 2013. *Youth Resistance Research and Theories of Change.* New York: Routledge.

Uline, C., and M. Tschannen-Moran. 2008. "The Walls Speak: The Interplay of Quality Facilities, School Climate, and Student Achievement." *Journal of Educational Administration* 46, no. 1: 55–73. https://doi.org/10.1108/09578230810849817.

Unger, R. K. 2000. "Outsiders Inside: Positive Marginality and Social Change." *Journal of Social Issues* 56, no. 1: 163–79.

U.S. Bureau of Labor Statistics. 2011. "Quarterly Census of Employment Wages." Last modified September 2020. http://www.bls.gov/cew/datatoc.htm.

Valla, J. M., and W. M. Williams. 2012. "Increasing Achievement and Higher-Education Representation of Under-Represented Groups in Science, Technology, Engineering, and Mathematics Fields: A Review of Current K-12 Intervention Programs." *Journal of Women and Minorities in Science and Engineering* 18, no. 1: 21–53.

Villegas, A. M., and T. Lucas. 2002. *Educating Culturally Responsive Teachers: A Coherent Approach.* Albany: State University of New York Press.

Villenas, S. 1996. "The Colonizer/Colonized Chicana Ethnographer: Identity, Marginalization, and Co-optation in the Field." *Harvard Educational Review* 66, no. 4: 711–31.

Virkkunen, J., D. S. Newnham, P. Nleya, and R. Engeströöm. 2012. "Breaking the Vicious Circle of Categorizing Students in School." *Learning, Culture and Social Interaction* 1, no. 3: 183–92.

Wajcman, J. 2000. "Reflections on Gender and Technology Studies: In What State Is the Art?" *Social Studies of Science* 30, no. 3: 447–64.

Wann, T., L. Hayes, G. Marshment, C. Marcum, M. Meiklejohn, and P. Branscum. 2015. "Native American Childhood Obesity Prevention Interventions: A Systematic Review." *Vulnerable Children and Youth Studies* 10, no. 2: 118–30.

Wanzo, R. 2009. *The Suffering Will Not Be Televised: African American Women and Sentimental Political Storytelling.* Albany: State University of New York Press.

Warschauer, M. 2000. "Language, Identity, and the Internet." In *Race in Cyberspace*, edited by B. E. Kolko, L. Nakamura, and G. B. Rodman, 151–70. New York : Routledge.

White, J. W. 2011. "Resistance to Classroom Participation: Minority Students, Academic Discourse, Cultural Conflicts, and Issues of Representation in Whole Class Discussions." *Journal of Language, Identity and Education* 10, no. 4: 250–65. https://doi.org/10.1080/15348458.2011.598128.

Willett, R. 2008. "What You Wear Tells a Lot about You: Girls Dress Up Online." *Gender and Education* 20, no. 5: 421–34. https://doi.org/10.1080/09540250701797242.

Willis, J. L. 2009. "Girls Reconstructing Gender: Agency, Hybridity and Transformations of 'Femininity.'" *Girlhood Studies* 2, no. 2: 96–118.

Wing, J. M. 2006. "Computational Thinking." *Communications of the ACM* 49, no. 3: 33–35.

———. 2008. "Computational Thinking and Thinking about Computing." *Philosophical Transactions of the Royal Society A: Mathematical, Physical and Engineering Sciences* 366, no. 1881: 3717–25. https://doi.org/10.1098/rsta.2008.0118.

Winkle-Wagner, R. 2009. *The Unchosen Me: Race, Gender, and Identity among Black Women in College*. Baltimore: Johns Hopkins University Press. http://muse.jhu.edu/books/9781421402932/.

Yee, N., and J. Bailenson. 2007. "The Proteus Effect: The Effect of Transformed Self-Representation on Behavior." *Human Communication Research* 33, no. 3: 271–90. https://doi.org/10.1111/j.1468–2958.2007.00299.x.

Yevseyeva, K., and M. Towhidnejad. 2012. "Work in Progress: Teaching Computational Thinking in Middle and High School." In *Frontiers in Education Conference Proceedings*, IEEE, 1–2

Index

101–102, 106–108; Montserrat and, 27–28, 37, 149–151; Native American students in, 123–142; outcomes for girls in, 81–86, 144–154; ownership taken by girls in, 19; physical space for, 45–47, 62–63; power and, 8–10, 19, 62, 84–85, 154; presentation at MIT, 80–81; producing more than digital products, 62–66; reasons to join, 31–39; recruitment of girls for, 31–39, 57–58, 90, 110; relationality and context of, 10–11; Sonia and, 129–135; success of, 157; ten years later, 148–151; ultimate intent of, 52–53; university space for, 17–18; unsuccessful participants in, 39–44; values of, 154; voices of participants in, 47–50, 82–83, 142–143, 154; Yvette and, 54–80; Zaire and, 111–122
conflict and love, 67–70, 73
Corsaro, William, 1
Cox, A., 146
Crabtree, R., 69
Crenshaw, K., 90–91
critical feminist pedagogy, 105
critical inquiry, 12–13, 17
critical pedagogy, 13, 70–73, 90, 105
critical praxis, 12–13, 17
cultural connectedness, 49–50
Currie, D., 78

danceLogic, 3
"dangerous dignity," 57
Denner, J., 146
Dillard, C. B., 121
Donetta, story of, 20–23
Du Bois, W. E. B., 156
Duckworth, A., 11

education: conflicting trends in, for women of color, 2004–2008, 4; federal policies on, 2; Reggio Emilia approach in, 1–2, 35; "special needs," 2–3
Elena, story of, 115–123
escapism, 152
e-zines, 5–6, 25

Facebook, 2
feedback from parents and students, 24–25
Fine, M., 79
Fordham, S., 83–84, 97
Freeman, C., 99

Gay, Geneva, 3
Generation STEM, 99

Gibson, K. S., 53
Girl Effect, 5
Girl Go Techbridge, 4
girls and women of color: becoming peers and sharing stories, 115–123; conflict and love among, 67–70; at historically Black universities, 23–24; individualism of, 56–57, 60–61; interpreting instructional interactions, 106–107; microaggressions against, 9; needing space for learning, 20–23; out-of-school programs for, 3–4; power, 154; power of, 8–10, 19, 62, 84–85; raced-gendered-classed lens of silence and, 97–100; reasons for joining COMPUGIRLS, 31–39; stereotypes of, 30–31, 56–57, 61, 87, 91–92; stereotypes of beauty and, 112–115; underrepresented in STEM, 2, 99
Girls Creating Games, 4
Girls Empowerment After-School Programs, 3
Gonick, M., 12, 62
Google, 2
GPA and COMPUGIRLS applicants, 58–62
graffiti, 47–48
Green, G. P., 61
Greene, Graham, 72
Guzman, B., 146

Haines, A., 61
Harris, A., 61, 151
Harris-Perry, Melissa, 82–83, 91
Harvard Educational Review, 124
hooks, bell, 67, 148
Howard University, 23

individualism, 61
informed defiance, 57
intersectionality, 8
Intersectionality as Critical Social Theory, 156

Jade, story of, 140–142

Kahne, J., 79
Kelly, D. M., 78
Kelly, story of, 37–38, 148–149
Kids-in-Tech, 4
Kwon, S. A., 100

labels and stereotypes, 30–31
Ladson-Billings, Gloria, 3
Laura, mentoring by, 73–75, 85–86

73; critical pedagogy and, 70–72; emergence as leader, 77–79; introduction to COMPUGIRLS, 54, 55–58; lasting impact of COMPUGIRLS on, 81–86; mentoring of, 73–76; participation and progression through COMPUGIRLS, 63–66; perspective and viewpoint of, 76–80; presentation at MIT, 81, 115; public speaking and travels by, 81–82

YWCA, 3

Zaire, story of, 111–122
Zelman v. Simmons-Harris, 1

KIMBERLY A. SCOTT is a professor in the Women and Gender Studies Department at Arizona State University and the Founder/ Executive Director of ASU's Center for Gender Equity in Science and Technology. She is coauthor of *Kids in Context: The Sociological Study of Children and Childhoods* and coeditor of *Women Education Scholars and Their Children's Schooling.*

DISSIDENT FEMINISMS

The University of Illinois Press
is a founding member of the
Association of University Presses.

_____

University of Illinois Press
1325 South Oak Street
Champaign, IL 61820-6903
www.press.uillinois.edu